THEATRE SOURCES DOT COM

A Complete Guide to Online Theatre and Dance Resources

Louis E. Catron

HEINEMANN
PORTSMOUTH, NH

Heinemann
A division of Reed Elsevier Inc.
361 Hanover Street
Portsmouth, NH 03801–3912
www.heinemann.com

Offices and agents throughout the world

© 2001 by Louis E. Catron

Library of Congress Cataloging-in-Publication Data
Catron, Louis E.
    Theatre sources dot com : a complete guide to online theatre and dance resources / Louis E. Catron.
      p. cm.
    Includes bibliographical references.
    ISBN 0-325-00382-3
    1. Theater—Computer network resources—Directories. 2. Dance—Computer network resources—Directories. I. Title: Theatre sources.com.
II. Title: Theatresources.com. III. Title.
PN2052 .C38 2001
025.06'792'0973—dc21

                                                    2001039647

Editor: Lisa A. Barnett
Production: Vicki Kasabian
Cover design: Jenny Jensen Greenleaf
Typesetter: Tom Allen
Manufacturing: Steve Bernier

Printed in the United States of America on acid-free paper
05 04 03 02 01 DA 1 2 3 4 5

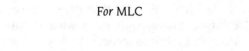

For MLC

"On a day no different than the one now dawning, Shakespeare sat down and started Hamlet, Leonardo stepped to an easel and made the first strokes of the Mona Lisa, and Beethoven took out a sketch book and began the Ninth Symphony."

—adapted from Robert Richardson,
Emerson: The Mind on Fire

CONTENTS

CONTENTS

ACKNOWLEDGMENTS

To my colleagues who generously gave comments and suggestions, my thanks. I am especially appreciative to several in particular. To Richard Palmer, for always being ready to read and comment on the current manuscript in progress, I am once again grateful. To David Dudley, for his willingness to discuss the tricky morass of copyright, especially applied to Sound, my sincere gratitude. To Joan Gavaler, my thanks for suggestions to the Choreographer and Dance sections. To Matt Cohen, who patiently guided me through Internet practices, I am in debt.

I must especially thank the people at Heinemann who make an author's life a joy. Vicki Kasabian skillfully shepherded the book through production. And Lisa Barnett, as always, had constant good humor, sage advice, and thorough professionalism.

INTRODUCTION

When it started, I hadn't thought that *Theatre Sources Dot Com* would become a book. Like a number of theatre and dance people, I imagine, I had a collection of websites that were stored more or less randomly in my bookmark file. Sensing that I surely was missing significant sites, I started asking for suggestions from others—theatre professionals, former students now active in the field, faculty colleagues, current students, webmasters, even newspaper columnists who specialize in advice about the Net. I was quite surprised to discover that the majority of them had little knowledge of the rich variety of theatre materials that existed in the cyber world, had not discovered even basic sites like *Theatre Central* and *Artslynx*, were unaware that online access was available for places as diverse as the U. S. Copyright or Samuel French, and did not know that directories like *Lycos* or *Yahoo!* have many theatre and dance sites a few clicks from their home pages.

The people I asked for advice were, it turned out, eager for me to feed them the information I'd accumulated. When it started, then, this book was a series of handouts for students, colleagues, friends, and even some strangers. Handouts about search engines. About basic directories. About sites for specialized areas like playwriting, dramaturgy, design, acting, dance, and more. About finding a job. About discount tickets, less expensive books.

In what I see as an interesting coincidence, this use of handouts is the way my other books started. The advantage is that the materials are "user tested." They've been circulated and they received helpful comments and suggestions.

As a result of that testing process, what you'll find in these pages is very specific information, not merely a list of sites. Each site's name and address is listed, and each is described, some in detail. Selected sites are labeled "author's choice" for their depth and expertise.

I made every effort to find all of the "best" theatre and dance sites (and a few more), but I can't promise that *Theatre Sources Dot Com* has *every* top theatrical site, and no doubt you will be surprised that I missed this or that one. Nor can I promise that all the sites listed in this book will be alive when you visit them, but I do assure you that each was in excellent operational health when this manuscript was prepared.

I can promise, however, that you will find valuable suggestions here.

To keep the book updated, Heinemann has arranged for a special website that you can access: <*www.heinemanndrama.com/theatresources/*>. There you'll find birth notices about new sites and funeral announcements about those that die.

The book's chapters are organized by interest areas—playwrights, dancers, actors, and so forth—but please remember that very often a site has a depth of material that defies easy classification. A site for, say, actors will likely have fine materials for dancers. A site for scenic design usually will also contain information for costume, lighting, sound, props, and tech. A place that discusses auditions can have information not only for actors and dancers but also for technicians and designers. That pattern is repeated for each specialization. You'll find that the descriptions indicate those variations.

The advantage is that the book has done the surfing for you. More than 750 sites for dance and theatre are listed, and given the way one site will list a numerous other sites, the total compounds to a staggering amount.

I hope *Theatre Sources Dot Com* will help you reap the riches waiting on the Web.

1

Welcome to the World Wide Web

For those of us in theatre and dance, the World Wide Web is fast becoming—no, already *is*—a vast encyclopedia larger than ever dreamed, a warehouse of ideas and facts, a source of endless opportunities waiting to be collected, and a place of enriching and exciting discoveries about our art. The Internet is a wonderful thing. Designed by the Defense Department to provide uninterruptible communications, it has become a global network for everyone. Although some of us wryly think that the "uninterruptible" goal is yet to be achieved, it is a phenomenon now and can only grow in power—power *you* can use in countless ways to improve your theatrical knowledge and skills, form links with like-minded people, find jobs, increase your knowledge of dance and theatrical happenings around the world both past and present, and much, much more.

RICHES ON THE NET: THEATRE AND DANCE IN THE U. S. AND CANADA

The Net can provide amazing riches—if, of course, we can find appropriate sites. That's the purpose of this book: to guide you to the sites that wait for you, whether you're involved in dance or theatre, and whether you live in the U. S. or Canada. What sorts of riches are out there? Here's one example of the sort of information you can glean from searching the Net:

> Employment of actors, directors, and producers is expected to grow *faster than the average for all occupations* (emphasis mine) through the year 2006. . . . Growing numbers of people who enjoy live theatrical entertainment for excitement and aesthetics will attend stage productions. Touring productions of Broadway plays and other large shows are providing new opportunities for actors and directors.

Encouraging news, isn't it? That's the official U. S. government prediction of the Occupational Employment Outlook. For more information, go to

<*www.fedstats.gov/*> and conduct a search for *actor*. By the way, if you want governmental information about salaries and job descriptions for show-biz folk, the Net—*fedstats* in this instance—is a good place to look.

That's only one example of what we can find because this international cyber community of linked computers has an amazingly large number of sites. How large? In 1998, a research group found 275 million distinctly different pages on the Net. To put that figure in perspective, that's more individual sites than the entire U. S. population, which was (according to a Net search) estimated at 272.6 million in 1999. Those researchers concluded that the Net is growing at the rate of some 20 million pages *per month*, doubling in size in only *nine months*. Two years later a new report by Inktomi and the NEC *Research Institute, Inc.*, said the Web had grown to more than one billion unique pages (for that story, see <*www.inktomi.com/webmap/*>). Each day the Internet—actually a network of networks—connects an estimated 15 million users in some fifty different countries. Even more rapid growth is in store. It is one of humanity's most amazing developments, and all of it is there waiting for theatre workers to use.

The Net and the Web

A brief technical clarification. Many of us use the terms Internet and Web interchangeably as if they are synonymous, but in fact they're two separate e-entities. The Internet is the global association of computers that carries data, allowing exchange of information. The World Wide Web is a collection of documents that can interlink because they work together using a specific Internet convention called HTTP, or HyperText Transfer Protocol, which are standardized rules for exchanging text, sound, and images. Web pages can be exchanged over the Net because browsers (which read the pages) and Web servers (which store the pages) both understand HTTP. As theatre does not exist without an audience, so the Web can't survive without the Net, but the Net exists independently of the Web.

That technical distinction being made, however, this book will follow common usage and use Net for both. We're deliberately avoiding tech jargon. Just as you don't have to know how a combustion engine works in order to drive a car, so, too, you can use the Net without knowing its history or how it is constructed.

Your Discoveries on the Net

What can you discover on the Net? No matter what your theatrical interests are—whether you are a playwright, an actor, a director, a designer, a manager, or a technician—there are sites out there for you. Here's an abbreviated list that indicates some of the Internet possibilities for theatre and dance people.

- Lists with details about job opportunities (this book includes more than 40 sites for theatre and dance jobseekers!), auditions, and conventions.

- News about theatre—Broadway, other cities and countries, community theatres, educational institutions, and more.
- Contact information for theatrical companies.
- Location guides to find individuals who work in theatre.
- Details about schools, workshops, and training.
- Access to professional organizations like Equity, academic groups like American Theatre in Higher Education, and so forth.
- Specialized sites with news and information for managers, actors, dancers, playwrights, directors, choreographers, designers, technicians.
- Opportunities for online education and training.
- Announcements about awards like the Tony or Obie.
- Statistics about Broadway box office income, longest-running shows, those shows slated to close, even those shows currently offering discount tickets.
- Photographs and drawings of costume, scenic, lighting, and makeup designs.
- Scholarly information about classical history and modern developments.
- Fan sites for musicals, plays, performers, plus interviews with outstanding theatre people.
- Research facilities, online libraries, and encyclopedias.
- Companies ready for your business with catalogs and online ordering for technical supplies, makeup, lighting equipment, scenic paint, sound, and other items.
- Collections of plays.
- Chat rooms to ask questions and discuss your interests with like-minded people.
- Online locations where you can order scripts, books, posters, theatrical memorabilia, and gifts for opening night presents.
- Sites where you can post your résumé for employers to consider.

Whew! And there is yet more. Much, much more. So much more that it's difficult to say what you *can't* find on the Net.

THE PURPOSE OF *THEATRE SOURCES DOT COM*

In the following chapters, you'll find a list of selected helpful websites for theatre and dance, in the U. S. and Canada, to guide you through the cyber mazes. The next chapter starts with a list of recommended search engines, then discusses "best" general sites to start your search. The bulk of the book deals with specialized sites for theatre and dance interests.

You don't have to be a 'puter wizard. You don't have to own the latest multigigahertz blazing box with all the bells and whistles, though of course that would be nice. Furthermore, because so many public libraries and campus computer labs give you free access to the Internet, you don't have to even own a computer at all.

INSIDE THIS BOOK

A tally of the number of sites listed in all chapters adds up to some 750 *sites for theatre and dance.* The sites aren't merely listed; they are described. In addition, you'll find annotations and notes along with guides to help you maneuver through them most effectively. Many of those sites contain links to yet other pages, doubling or tripling your e-access to theatre and dance.

Regardless of what interests you specifically, you'll find valuable e-destinations in these chapters. For example, there are *more than 40 sites that list theatre jobs . . . almost 90 for acting and dancing . . . close to 200 sites for design and tech . . . 81 for playwrights . . . 50+ for theatre management.* In addition, there are *more than 40 recommended best sites for theatre,* and most contain links to acting, dance, design, tech, and so forth. Looking for books or theatre gifts? That chapter has *more than 70 listings* for you.

The Net is a wondrous world, indeed. Its riches await you.

2

Search Engines for Theatre

To find the information you want on the Net, you'll need an intelligent and professional guide to escort you through the cyber labyrinth. An e-stage manager, so to speak. Enter stage right, bowing helpfully, your friendly *search engine*.

Think of a search engine as a cybernetic octopus with tentacles in computers all over the world. This wizardly creature's e-suckers pluck out materials otherwise hidden in the Internet maze. Providing you type in the correct word(s) and follow its search rules and techniques, the engine deftly locates the precise Net sites that deal with what you requested.

That's the theory, anyhow. Not the reality. Recent studies have shown that even the most powerful search engines can't find all relevant materials on the Internet, and an engine's search for a given topic may miss 50 percent—perhaps even more—of pertinent sites. With over a billion pages and more added daily, who can fault the omissions? What's more, those apparently friendly guides have quirky tastes and may ignore the very site you wanted. For those reasons, experienced Netters expect to use several search engines on the premise that one of them will uncover materials that others missed.

It's certainly easy enough to find engines. There are a staggering 3,500+ search engines, and the list is growing with new technology. At the same time, some engines disappear into the cyber equivalent of a black hole. Others merge with companions. The American big-business merger mania is alive and well on the Net, and it's hard to keep up with the changes. Recently, for example, the search utility maker *Intelliseek* acquired meta-search engine *ProFusion*; *Go2Net* bought meta-search site *Dogpile* in a $55 million deal; and *Cnet* took *SavvySearch* for $22 million. Will these changes bring improvements? We can hope, of course.

Whatever the number of engines, none of us wants to play with so many. We need a method to select the ones that fit us best. This chapter gives you suggestions, starting with a brief, nontechie discussion of types of search engines. It then list sites that help you find and evaluate engines. It concludes with recommended engines you might want to try. Some are marked "author's choice"—a personal favorite I think you would like.

THREE BASIC TYPES OF SEARCH ENGINES

Depending on their mode of searching and where they get information, search engines fall into three basic categories according to their operational techniques:

- **Meta-Search or Multiple-Search Engines.** These search a number of engines and compile the results. The best of them eliminate duplication. Examples include *Dogpile*, *Momma* (how can you not like engines with those names?), *ixquick*, *Starting Point*, and *ProFusion*. (Web addresses and more details appear later in this chapter.) There's no agreement about which is the "best," but sites that evaluate search engines give high marks to *ixquick*. I've grown used to *Google*, and although it isn't evaluated as a top engine, habits are hard to break. While the advantages of meta-engines are clear—a chance to dig into so many engines at once—they also have disadvantages. For example, they are so dedicated to replying quickly that the total number of results can be limited, which means they don't give full coverage. Also, most mega-search engines are popularity-oriented: they will pull in only the top 10 or perhaps 20 hits from the individual engines, which means we get fewer responses than we would using the solitary searcher. Finally, too few look in the *Inktomi* database, which is the largest on the Net.
- **Search Engines.** These examine their own database of hyperlinks. The larger that base, the more links the engine will find. Quantity isn't necessary always good: We want relevant links and we don't want duplications. Examples of searchers in this category include *AltaVista*, one of the largest; *Lycos*; and *Excite*.
- **Directories (sometimes called Classified).** Websites are listed by categories such as finance, health, and arts. Engines in this group organize their search by looking at such groups. Some review or rate sites they find. Examples include *Yahoo!* and *LookSmart* (humans compile the sites, not computers).

To most of us nontechies, the distinctions between types are less important than the results. We'll probably lump all three under one generic name,

"Search Engine," and expect whatever device we use to bring us the precise site we wanted. After all, we're in theatre, where optimism is what keeps us going. The trick is to find a few that work consistently well for us, and to remember that others are out there that may uncover new materials.

SEARCH ENGINES TO SEARCH OUT SEARCH ENGINES

We tend to work with a given search engine for a period of time. If it works fairly well, it becomes our "favorite." However, if we don't experiment with new ones and judge strengths and weaknesses, we may be losing out on technological improvements. Certainly the new meta-search engines are so powerful that they deserve our attention.

If you're going to look for your ideal search engine, why not use a search engine? Here are sites that help you find and evaluate the various engines available. Time spent looking through these reference materials will help you decide just what search engine is best for your needs. Note that some also offer tips for effective searching.

> **The Invisible <http://>**
> This book follows popular convention and omits the prefix *<http://>*, unless the site is not on the World Wide Web and therefore does not start with *<www.>*. When you type an address into your browser's location window, remember to include the *<http://>*.

GUIDES TO SPECIALIZED SEARCH ENGINES
www.searchability.com/
This is a guide to guides, a sort of coach for users. The home page says that it is a "complete list of guides (with descriptions) to thousands of search engines covering hundreds of subjects." You'll find links to more than 30 different guides that discuss search engines. This is no mere listing of sites. Instead, there are excellent detailed annotated descriptions, candid and forthright, of each guide. The discussions are neatly organized by Subject Coverage, Search Engine Information, and a quite helpful Especially Useful For category that helps you decide if particular guides are user-friendly for your particular needs. The menu on the left part of the home page allows you to select guides for particular information, such as academic areas, children's engines, popular topics, regions, and so forth.

Scrolling down the home page leads you to text descriptions of specialized guides, and you may want to start with *Internets*, which "covers an astounding variety of subjects, encompassing every field or subject you can think of—from the frivolous to the scholarly." At *Internets*, use the categories pop-up, second from the top, and click on Entertainment. That leads you to another menu where you can select Theatre (or you can go there directly by typing this in your browser: *<www.Internets.com/stheatre.htm>*). You're led to searchable databases.

Those Weirdo Net Codes

An explanatory word for those getting their feet wet in Netting. A Net address—those cryptic-looking letters and punctuation marks like *http://altavista.digital.com/*—is the site's Internet address, as unique as a fingerprint.

There is a logic at work here. **HTTP** refers to Hypertext Transfer Protocol, the cyber-system that moves pages over the Net.

The middle portion—in our example, *altavisita.digital*—is the specific name of the individual or company.

The ending letters—"extensions" in 'puter-speak—identify the generic nature of the host, such as *.com* (the host is a commercial organization); *.edu* (educational institution); *.gov* (federal or state government); *.net* (a Networking organization); or *.org* (a nonprofit organization).

Those codes are necessary to open sites from your basic browser. For example, if your browser is Netscape Navigator, look at the top of the home page and you'll see a thin horizontal box marked *location* that contains similar-looking entries that describe your current location. Use your mouse to single-click that box and it will turn a different color. Type the full *AltaVista* address, hit enter, and you'll be transferred to that engine. (Notice that as you type, the word *location* changes to *go to*.) You can follow that procedure to find any site. Because one mistake makes the search worthless, type entries carefully.

Actually, however, Netscape is pretty smart. Often, all you need to do is type the name of the site if you've visited it before. For example, merely typing *Amazon*, without the full coded address, will take you to that bookseller's site if you've been there before.

All of this really is much easier than it sounds. If you're having difficulties, enlist the aid of a friend. Better, grab the 10-year-old kid next door. Kids have gene mutations that allow psychic knowledge of cyber activities.

INTERNET QUICK REFERENCE—Searching the Web
www.indiana.edu/~librcsd/resource/search-list.html#gen

Indiana University Library offers a clean, efficient index to search engines. You'll find valuable facts by looking in such categories as Search Engine Information, Directories and Subject Guides, Special Search Engines, Meta Search Engines, or Portal Guide.

SEARCH ENGINE SHOWDOWN
http://searchenginesshowdown.com/

Calling itself "The User's Guide to Web Searching," this excellent site gives you details you never suspected existed. Did you know that some engines bring up dead links? *Showdown* will tell you which do that and how many corpses they list. For example, the last time I looked, *AltaVista* had the unhappy honor of leading the pack with almost 14% deceased locations. Do you know which engine to use for what purpose? Examine Search Strategies. Have you heard arguments about this or that engine being the best? See Features of Web Search Engines and make up your own mind. Which engine will produce the most unique results? According to the *Showdown* report, *AltaVista*, *Excite*, and *Northern Light* found the most pages that none of the other search engines located. Check them out at these addresses:

AltaVista: *www.altavista.com/*

Excite: *www.excite.com/*

Northern Light: *www.northernlight.com/*

Perhaps the most valuable file here, though, is called Learning. Subdivided into Strategies, Reviews, Books, and On the Net, the entries will help you search the Net more effectively.

SEARCH IQ

www.searchiq.com/directory/multi.html

This site ranks meta-search engines—tools that examine a number of databases, in effect a search of search engines—and ranks them with an "IQ score" based on thoroughness, speed, efficiency, and ability to weed out repetitious listings of sites. For instance, it gives its highest score to *ixquick*, saying it is better than others in terms of finding relevant materials. Better, it avoids duplications—it lists only once the sites it reports that various engines found. *Search IQ* discusses others, too. For example, in descending order of power, it likes *Dataware*, although slower than some others; *Zworks*, which is similar to *ixquick*; *RedeSearch*; *BigHub*; *C4*; *InfoZoid*; *CNetSearch.com*; *Karnak* (very, very slow, but notably thorough), and more. *MetaIQ* has an unusual "Ask an Expert" to aid your search. Check them out at these addresses (and see my extended descriptions later in the chapter):

ixquick: *www.ixquick.com/*

Dataware: *http://queryserver.com/web.htm*

Zworks: *www.zworks.com/*

RedeSearch: *www.redesearch.com/*

BigHub: *www.thebighub.com/*

C4: *www.c4.com/*

InfoZoid: *www.infozoid.com/*

CNetSearch.com: *http://search.cnet.com/*

Karnak: *www.karnak.com/*

MetaIQ: *http://server15.hypermart.net/searchitall*

SEARCH ENGINES EVALUATED
http://libweb.uncc.edu/library/engines.html

Listed by the library at the University of North Carolina, Charlotte, the evaluations of search engines are clear and efficient. It gives its highest rating to the meta-search engine *ProFusion* (<*www.profusion.com/*>). Highest rankings for search engines go to *Google* (<*www.google.com/*>) and *Northern Light* (<*www.northernlight.com/*>).

SEARCH ENGINES WORLDWIDE
www.twics.com/~takakuwa/search/

Created and maintained by Toyo Takakuwa, *Search Engines World Wide* has entries for 1,045 directories and search engines representing 130 countries and five regions. Scroll down the left menu to the country of your choice. For the U. S. there are more than 180 engines listed with their logos. (Be patient for the download.)

RECOMMENDED SEARCH ENGINES

While there are partisan arguments about which is the "best" engine to explore the Net, there's agreement that engines like *Yahoo!* and *AltaVista* are well known and rated highly. But you needn't use *Yahoo!* if you also use a meta-search engine, because almost every meta draws from it.

A good approach is to start with a list of searchers, such as those listed in the following section, and develop your own list of favorites. The list is a compilation of research and personal use.

Internet searchers place their favorite search engines on their personal "bookmark" page. Likely you will find that the engines listed here are significantly important to deserve bookmarking. Let's start with meta-engines that compile information from a number of other engines.

Meta-Searchers

Because meta-searchers look through many search engines all at once, they are more apt to guide you to your target. Here is a list of some of the best.

IXQUICK
http://ixquick.com/

AUTHOR'S CHOICE This is an attractive site. With no annoying drop-in ads or cutsie animations, the opening page is clean and briskly efficient. It calls itself "the world's most powerful metasearch engine," and *ixquick* is rated as the most comprehensive meta-search engine. It searches 14 other engines (like *AltvaVista*, *Yahoo!*, and *InfoSeek*) and reports its findings to you, noting which search engine found the site. To indicate relevancy, it gives each site one star for each search engine that placed the site in the "top 10." This ranking often surprises me, and may need some refinement. In any case, popularity isn't necessarily what we want because some sites we seek may not rank that highly.

ZWORKS
www.zworks.com/

The opening page is rather cluttered with ads, and sometimes *Zworks* opens with that ubiquitous Punch The Monkey ad that makes me want to punch something, all right. Although ads are plentiful, *Zworks* offers no search tips or information about its services. It searches 10 engines (such as *Yahoo!*, *Northern Light*, and *Direct Hit*). *Zworks* is efficient and similar to *ixquick*, but I found it tends to be slower.

REDESEARCH
www.redesearch.com/

RedeSearch says it is the "next generation search engine." It examines 10 popular search engines (such as *Lycos*, *WebCrawler*, and *Yahoo!*) and gives you the results for each, one at a time. It lacks the speed of *Inquick*. Once loaded, it is easy to use.

C4
www.c4.com/

"Total Search Technology" proclaims the opening page, which offers various sites and an opportunity for you to personalize the site. It encourages you to ask questions as you would to a human and offers free e-mail, but it doesn't give you search tips. Apparently it will search up to 16 engines at a time but it doesn't list them. Rather annoyingly, its first response to a search is an invitation for you to join C4. That screen drops away after a while and you'll see the results of the search; each site is labeled with the logo of the search engine that found the location. It doesn't filter out duplications, and even the Boolean search (described later under Common Search Techniques) pulls up nonrelated sites.

KARNAK
www.karnak.com/

AUTHOR'S CHOICE *Karnack* is an unusual engine. It seeks thoroughness more than speed, and it uses hundreds of websites to dig far more deeply into topics than do other engines, at the same time eliminating dead sites and duplications. Calling itself "the library of infinite knowledge," its home page appropriately is an illustration of a handsome building that symbolizes research. It offers free Guest Services and Member Services. Monthly costs for the latter range from $9.99 to $49.99 depending on the number of research topics you need. Members receive e-mail updates, and information is stored at the site. The free Guest Services give you similar access but without the storage capabilities. Queries may take up to 20 minutes—which is why it e-mails you its findings—but the machine is actively searching to produce you the finest results. All in all, *Karnak* is a serious researcher's dream, and I wish I'd discovered it earlier.

DOGPILE

www.dogpile.com/

Dogpile illustrates the rapid technological evolution. It was one of the first mega-engines, and I was impressed with its capabilities when I first started using it. I still have it bookmarked, but the other engines I've listed are flashier with improved qualities. *Dogpile* examines three databases at a time, then asks you if you want it to search more. That is more cumbersome than newer meta-engines that open all databases at once. *Dogpile* also does not filter out repetitions, which get boring.

Dogpile also illustrates another trend with search engines: the merger. *Go2Net* gobbled up *Dogpile*. What that means to the two engines remains to be seen.

PROFUSION

www.profusion.com/

ProFusion is a specialized meta-search engine. It looks for five subjects. There is Entertainment—the section that interests us—as well as Health, MP3 Music Files, Sports, and Young People. It looks through nine engines, and you can select the ones you think may be most helpful.

GOOGLE

www.google.com/

Google makes heavy use of link popularity as a primary way to rank websites. It also has a technique of link analysis that leads it to search an estimated 300 million pages on the Web, more than any other search service. *Google* recently connected with *Netscape*, greatly increasing its audience. I've found that sometimes it helps to hit "reload" on its home page, giving it an e-jolt to perform.

Search Engines and Directories

Although the mega-search engines certainly have advantages in scope, the engines that examine a personally constructed database often have more depth. They will dig up more sites than the megas, which select perhaps only 10 from other engines. Many have Advanced Search buttons, which allow you to design your search. Some of the better engines are listed here.

ALTAVISTA

http://altavista.com/

AUTHOR'S CHOICE In terms of number of pages indexed, *AltaVista* is one of the largest search engines. It also has a wide range of search commands and operates efficiently. As a result, researchers think of it as a favorite engine. It also has an *Ask AltaVista* command, which really is using the *Ask Jeeves* engine. Expect its first few selections to be the most applicable to your search topic.

HOTBOT

www.hotbot.com/

HotBot recently added *Direct Hit* to its search technique. This system keeps track of what pages users select and how long they spend on such pages—what is known as "click-through data"—making it a popularity gauge. It continues to use *Inktomi*, known for its depth of coverage, but now those matches are listed following the *Direct Hit* responses.

LYCOS

www.lycos.com/

AUTHOR'S CHOICE Although the opening page is busy with offers and ads like the typical portal machine, *Lycos* is an effective, fast search engine. Helping you quickly decide which sites you want to open, it lists them by categories such as Popular, News Articles, or Websites. The feature called My Lycos allows you to personalize the page.

Lycos is engineered to be helpful. Results of some searches are selected by Lycos editors and other times the engine lists findings by popularity, based on user traffic. In either case, other sites also are listed from the complete *Lycos* catalog. Often the engine anticipates your needs and gives you categories or featured sites.

Lycos also has a huge collection of dance and theatre sites. From its opening page, click Arts and Entertainment. The next menu lists a number of folders. When I last looked, Dance had 3,436 sites, and Theatre had 3,244. Many sites are individual's Web pages, valuable to help you decide how to fashion your own home page.

EXCITE

www.excite.com/

Although its home page is typical of portal sites—cluttered—*Excite* works quickly and efficiently. For this engine, like many others, don't assume it uses Boolean; check its Help facility. Note that one special feature allows you to search by category as well as keyword. It also offers voice mail, e-mail, and current news.

NORTHERN LIGHT

www.northernlight.com/

Northern Light has one of the largest indexes of all engines, and organizes its findings by categories. It remains a favorite among those who do serious research. Take advantage of its Custom Search Folders, which pop up after you initiate a search. In those blue folders are categories that the engine thinks are relevant to your topic.

YAHOO!

www.yahoo.com/

Undoubtedly the best known search engine, *Yahoo!* has an advantage that some other engines lack: humans. It employs some 150 editors who work to put sites into categories or directories. So far they've put together more than one million sites.

GOTO

www.goto.com/

GoTo has a different theory than the other engines—if you're a webmaster, you can buy popularity. *GoTo* sells its main listings, and companies pay premiums to be placed higher in the results. *GoTo* believes that improves relevancy. It also should eliminate the problem of encountering dead sites, because people won't pay *GoTo* if their sites are defunct.

DIRECT HIT

www.directhit.com/

This is a popularity engine. *Direct Hit* judges what sites users decide to open. The sites most often selected are ranked higher in *Direct Hit's* results. A nice idea—if you believe those other people have good taste.

INFOMINE

http://infomine.ucr.edu/cgi-bin/search?arts

Some search engines are specialists. *Infomine* is designed to collect information on visual and performing arts, which makes it an excellent engine for you to try. A resource of the University of California, it has a scholarly approach.

COMMON SEARCH TECHNIQUES

Deciding which engine to use and accessing it is the first step. The second is getting used to its system and eccentricities. To get the most out of your search, note each engine's statements about its method of searching. For example, does the engine use Boolean algebra, with its system of AND and OR and NOT to determine which words to include or exclude? Perhaps the engine prefers quotation marks to indicate a phrase? Check each engine's front page for handy tips about its system.

Note that some engines give you an option to "find other sites like this one." That option usually appears on a small line following its listing of a site. If a given site is especially helpful, try clicking that "other site" announcement.

Also see if you can take advantage of an engine's particular topic groupings, shown on its first page. For instance, from the front page of *Yahoo!* you can click Arts and Humanities, then Performing Arts, which allows you to choose from several dozen entries such as Awards, Dramaturgy, Musicals, Shows, Theatre Companies, and even Vaudeville. *Yahoo!* also has an Entertainment Guide that incorporates a broad universe of materials, with theatre in the Performing Arts division.

The engines' selective guides are helpful. *Lycos*, for instance, offers the "top 5%" theatre sites. Once you've entered *Lycos*, you have two ways to access those selections. You may select Top 5%, then Culture, and finally Theater. Alternatively, you can click on Top 5% and then type in *theatre* in the search blank. Interestingly, each gives you different results. Quirky critters, these engines.

BARE BONES 101—A Basic Tutorial on Searching the Web

www.sc.edu/beaufort/library/bones.html
You find more detailed search techniques on—where else?—various websites. I mentioned earlier that *Search Engine Showdown* (*<http://searchengineshowdown.com/>*) gives good advice. *Bare Bones* is another site that can help you develop your techniques.

From the University of South Carolina's Beaufort Library comes this "tutorial" in 20 parts. Well-organized and user-friendly, this is an excellent place for getting used to Web searches. The description encourages you to plunge in:

> **Tip: Family Relatives**
> When you find a site you like, you can use your browser to look for similar pages. On Netscape, look in the upper right-hand corner for a button marked "What's Related." Click it and you may find lists of comparable places.

You can zip through these lessons in no time, any time. They are very short and succinct; each can be read in a few minutes. Feel free to jump in wherever you like, skip what you don't want to read, and come back whenever you need to.

The information contained in the following lessons is truly "bare bones," designed to get you started in the right direction with a minimum of time and effort. For more comprehensive and detailed help on searching the Web, consult our recommended list of sites in Lesson 20 at the end of this tutorial.

Don't let the apparent simplicity fool you. "Bare Bones" or not, even experienced websters are likely to find valuable tips. Most of us, I suspect, learned Web searching by plunging in on our own, and while we have a good knowledge of *some* search techniques, in our self-education process we probably skipped significant basic information. This tutorial can fill in those gaps.

These friendly search-and-find octopi will help you locate about every general page on the Web. If you want to locate additional search engines, try exploring such sites as *Argus Clearing House Internet Searching Center* (*<www.clearinghouse.net/>*).

3

40+ Best Sites to Start Searching for Theatre

An introductory caveat is important before discussing the "best" sites to gain theatrical riches: One person's selection won't be the same as another's, and undoubtedly you already have a list that works for you. Fair enough. Still, I suggest that you try the following sites; individually and collectively they can take you to an amazing number of theatre sites. No, not *every* theatre site on the Net. But a nice start. Almost every site has many links to others you may want to examine.

To select these primary sources I sought sites that were detailed, thorough, well organized, easy to access, and frequently updated. I searched out sites with depth and rich materials, and I especially looked for those that offer varied experiences. The Web pages listed here are regularly tended, an important criterion because too often sites are out of date, languishing unloved in cyber loneliness. I also chose sites that loaded relatively quickly. Attractiveness and design, while important, weren't major criterion, but most of these "best" sites are nicely engineered.

Later chapters will list sites according to specialization—Acting, Directing, Playwriting, Design, Research, and more. This chapter focuses on broad resources that you may wish to explore. The 40+ sites are divided into five groups:

- ◻ *Best sites for theatre specifically.* Fourteen outstanding theatre locations.
- ◻ *Web rings.* Fourteen different rings, each consisting of sites joined together by a common topic, such as tech theatre, playwriting, and costumes.
- ◻ *Directories of directories.* Ten master conglomerates with huge quantities of theatrical information.
- ◻ *General sites that promise to answer your questions.* Three general sites that often can be surprisingly helpful.
- ◻ *Newsgroups.* This category accounts for the + in the chapter title because the number can't be specified. There are dozens of discussion forums that you can surf.

These sites are full of theatrical nooks and crannies to explore. Each site is listed in this chapter with an address and detailed description. For a wealth of theatre sites, you can start your search with the richly informational *Artslynx*, an extremely well-organized tool. You might then move next to *Theatre Central*, *Scott's Theatre-Link Dot Com*, and *Drama and Theater Connections*. For show biz information about theatrical techniques and practices, shows now playing, and the professional, regional, and amateur scenes, look at *Playbill on-Line* and *Talkin' Broadway*. For authoritative sources and research, go to *McCoy's Guide to Resources in Theatre and Performance Studies*, *The Encyclopedia Britannica*, and *Theatre and Drama Virtual Library*. Canada's *CultureNet* illustrates the best of a national focus on its culture, and *Canadian Theatre WebRing* is a rich series of connected links.

After those, look next at the 10 "conglomerate" directories of theatrical sites, which contain lists of lists. In these you'll need to explore the entries to search out the information you seek. Sites like *About.com*, *AltaVista*, *HotBot*, *Netscape*, *Lycos*, and *Yahoo!* offer categories of nearly everything the world experiences. *Performing Arts Links* and *Performing Arts Online* are more directly aimed at our specific interests.

Finally, see if three nontheatre broad-based sites can help you. Pose questions to *Info Please*, *Ask Me*, and *Ask Jeeves*.

All links were alive and well when I last checked them, but the World Wide Web is a fluid creature and things fluctuate. (Hey, this is the Net, consistent in its changes!) If there's a moral here, it's that when we find a site we respect, we should give the webmasters positive feedback and support to help keep it alive.

> **Security Alert—
> Ordering Online**
> Sites often have online ordering facilities for you to purchase tickets, books, or gifts, or to make travel reservations. Please be careful. Identity theft is becoming more prevalent, and you want to avoid putting yourself at risk.
>
> Double-check the security arrangements the site says it has, and do not give your credit card or other personal information until you are certain you are protected. Also use your Web browser's particular security indicators. If you use Netscape, for example, note the padlock on the top tool bar. For information, click your browser's Help feature and then Security.

14 SITES SPECIFICALLY FOR THEATRE

With some trepidation, I list the following 14 sites in order of value. Of course, you may rank them in different order. As experienced Netters know, this list is larger than it may appear—each individual site contains numerous links to additional sites that can be helpful. Prepare to surf.

INTERNATIONAL ARTS RESOURCES—ARTS LINKS TO THEATRE, DANCE, MUSIC, AND MORE FROM ARTSLYNX

www.artslynx.org/

—or take a short cut directly to the theatre location—

ARTSLYNX INTERNATIONAL THEATRE RESOURCES

www.artslynx.org/theatre/index.htm

AUTHOR'S CHOICE Think of Lynx as *links* and you understand this site. With a neat and well-organized series of connecting icons, *Artslynx* has master folders for Dance, Visual Arts, Writing, Film, Arts Administration, Music, Arts of Social Responsibility, Education, and Arts Advocacy. All are rich in resources. *Artslynx* also is well-engineered—it connects quickly and effectively.

Alphabet Soup is the webmaster's connection to an "amazing list of arts support organizations" that, he says, makes sense of the arts. There you find organizations listed by their acronyms. They range from American Arts Alliance to Young Audiences, including some from countries such as Canada, Britain, and Japan. Most have links to the group's headquarters. Some have such intriguing titles that you feel compelled to investigate. Center for Cognitive Studies of the Moving Image?

Arts of Social Responsibility is an intriguing and well-named page. It has entries for Art Therapy, Arts Access, Arts for People with Disabilities, Arts of the Oppressed, and Feminism and Women's Arts Resources and Connections. Each has a number of sources. For example, the entry for Health and Rehabilitation Issues such as Alcohol and Drugs takes you to a number of sites, including The Improbable Players, a professional touring theatre company based in Boston, that gives performances about alcohol and abuse, especially insightful because the actors are recovering addicts.

The *Artslynx* theatre section is a joy. From the home page click on Theatre (or go directly to <*www.artslynx.org/theatre/index.htm*>) and you will find helpful information about Books, Children's Theatre, Acting, Combat, Costume Design and History, Performance, Design (Makeup, Scenic, Lighting), Dramaturgy, Musical Theatre, Puppetry, Fight Direction, Playwriting, Technical Theatre, and much more.

Students, dramaturgs, and researchers looking for informational materials will want to use its links to Theatre Libraries and Research Resources, plus Theatre History Resources, where you'll find libraries and collections. For the theatre buff, it has a special This Month in Theatre history link. For those seeking jobs, there are links to Employment and Jobs, but when I last visited, there were the same 12 hookups under both.

All in all, *Artslynx* is a model of thoroughness and excellence. Using it is easy, rewarding, fun.

THEATRE CENTRAL

www1.playbill.com/cgi-bin/plb/central?cmd=start

Easy to enter from *Playbill on-Line* (below), *Theatre Central* is a well-maintained and comprehensive searchable web of links to theatre. Many experienced theatre Netters would place it first in this list of "best" sites, and certainly it is a principal place to visit to find information about stars, productions, and current theatrical news.

Theatre Central claims it has "the largest compendium of theatre links on the internet," and you aren't likely to argue when you see its depth of coverage. From the home page click on Sites and you'll find a long menu that is organized under headings such as Celebrity Sites, Dance, For the Playwright, Musical Theatre Sites, Professional Theatre Companies, Stagecraft, and Stage and Technical Crew.

Actors will want to go to Sites to check Audition Notices and to look at news about productions and casting. You'll find a lengthy list of possibilities across America and Canada, as well as in other countries, such as Germany and Australia.

Andrew Kraft updates *Theatre Central* regularly, so you'll find last-minute information. It includes an up-to-date calendar of international theatre events and related message and chat boards.

Do you want to find a specific theatre artist who has a Net presence? Try Connections, a central resource for contacting and communicating with theatre artists throughout the world who have specific interests or background. You have two ways to see if that artist has a site. First, the Directory search engine allows you to look by keywords for professionals who are interested in Musical Theatre, Dramaturgy, Directing, or a number of other interests. The lists are long. Clicking a given name will lead you to a brief biography and a hookup to a website. Alternatively, you can browse the entire list, although you may have time to get a cup of coffee while you wait for it to download. You can add your theatre's link or put yourself in the Connections list.

PLAYBILL ON-LINE—The Theatre Source on the Web for Broadway Theatre Information

www1.playbill.com/playbill/

When you attend a Broadway show, you receive a booklet that contains the production's program and other information. That booklet is an edition of *Playbill*. This is its cyber kissin' cousin.

The Broadway part of the site's title, however, is misleading because *Playbill on-Line* is not restricted to Manhattan theatre. While it has definitive listings for current theatre productions both on and off Broadway, it also offers guides for sites throughout the United States (including summer stock, regional theatres, and national touring shows), London, Canada, and other countries. The site has online facilities for you to arrange travel packages and tickets.

One of the major theatrical sites—and of impressive size—*Playbill on-Line* is especially valuable because it has so many entries and, more important, because it is regularly updated. Folders lead you to Late News on the shows now playing as well as people, productions, and awards. Theatrical Listings are complete. There even is information about New York hotels and seating charts of major theatres. Of special note is the Casting and Jobs folder.

Playbill on-Line has up-to-date information about openings, shows now offering discount tickets, and details about important theatrical awards such as the Tony and Obie. You can find how Broadway shows are faring financially. Its college database, although a bit limited, is helpful for those seeking information about educational institutions. Feature articles about shows, a searchable list of biographies, and a chat area are nice additions.

Mixed with the factual information are chatty columns and interviews with significant people in the theatre. Diva Talk, for example, is a weekly column that worships popular stars, and Brief Encounter contains an interview with significant personalities. One such interview is with Marni Nixon, one of the best-known unknown movie songsters and an accomplished live performer. She was the unaccredited voice you heard singing for Deborah Kerr (*The King and I* and *An Affair to Remember*), Natalie Wood (*West Side Story*), and Audrey Hepburn (*My Fair Lady*). This site also leads you to fan sites.

Here, too, you'll find commercial sites such as *Tele-Charge* to help you buy tickets for New York and London plays. You can purchase tickets online (members receive discounts); order books from the Dramabook Store, known for its rich theatre collection; and find gifts at One Shubert Alley, which offers theatrical memorabilia such as posters, T-shirts, music scores, mugs, and so forth.

From this site you can access *Theatre Central* (described earlier).

DRAMA AND THEATER CONNECTIONS
http://libweb.uncc.edu/ref-arts/theater/

Compiled by the J. Murrey Atkins Library at the University of North Carolina, this guide to theatrical websites has a librarian's crisp organizational system. Among the entries you'll find are Actors and Acting, Jobs, Biographies, Electronic Indexes, Electronic Journals, Theater and Drama Research, Plays and Playwriting, Costume and Scene Design, Lighting, and Shakespeare.

Actors and Acting leads you to Star Bios, subdivided into actors, actresses, and comedians (but, strangely, not singers or dancers). Performance Art offers mime, clown, and performance art sites.

General Sites and Links is a selective list of places you may want to visit to discover theatrical activities in America and other countries. Research Tips leads you to a Comprehensive Research Guide, valuable although needing an update. Directly applicable to the UNC library, the guide is easily adapted to other libraries.

ENCYCLOPAEDIA BRITANNICA
www.britannica.com or *www2.britannica.com/*

The *Britannica* has had an interesting recent e-history, one that, frankly, has me confused. In late 1999, when it announced it was making its complete works available online *at no cost*, the resulting surge of hits jammed the site and the webmaster had to reorganize to handle the heavy traffic. The heavy influx of visitors is not surprising. The print version of *Britannica* has long had an enviable reputation for scholarly excellence, and for it to make its resources available—free!—on the Net was remarkably generous.

The *Brit* then grew. In a year it featured a lively page full of contemporary events, and entry was via *<www.eblast.com>*. It wasn't your grandfather's *Brit*. On that page, for example, you'd see an article about Brittany Spears' belly button (yes, really!) or annotations of Dennis Miller's football commentary. These articles were not merely about mod happenings; they were clever and well-written scholarly pieces, tracing, for example, the way various cultures made the belly button a ritualistic icon or the literary references inherent in Miller's comments. At that time the *Brit* had a very large number of editors—apparently more than 40, to judge by one editor's comments to me—and it actively recruited freelance writers. Those contemporary event pages were full of rich detail.

More recently, the dot-com disappointment struck the *Brit*. The editorial staff was severely downsized, and a stable of writers disappeared. The result was the loss of *e-blast* and the lively page.

What does this series of events mean? I suggest we should keep checking the *Britannica* site to see how it evolves. With or without that contemporary page, this is a primary source for information.

From the home page, use its efficient search engine and you'll find excellent reference materials. The *Brit* has a marvelous way of listing reference materials. Of course you'll find its own articles, all scholarly and definitive, but you'll also see authoritative websites, periodicals, and added information.

> **More Sources of Encyclopedias**
> A number of other excellent encyclopedias are online (an *AltaVista* search found 5,209,415 pages!). For example, *Encyclopedia.Com* is an e-version of the Columbia version (*<www.encyclopedia.com/>*); although free, it does require you to register. It also wants to send you ads, but it gives you an opt-out clause. *Encarta* (*<www.encarta.msn.com/>*) can be a helpful reference. Canadians will want to look at *The Encyclopedia of Canadian Theatre*, although despite its name it isn't limited to theatre (*<www.canadiantheatre.com/>*).

TALKIN' BROADWAY

www.TalkinBroadway.com/

Whatever you are looking for regarding theatrical events on Broadway and off Broadway, plus information on selected geographic regions outside of New York, likely it is here. This regularly updated site is large and thorough, and some 30 different contributors keep it rich and lively. There are reviews of shows in New York and around the United States as well as in Canada and London. You also can look at informative guides to restaurants or read interviews with significant theatrical folk.

Talkin' Broadway says that its "purpose and goal is to promote and support live theatre and the theatrical arts in both the cultural and political arenas," and it reports that it has thousands of daily readers, with expectation of growth. No doubt those theatre Netters are attracted by the breezy atmosphere, wide variety of offerings, authoritative expert opinions, and insight into individuals and shows.

Broadway 101 is a historical trip through the Great White Way. Arranged by decades, Robert Rusie starts in 1810 and relates the development of the fabled theatrical center. Colorful illustrations help you envision the growth of theatre. The Broadway of Yesteryear Gallery has photographs and prints ranging from 1650 to 1905. Browsing the gallery and reading Rusie's history is required for all theatre buffs.

What's New at the Rialto? is a frequent column of theatre events, people, and productions. Author V. J. arranges for interesting and witty interviews with people you'd like to know better, and at the bottom of the page is a link to past Rialto columns, all worth exploring. (Okay, honest and full disclosure here. They interviewed me for my book *The Power of One*—<*www.talkinbroadway .com/rialto/past/2000/4_9_00.html*>—so I could be prejudiced. Certainly I felt honored because interviews usually are with well-known stars. But I can testify that I was impressed with the professionalism of the interview technique, and I now read the interviews with increased respect.)

On the Boards lists all Broadway productions (there is a companion off-Broadway location), most linked to reviews. For all, you can click on one of the ticket ordering companies.

The Regional page has reviews of theatrical productions in major cities such as Toronto, Pittsburgh, Washington, Atlanta, Seattle, St. Louis, San Francisco, Los Angeles, Phoenix, and St. Louis.

There is a lively, high-volume chat board that is populated by knowledgeable fans with passion, and you'll also find shopping information and current awards. Spotlight On has regular biographical sketches of significant theatrical artists. Sound Advice comments on cast albums. Broadway Bound is an ongoing column in which Michael Reynolds creates a dialog between two people to chronicle his development of a musical, in the process giving excellent advice about the playwriting process. (I suppose full disclosure again is in order: In two columns [*<www.talkinbroadway.com/bound/10.html>* and *<http://talkinbroadway.com/bound/12.html>*] Reynolds mentions a couple of my playwriting books. I would've enjoyed his columns even if he hadn't.)

The Internet Theatre Database alone would make this an outstanding site. It states its mission simply: "The Internet Theatre Database is to provide all aspects of theatre information free of charge." A four-person staff is accumulating the materials, and so far they have recorded basic information on most Broadway shows since 1975 and most musicals for the past 50 years. When I last visited they reported they had entered several thousand Broadway shows and about 70 off-Broadway shows.

McCOY'S GUIDE TO THEATRE AND PERFORMANCE STUDIES
www.stetson.edu/departments/csata/thr_guid.html

Maintained by Ken McCoy at Stetson University and regularly updated, this guide consists of his selections of significant sites that fit his criteria: unique or interesting, somewhat off the beaten path, or examples of well-managed and productive sites. The outline organization is admirable and easy to use.

Valuable are his two lists of guides. First, Places That Help Me the Most has 16 interesting sites (including one for knots!). Second, Other World Wide Web Resources by Topic is thorough and put together with logical divisions ranging from actors to technical theatre, arts management to Shakespeare.

Researchers, students, and dramaturgs will like Finding Primary Materials, which reflects McCoy's interest in scholarship and will take you to electronic and print materials. Potpourri: The Best of the Rest is an eclectic mixture of sites, many with such interesting descriptions that you're likely to surf around.

He also has an international vision, guiding you to sites from or about other nations.

CULTURE NET (Canada)
www.ffa.ucalgary.ca/

This is an excellent site that could be a model for other countries. Its dedication to promoting national cultural richness undoubtedly helps all Canadian arts programs. I found no other country with such a strong site. Too bad. A site like this demonstrates a country proud of its diverse artistic activities.

Calling itself an electronic window on Canadian culture, *CultureNet* is a list of links for Canadian Networks and serves individuals and organizations from all areas of Canada and from all cultural disciplines. It is available in both English and French versions.

It has a cultural events calendar with a fast and efficient search engine, and when I last visited the site it listed almost 300 events from 340 different towns. There is an impressive list of organizational and individual members.

THE WWW VIRTUAL LIBRARY—Theatre and Drama
http://vl-theatre.com/

The master home page—*The Virtual Library*—is an overview of various sites. This *Theatre and Drama* section is one category, and it says that it now records more than one million hits a year. Worth noting is its commitment to keep information current: It updates the site daily.

WWW *Theatre and Drama* offers links to resources in more than 40 countries. From its home page you select categories such as Academic/Training Institutions World Wide, General Organizations and Resources, Plays in Print, or Theatre Companies World Wide. Each category contains numerous connections. For example, General Organizations holds well over 100 links that represent such countries as Africa, Australia, Belgium, Canada, England, France, Germany, Italy, Scotland, Wales, and the United States.

For international study, click on Theatre Companies World Wide. From Argentina to Venezuela, you'll find 42 different countries listed.

A highlight is an excellent Plays on Line, which uses an alphabetical guide to playwrights from across the world. Strong, too, is its effective search engine. You'll also find guides to Academic and Training Institutions, Newsgroups, and Theatre Journals, Studies, and Articles.

This is a detailed and important site. Some patient surfing here very likely will help you find information on a wide range of theatre topics.

SCOTT'S THEATRE-LINK.COM
http://theatre-link.com/

A rich collection of sites and resources, *Scott's* says it is "Your complete guide to all aspects of theatre on the Net!" Oversell? Well, let's call it enthusiasm, and at any rate *Scott's* is a thorough site designed to help you find the virtual information you need.

Scott's offers an Index that it describes as an organized way to find what you're looking for, saying that it contains many thousands of theatre-related sites. Among the topics are academic theatres, casting and auditions, and Broadway and London's West End theatres. Helpful areas include News and Information, Goods and Services, Theatrical Unions, Plays and Playwrights, Research Sources, and Shakespeare. Alternatively, you can search its database.

There's an active message board for questions and discussions. When I visited, there were many questions asking for help finding a particular play or an audition piece. Answers were direct and helpful.

If you're looking for a job, check *Scott's* Theatre Design and Technical Jobs Page. It also can lead you to National Theatre Design Archive, Dance and Musical Theatre, and a U. K. Theatre Web.

If you have a website, *Scott's* invites you to add a link to it. You get a password that gives you access to your entry so you can make changes.

CANADIAN THEATRE WEBRING
http://members.nbci.com/theatre2/cdntheatrewebring.htm

A Web ring, speaking generally, is a system that supports a nearly unlimited number of separate but connected sites across the Internet, each feeding the others. The theory of a Web ring is that it provides an easy way for visitors to navigate the Web to find sites that have similar interest areas.

We have two ways of accessing the connected sites. One is usually found at the bottom of the ring site, and it allows you to move forward or backward, sending you to the next member site. That's a crapshoot: You don't know where you'll go. The other method of accessing is through the ring's directory.

The webmaster of the *Canadian Theatre Webring* shows admirably high standards in the site's introductory statement about progress and plans for the future. Significantly, several candidates seeking to join have been rejected because they do not address the site requirements, and there is a system that automatically checks all member sites are alive and well. These steps suggest a healthy approach to make this an important ring.

More than 60 different sites were present when I looked. They include professional and amateur theatrical organizations, schools, vendors of theatrical supplies, and organizations. For example, Services Guide is a directory of businesses, organizations, and individuals that provide products or services to theatre. Stage Door Toronto describes the many productions offered by a host of that city's theatre companies. Representative of service organizations is the Toronto Theatre Alliance, which represents Toronto's professional theatre and dance companies. Each site provides more links.

ASSOCIATION FOR THEATRE IN HIGHER EDUCATION
www2.hawaii.edu/athe

ATHE is an organization of individuals and institutions that band together to promote excellence in theatre education. Many members teach theatre in colleges and universities, and at ATHE annual conventions they participate in panels and discussions on a broad range of topics connected to educational theatre.

Although its website seems quite limited for such a significant national organization, it does offer links to a variety of its publications (click on Resources).

THEATRE RESOURCES—Rhodes
www.rhodes.edu/Theatrehtmls/theatrenet.html

Rhodes College in Memphis gives us an efficient list of sites in six basic categories: General Collections, Technical Resources, Drama Resources, Awards and Reviews, Theatre Home Pages and Guides, and Electronic Journals, Listservs, and Reference. Although relatively brief in comparison to some megadirectories, the contents are valuable.

Because the links at the top of the page don't fully describe contents, you might want to ignore them and instead scroll down. You'll find that General Resources is well-named: In this potpourri there are links for acting, sites based in Canada and the U. K., theatre history, and more.

Notice that at the top of the page above the title is a link to Internet Resouces. Worth exploring, it will lead you to Metasites, Resources by Subject, and Selected New Websites (frequently updated).

THE THEATRE RESOURCE
www.theatre-resource.com/

Want to see ambition? Look at *Theatre Resource's* statement of goals. Webmaster Darleen Viloria says:

> This is an attempt to put you in touch with virtually every theatre person and organization with a presence on the Internet. An overwhelming task, I know, but it is all about education—yours and mine. I especially like the twist in the following sentence: After all, it's true what they say about this business: It's all about who you know.

The site is determined to help you know. Although new, it shows every promise of continuing to grow. It is frequently updated.

You have your choice of left or right menus—strangely, both are the same—to access a number of sources: Theatre Organizations; Regional; Theatre Training; University; Research-Inspiration; Theatre Jobs; For Actors, Directors, Playwrights; Theatre Business; Your Local Scene. Each leads you to selected sites, briefly annotated. The People/Webrings should become a significant contribution to Viloria's goal of listing theatre folks on the Net.

14 WEB RINGS FOR THEATRE

Web rings consist of a number of interlaced sites that share a mutual interest or common theme. One ring may focus on, say, costume pages; another may deal with playwriting; yet another may consist of sound design; and so forth. Rings are more effective if the webmaster approves proposed sites for relevance before adding them to the ring. Most rings are made up of individuals; in some rings, however, there also are theatre companies and suppliers.

Each ring site has a box for you to click to go to the next or previous site at random. Alternatively, you can view the whole list and select a specific site you want to visit.

Sizes of theatre rings seem to vary, from only half a dozen or so to 50 or more. The rings listed here will, collectively, lead you to hundreds of sites. Here you see just the title and the URL, but the rings are described throughout this book in appropriate chapters. When the title isn't self-explanatory, I've added a descriptive note.

THE ART OF THEATRE WEBRING
www.geocities.com/Broadway/Stage/9496/aotwr.html

THE BOSIP WEBRING—Backstage, On Stage, and In the Pit
www.webring.org/cgi-bin/webring?ring=frenetics;id=39;next5

CANADIAN THEATRE WEBRING
http://members.nbci.com/theatre2/cdntheatrewebring.htm

THE CASTING NETWORK.COM, INC.
www.thecastingnetwork.com/webring.html

By actors and for actors, this ring provides comprehensive databases of auditions, casting directors, talent agents, and the like.

THE COSTUME WEBRING
www.marquise.de/webring/costumering.html

DESIGN IMAGE ONLINE
www.performance-design.com/dol/desimage.html

For all designers—scene, lighting, costume, sound. Includes CAD and computer graphics.

THE GAFF TAPE WEBRING
http://members.aol.com/thegoop/gaff.html
Tech theatre.

THE GARB'N FROCK RING
www.geocities.com/Paris/4440/costuming.html
Costumes, including commercial sites.

MAKEUP ARTIST WEBRING
www.geocities.com/Hollywood/Hills/5829/myring.html

LA RONDE—The Playwright's Ring
www.pipeline.com/%7Ejude/AboutLaRonde.htm

TECHNICAL THEATRE RING
http://icdweb.cc.purdue.edu/~jfrederi/hiddenworld/webring.html

THEATRE AND CONCERT LIGHTING DESIGNERS WEBRING (Also appears as Stage and Concert Lighting Designers)
www.geocities.com/Broadway/Stage/5429/ldringhm.htm

THEATRE SOUND DESIGNER AND COMPOSER RING
www.ashland.net/madrone/tsound_ring.html

THESPIAN THEATRE WEBRING
www.geocities.com/Broadway/Stage/1425/thespian.html

YAHOO! WEBRING
http://dir.webring.yahoo.com/rw

Yahoo! here lists Web rings in all categories. For theatre, use the search engine. Alternatively, click on Entertainment and the Arts and then select from the various categories such as Performing Arts or Actors and Actresses. Playwrights can click on Books and Writing to find rings.

10 CONGLOMERATE CATEGORY SITES

Perhaps this category could be called "database sites." Or "what you were looking for but didn't know you wanted." Or "everything including the kitchen sink."

The 10 sites listed here are links of links, directories of directories, master locations that have put together categories of sites—such as Finance and Entertainment—according to some master plan. Here we look at the categories of theatre directories.

ABOUT.COM
www.about.com/

"The Network of sites led by expert guides," this site features a potpourri of news, humor, tips, and more. Its front page offers an index of 28 categories such as Finance and Investing, People and Relationships, and Pets. Clicking on Arts and Literature takes you to an index (<*http://home.about.com/arts/index .htm*?PM=59_0201_T>). There you'll find topics such as American Theatre, Ballet and Dance, British Theatre, and Performance Art (along with Classical Music, Jazz, and Magic and Illusion).

Inside the American Theatre file are numerous subjects, from Actors to Women's Theatre. The site also has chatty bits of information, such as what to do if someone is talking during a performance (politely ask 'em to knock it off) or how to see a Broadway show for free (slip in during the hubbub of the intermission).

ALTA VISTA: THEATRE
http://dir.altavista.com/

AltaVista has one of the better categorizations, and its organization is logical and accessible. From its home page, click Arts and Entertainment. At the next page, click Arts and Culture, then choose Musical Theater, Theater, or Dance.

You'll find Advocates, Community Theater, Costuming, Dinner Theatre, Directing, Dramaturgy, Education and Training, Experimental, Improvisation,

Link Directories, Musicals, NYC Off Broadway, People, Physical Theatre, Plays, Production, Reference, Reviews, Listings and Articles, Shakespeare, Shows, Special Effects Makeup, Stage Managers, Stage Movement, Stagecraft, Technical, Theatre Shops, Theatres and Troupes, and Tickets.

Despite the number of entries, however, there are conspicuous holes. Among the missing were Acting, Sound Design, and Playwriting.

HOTBOT

http://dir.hotbot.lycos.com/Arts

HotBot has so many entries you could spend a couple of days surfing. The address here takes you to Arts & Entertainment, where you have choices— and choices and choices. This section of *HotBot* constantly grows, and each time I visit I find that the number of listings has increased. The last time I visited, Performing Arts had 10,422 sites (an increase of about 800 in a week), and its Theatre division had 3,244.

Click on Theatre and you'll find 35 categories, similar to *AltaVista* and also omitting Acting and Playwriting (although there is a large list of playwrights) but including Sound.

LYCOS

www.lycos.com/

I discussed *Lycos* in the previous chapter. Now we can look at its lists for theatre and dance. On the opening page, scroll down a bit and you'll see categories such as Travel, News, Autos, and so forth. Clicking on Arts and Entertainment takes you to another menu, where you find Dance (3,436 listings), Performing Arts (10,042), and Theatre (3,244). Performing Arts is the one to click. It lists Acting and Mime, but the Theatre site does not (you can go there directly with this address: *<http://dir.lycos.com/Arts/Performing_Arts>*). The basic lists of ingredients are similar to *AltaVista* and *HotBot*, but the contents vary in some cases. You also can scroll down to find valuable hand-picked sites that the *Lycos* editors recommend and describe briefly.

NETSCAPE

http://directory.netscape.com/Arts/Performing_Arts/Theatre

Many of us use *Netscape* as our basic browser, although perhaps fewer use the My Netscape feature (*<http://my.netscape.com>*). It has 15 Search Categories, such as Arts, Computers, Games, Health, or Sports.

Clicking on Arts (*<http://directory.netscape.com/Arts/index.html>*) leads you to almost 40 subjects, from Animation to Writers' Resources (and let's not get involved in wondering if they are all "arts"). You then select Theatre, which has a staggering 2,525 entries. Once there you may be mystified by the organization—I was—but a bit of patient scrolling will allow you to find areas you want. Note the international entries.

PERFORMING ARTS LINKS—INDEX

www.theatrelibrary.org/links/index.html

AUTHOR'S CHOICE This index is neatly organized, updated regularly, clean, attractive in its logical arrangement, and thorough in its coverage of international links. It is arranged in master categories of Cinema, Dance, Theatre, and Reviews.

Each category has sites in logical patterns. For the theatre group, for example, there is a heading for Actors, followed by a box of links to General, Local (Great Britain and the United States), Mailing Lists, and Personal Pages.

The pattern continues for Genre, History, Plays and Playwrights, Costume and Set Design, and Technology. It concludes with Mailing Lists, Newsgroups, and Libraries: General Resources.

The international flavor is strong. For example, Local lists almost 30 countries.

The theatre section (<*www.theatrelibrary.org/links/ActorsHistory.html#theatre*>) is an unusual site with unique ingredients. The home page starts not with a flurry of visuals but instead moves immediately to an index of links. There you discover the major strength of this site: It lists materials not found on other mega-directory sites or through usual Web searches.

It is effectively organized, primarily on historical materials that are subdivided into Ancient Theatre, Medieval Theatre, 15th–18th Centuries, and 19th–20th Centuries. There also is information for actors and playwrights. Maria Teresa Iovinelli, your hostess, apparently revises and updates the site frequently.

PERFORMING ARTS ONLINE

www.PerformingArts.net/Links/i-nlinks.html

Links that are "relevant to the Performing Arts Industry" are here, subdivided into Performing Artists (Dance, Music, and Theatre) and Organizations, Teachers, and Resources. Additionally, there are interesting sites from numerous countries.

The home page says there are several hundred links. That's an underestimate. But you'll want to be discriminating as you search because many of the personal sites in the four Performing Artists categories are, sadly, pretty much fluff stuff.

Better are the categories that deal with broader topics: Performing Arts Organizations; Performing Arts Management; Performing Arts Schools, Colleges, Workshops; Performing Arts Resources; and Performing Arts Links. These materials justify listing this site in a chapter of "bests."

WORLD WIDE ARTS RESOURCES—VISUAL ARTS, PERFORMING ARTS, AND RESOURCES

http://wwar.com

Although apparently more heavily weighted toward the visual arts, you find links to Dance and Theatre when you scroll down to Performing Arts. Both lead to other links. The Theatre section has entries for a number of subdivisions, such as acting, design, playwriting, producing, and—oops, WWAR, engage your spell checker—"coreography." There also are entries for Talent Agencies, Youth Theatre, and Companies. An alphabetized listing includes links you'd expect to find in the basic categories.

While it has fewer links than you'll find on other conglomerate sites, you're likely to find some that aren't uncovered elsewhere. You also can go to a Chat, subscribe to the free Arts News, and see Arts Resumes.

YAHOO!

www.yahoo.com/

Yahoo! has pages—and pages and pages!—of directories with an absurd lack of organization, rather as if the selection-organization process is assigned to a robot that is a few chips shy of a full operating system. Once you do manage to find the theatre location, there are only nine sites listed. The trick is to search out these other places:

Yahoo! Drama Resources

http://dir.yahoo.com/Arts/Humanities/Literature/Genres/Drama

Here the categories are Greek Tragedy, Playwrighting (someone please tell the Yahoos! that those who write plays are "playwrights" and the act of writing plays is "playwriting"), and scripts.

Yahoo! Costuming

http://dir.yahoo.com/Arts/Design_Arts/Stagecraft/Costuming

It says Costuming, but the robot probably was playing SimCity when it put this index together (a better directory for costumes is described next). You likely won't be interested in Furry or Halloween, and there are no entries under Costume History, Fashion, or Makeup. Perhaps Masks, Organizations, and Web Directories can be useful.

Yahoo! Design Arts

http://dir.yahoo.com/Arts/Design_Arts/Stagecraft

Here you can find more than 50 sites for Costuming plus a few entries for Lighting (five sites) and Set Design (one).

Yahoo!—Performing Arts

http://dir.yahoo.com/Arts/Performing_Arts

Along with other Circus and Historical Reenactment categories— these are "arts"?—there are theatrical categories such as Performance Arts (with 97 listings), Stage Combat (24), Street Performance (29), and Theater (2,134). It sounds huge, but once you enter it you'll note that for such aspects of theatre as Acting, Stagecraft, Lighting, Costuming, Playwriting, and Plays, the number of sites is zip. Nada. *Yahoo!* logic at work: no entries at all. The large sites are Theater Companies (976 sites), Musicals (521), Education (145), and Youth Theatre (81).

THE OPEN DIRECTORY PROJECT
http://dmoz.org/Arts/

This site, which is staffed by a number of volunteer editors, seems to be growing rapidly. The last time I visited, it had slightly over 3,000 sites for Theatre and 400 more for Dance.

DOZENS OF NEWSGROUPS

Bulletin boards, discussion groups, forums, newsgroups—these lively exchanges of information have had different names since they were founded back in BI, the dark ages Before the Internet, e-mail, and all the e-world we now take for granted. Those early groups were disorganized until *Deja.com* brought e-order by making a hierarchy of subjects that cover what seems to be a zillion topic areas and subdivisions. That is the *Usenet* and its many *alt* bulletin boards, such as *alt.stagecraft* and *alt.acting*, where people go to an interest group and make general comments, ask questions, state opinions. Patient surfing can help you find countless bits of info for theatre and dance.

Deja.com (described below) makes this statement: "It is said that the sum total of human knowledge is posted to Usenet every two weeks." That's a hard-to-believe stunner. With that I should add that you'll find displays of human ignorance because these forums are not moderated and people can post whatever they wish—spam, flames, wacko opinions without substance, and more. Call it Free Speech. Unlike sites we've mentioned, there's no webmaster, no one "in charge."

Still, many forums indeed do contain valuable information. Luckily for us, that's true for theatre and dance forums. You'll find enthusiastic, sometimes opinionated, posts, some from obviously highly experienced theatre workers and others from newbies. For more information about the *Usenet* and *alt.groups*, you may want to look at So You Want to Create an Alt Newsgroup at <*www.visi.com/~barr/alt-creation-guide.html*>.

DEJACOM USENET DISCUSSION SERVICE
www.deja.com/usenet

Deja.com is your portal to discussion forums. If you've never been on board Usenet, stop first at Learn the Basics (left-hand menu), where you'll find details about how it works. Important for you is information about searching for topics. Certainly the more proficient you are with the search engine and power search, the better your chances you'll find what you want.

The best way to start is to use the *Deja.com* search engine, appropriately the first thing you see on the home page. Valuable instructions next to the engine—Search Tips and Power Search—will help you find your path and prevent casual surfing. On the other hand, this place is a magnet for surfers, who can wander for hours through the labyrinth.

Using the engine to search for *theatre*, for example, will lead you to forums for musicals and tech, as well as *Star Trek* and movies. Dance takes you to one appropriate site, plus nonrelevant forums like scientology and quilting. Acting also gives you one discussion forum and—h'mm—there's scientology again, paired with British politics. Stagecraft pointed to two forums and something or other about vampires. You'll conclude that the search engine sometimes gets derailed, but it is at least partially successful.

Instead of the engine, you can look in the categories of forums. Under *alt*, for example, you'll find forums such as *alt.stagecraft* and *alt.acting*. In *rec.arts* you can see *rec.arts.stagecraft* (also *rec.arts.theatre.stagecraft*) plus acting and stagecraft. The more you experiment with the forums, the more tricks you learn. For example, the category search engine recognizes more entries under the *theater* spelling than *theatre*.

3 SITES TO ANSWER YOUR QUESTIONS

The previous websites were focused on theatre. The following three are broad-based and promise to answer questions.

ASK JEEVES
www.askjeeves.com/

I debated whether to include *Ask Jeeves* in this list of "best" sources. It is a bit lightweight. Still, it is the program that *AltaVista* uses to answer questions, and it can lead you to interesting sites. For example, try clicking on the Entertainment channel and then asking, "What are the best theatre sites?" *Jeeves* quickly gives you choices to investigate, such as "Where can I find education and career resources?" "What academic institutions offer programs?" "Where can I find publications?" or "Where can I find a concise encyclopedia article?" The search works well.

On the other hand, however, *Jeeves* has a dry sense of humor. Asking "An Acting career?" led to one helpful site ("Where can I find job listings for entertainment?"), but *Jeeves* also replied with two entries for finding information about job listings and career choices—not for theatre but for law. H'mm. Is *Jeeves* making a comment about lawyers?

ASKME.COM
www.AskMe.com/BusinessSplash.asp

Great answers from real people, the site claims, adding that 2.5 million people use the service. Registration (free) is required to participate. You select a category, pick an "expert," and ask your question. As you would guess, the effectiveness depends on both the quality of the question and the insight of the expert. To select an expert to ask, you can view thumbnail bios of those on call.

There are a number of categories ranging from Arts and Leisure to Travel. Hot Topics deals with the subjects de jour, and when I looked at them they included assorted areas like Academy Awards and Technology Stocks.

Theatre is within Arts and Leisure, as are Dance, Music, and diverse other subjects (even Cigars and Tobacco!). To bypass the various pages you can go there directly (<*www.AskMe.com/cat/ShowCategory_979_xp_1.htm*>). A bevy of experts is ready to answer questions regarding Acting, Actors and Actresses, Broadway Theater, Costuming and Scenic Design, Musical Theater, and so on.

What is the level of expertise? As you'd expect, it varies. You can read the public questions before deciding if you want to give a particular expert a try.

INFO PLEASE
www.infoplease.com/index.html

AUTHOR'S CHOICE This online dictionary, Internet encyclopedia, and almanac has a bit of everything, and in some cases a great deal more than you can find elsewhere. For example, when I was unable to open *Drama Desk* (<*www.dramadesk.theatre.com*>) to get details about Drama Desk Awards, I went to *Info Please*. Scroll down to Entertainment, click Performing Arts, and you find options for Broadway, off Broadway, and off-off Broadway seasons and statistics, as well as for Dance and Opera.

There's also a link to Performing Arts Awards—All-Time Top Tony Winners and Nominees, Recipients of Kennedy Center Honors, New York Drama Critics' Circle Awards, Outer Critics Circle Awards, Drama League Awards, Pulitzer Awards, Obie Awards, and—bingo! what I wanted!—Drama Desk Awards.

These 40+ sites put you in the fast lane. As you use them, you'll find most offer you access to so many sites you'll be pursuing links within links that are outside of links that circle . . . and that's surfing. It can get rich results.

4

Sites for Playwrights

The Net-wise playwright can find information about writing and new plays' production programs, attend playwriting courses and seminars (some free, others for a fee), and get general how-to advice. E-publication is possible, too, on scripts-on-line sites where new plays can be posted. There are valuable sites with tools for writers and information about writing style, locations for research for writers, manuscript format, and more.

You'll also find writers' forums that encourage discussions, questions and answers, and general chatter. These offer the camaraderie that comes with associating with other playwrights and writers, and it is possible for you to form cyber-buddy relationships. At times of writing stress and rehearsal frustration, knowledgeable sympathetic ears can be genuinely helpful.

ORGANIZATIONS AND PROGRAMS FOR PLAYWRIGHTS

The Web gives you access to informational pages about professional organizations that protect writers' interests, serve as advocates, and offer special services. Some provide legal counsel when the writer needs specialized assistance; several actively protect freedom of expression. For full-time writers who are self-employed and therefore not eligible for an employer's health and insurance plans, certain writers' organizations can fill in the gap.

THE DRAMATISTS GUILD OF AMERICA
www.dramaguild.com/
The professional organization for professional playwrights, composers, and lyricists in the United States, the *Dramatists Guild* provides standard contracts for commercial and noncommercial productions of plays, and it serves as the playwright's advocate in case of conflict with producers and directors. The *Guild* works for the rights of more than 6,000 international members; membership is open to anyone who has completed a playscript.

The site offers links in small type at the bottom of the home page. Among them are What Is The Dramatists Guild? Membership, Contracts, Special Events, and Symposia. The Business Affairs Department has legal experts to assist members with contractual matters. Theatre Connections/Theatre Links has a large number of sites, especially valuable if you're seeking a theatre in a particular geographic region. Significant for all theatre artists, not just playwrights, are the links to Dramatists Rights and Document of Principle.

PLAYWRIGHTS UNION OF CANADA
www.puc.ca/

The *Playwrights Union* is open to Canadian citizens who've had at least one play professionally produced. PUC represents some 335 members and distributes more than 2,500 Canadian plays. It actively promotes Canadian dramatists to other countries, and it publishes books and a bimonthly magazine called *CanPlay*.

As an advocate for playwrights, it lobbies governmental officials for theatre's health. One concept PUC supports fascinates this American: Canada's Public Lending Right, which compensates authors for use of their work in libraries.

The site offers access to its Catalogue of plays and has a form to arrange for their production. The Books button takes you to a healthy list of theatrical books.

PEN—American Center
www.pen.org/

With almost 130 centers worldwide, PEN is an international literary community composed of all writers—playwrights, poets, editors, essayists, fiction authors, biographers, historians, translators, philosophers, and critics. This site takes you to the American headquarters.

PEN is a strong advocacy organization, and perhaps you heard playwright Arthur Miller speak firmly in support of free expression in America and around the world. He was espousing one of PEN's major goals. PEN also encourages recognition of contemporary literature.

Characteristic of PEN's social concern was its recognition of an individual's unswerving dedication to First Amendment Rights, in this instance one who forcefully protected a college theatre's right to produce a controversial play, as PEN announced:

> Dr. William Holda, President of Kilgore College (Kilgore, Texas), is the winner of the 2000 PEN/Newman's Own First Amendment Award. Dr. Holda uncompromisingly protected the college's production of Angels in America, despite strong opposition from the community.

PEN quotes Dr. Holda's position: "If you allow a group to stop a play, where will it end? Can groups remove books from the library? Or curriculum from an instructor's course?"

Writers find especially valuable the *Grants and Awards* publication, which lists more than 1,000 grants available to authors. PEN also seeks to encourage young writers, has an active Prison Writing Program, sponsors authors reading from their works, gives annual literary awards, and publishes a *Handbook for Literary Translators*.

WRITERS GUILD OF AMERICA
www.writersguild.com/

A labor union, *The Writers Guild* represents more than 8,000 professional writers. It offers a List of Agents (*Guild* regulations prohibit listing agents who charge fees to read your materials), with keys to indicate if the agent will accept materials from new writers or only from those with acceptable references. If you click About Writers on the top menu, you'll find information about a Mentor program—free—that puts together experienced Hollywood film and television writers with new writers. Click on For Writers to find helpful links such as Research Links, The Craft, and The Business. You also will see a Standard Contract—Theatrical link, which takes you to various forms you can download.

WRITERS GUILD OF AMERICA, West   *www.wga.org*
WRITERS GUILD OF AMERICA, East   *www.wgaeast.org*

Although this book focuses on theatre, not film, and although WGA*West* and WGA*East* have some differences, they are important organizations we shouldn't ignore, and I can describe them both generally here. WGA (West and East) represents writers in movies, broadcast, and cable or other new technologies. Members also write for news as well as for animation and documentary programs.

Both sites offer a number of links that discuss membership, working conditions, and contracts, and both offer script registration (an important protection and, subtly, a way of calling a producer's attention to one's professional credibility). Both also have valuable tips, addresses, and contacts.

ASCAP—AMERICAN SOCIETY OF COMPOSERS,
AUTHORS, AND PUBLISHERS
www.ascap.com/

Over 100,000 artists—add to the above title "AND SONGWRITERS AND LYRICISTS"—are ASCAP members so they can receive its protection of their rights. It licenses members' works and sees that they are paid royalties for public performances of their copyrighted creations by negotiating license fees with the users of music, such as radio, TV, cable, bars, clubs, restaurants, shopping malls, concert halls, websites, airlines, orchestras, and more. To be sure fees

More Information About Playwriting

You will want to check the information in Chapter 13 about copyrighting your plays. *Theatre Center* lists a number of sites under For the Playwright (*<www1.playbill .com/cgi-bin/plb/central_res?cmd =show&code=2020>*). For example, you can find the Dorset Colony For Writers, which offers a retreat in Vermont, organizations in various states like the Greensboro Playwrights' Forum in North Carolina, and marketing information such as Market InSight for Playwrights. Also visit *Writers Guide of America* (*<www.wga .org/>*), especially Somebody Wrote That for Fun, plus Online Mentor Service and Research Links for information. *Writer's Union of Canada* (*<www.swifty.com/twuc/index.htm>*) offers writers a number of informational, helpful sites. *National Writers Union* (*<www.nwu.org/>*) is for freelance writers of all genres and actively protects their rights.

are paid, ASCAP has a complex system that monitors and surveys such users.

Membership is open to writers of musical compositions that have been commercially recorded, performed, or published (for more information, see the ASCAP site at *<www.ascap.com/membership/howjoin.html>*). There is no initial cost to join; annual dues are $10 for writers and $50 for publishers. Membership passes to the writer's heirs until copyrights expire.

THEATRE COMMUNICATIONS GROUP— Residency Program for Playwrights
www.tcg.org/

A dominant force in American Theatre, TCG works with the National Endowment of the Arts for the NEA/TCG Theatre Residency Program for Playwrights to support "new and established artistic alliances between playwrights, host theatres and their communities." It is an excellent concept. The program selects 12 playwrights, who receive $25,000 each and serve in residence at a host theatre where they develop new work and become an integral part of the local community. For more information and guidelines to apply, on the TCG home page click on Programs and Services, and on the next page click on Artistic Programs, which will lead you to various supportive activities, including the one for playwrights.

FINDING PARTICULAR PLAYWRIGHTS

Looking for a role model? Not surprisingly, playwrights delight in finding details about their writing idols. Unfortunately, not all are online—perhaps because they are modest or because they would rather write instead of spending hours (and hours and hours!) developing and maintaining a personal Net site. Still, the list of dramatists on the Net *is* growing, and the sites listed here can help you search for them.

THE DRAMATISTS GUILD OF AMERICA

www.dramaguild.com/

If you're trying to get in touch with a specific playwright, the *Guild* has links for Contact a Member, Members' E-mail Address, and Find a Member's Agent. The latter offers an alphabetized list of playwrights and their agents.

PLAYWRIGHTS UNION OF CANADA

www.puc.ca/

Click on Playwrights to open a neatly organized list of Canadian playwrights, which allowed me to find a long-lost personal favorite: Joanna Glass, author of *Canadian Gothic*, on my top-10 list of best one-acts.

THE WWW VIRTUAL LIBRARY—Theatre and Drama

http://vl-theatre.com/

Start by opening Theatre Studies, Article, and Resources, where you'll see a number of sites devoted to playwrights as you scroll down (and down and down). One special quality you find here is the Plays in Print, which leads to an alphabetical listing (the site doesn't tell you that the list is by title, not author).

LA RONDE—The Playwright's Ring

www.pipeline.com/%7Ejude/AboutLaRonde.htm

A ring is a group of sites that share a common interest or purpose. Once you enter one website of that ring, you can click on More to continue visiting similar sites. *La Ronde* puts together playwrights and encourages them to contribute synopses of work and cast requirements for play production, productions, articles or essays about playwriting, Net resources, and personal websites.

> **More Information About Locating Playwrights**
>
> Chapter 5 holds more keys to finding particular dramatists. Discussions of writers are found in *Theatre and Drama Virtual Library* and ELAC *Theatre*, discussed in Chapter 3. A fine source, too, is the *Encyclopaedia Britannica* (<*www.britannica.com/*>), where you can conduct a search by names or visit a section of its theatre listings and click on Comedy or Drama and Tragedy.

You may wish to explore this community of playwrights to discover what like-minded colleagues are doing. If it interests you, you can contact individual dramatists, perhaps starting an e-buddy relationship, or even join the ring.

ORGANIZATIONS DEDICATED TO PRODUCING NEW PLAYS

Playwrights differ significantly from novelists in many ways. For one thing, the novelist's goal is publication. For the playwright, publication is helpful but the primary objective is production. Too, when the novelist finishes the manuscript, it indeed is finished. Oh, sure, the novelist's editor may mark changes for revisions, but the book is done. In contrast, a playwright's completed script has many more steps ahead of it. A director and actors have to put it on its feet, transforming it from the page to the stage, submitting it to the crucible of audience response. Each step of that process almost certainly suggests yet more revisions. Playwrights need script development opportunities.

You'll find a number of cities across the country that have theatres that actively support playwrights' opportunities to develop the play. One popular process for new plays is the staged reading. While not a full-scale production—no scenery or production devices, and the actors carry scripts—nonetheless the reading brings the play to life and helps the playwright identify areas needing rewrites. Other theatres give full-scale production.

ACTORS THEATRE OF LOUISVILLE
www.actorstheatre.org

Founded in 1964, the *Actors Theatre of Louisville* has grown to be one of America's most highly respected professional theatre companies. It has won an impressive number of awards, and despite the *actor* reference in its title, ATL is a major force in American playwriting, due primarily to the dedication of its artistic director, Jon Jory, who started the Humana Festival of New American Plays, which annually showcases new plays, drawing critics from major theatrical cities. The New Plays program is responsible for the popularity of the 10-minute play, and it has given new respectability to the solo play and one-act forms. It also has premiered a number of significant new plays, as the site points out:

> The Humana Festival has premiered the Pulitzer Prize–winning plays *The Gin Game* (D. L. Coburn), *Crimes of the Heart* (Beth Henley), *Dinner With Friends* (Donald Margulies) and Pulitzer finalist *Keely and Du* (Jane Martin) as well as *Getting Out* (Marsha Norman), *Agnes of God* (John Pielmeier), *Lone Star* (James McLure), *In the Eye of the Hurricane* (Eduardo Machado), *Courtship* (Horton Foote), *Extremities* (William Mastrosimone), *My Sister in this House* (Wendy Kessleman), *Tales of the Lost Formicans* (Constance Congdon), *Danny and the Deep Blue Sea* (John Patrick Shanley), *Marisol* (José Rivera), *One Flea Spare* (Naomi Wallace), *Slavs!* (Tony Kushner), *The Batting Cage* (Joan Ackermann) and Y2K (Arthur Kopit).

Jory's retirement from ATL will be regretted, but his legacy ensures continued support of new playwrights. ATL's eagerness to find new plays is extremely attractive.

To find information about entering your play, at the home page click on Humana Festival (<*www.actorstheatre.org/humana/humanamain.html*>). You may want to revisit the site from time to time as ATL seems to work on its site frequently.

PLAYWRIGHTS HORIZON
www.playwrightshorizons.org/

New York's *Playwrights Horizon* points out it is "a writer's theater, and the only theater in New York City dedicated solely to the creation and production of new American plays and musicals." Its list of premieres is impressive:

> Plays like Wendy Wasserstein's *The Heidi Chronicles*, Alfred Uhry's *Driving Miss Daisy*, Jon Robin Baitz's *The Substance of Fire*, and Christopher Durang's *Betty's Summer Vacation*—musicals like *Sunday in the Park with George, Once on this Island, March of the Falsettos*, and *Violet*—were all discovered and developed here. That's because of our commitment to cultivating new American writers.

For information, at the home page click on the arrow. On the next page, click on Working with PH. You'll then see Writing Submissions. Because so many publishers, agents, directors, and theatre companies put up obstacles to playwrights sending scripts, one of the first things you'll note here is the statement "We accept unsolicited manuscripts." That friendly open attitude immediately makes *Playwright's Horizons* an unusual organization, and we can wish other producing companies shared that quality.

THE PLAYWRIGHTS' CENTER OF SAN FRANCISCO
http://playwrights.org/

Another illustration of a theatre's dedication to new plays is *The Playwrights' Center of San Francisco*, which specializes in staged readings of new plays by members, who help support the Center by paying an annual membership of $45. It says that since 1980 it has staged almost a thousand plays:

> the Center uses its acting company and directors to produce weekly readings of members' scripts, as well as the annual DramaRama contest in which the best scripts selected from a worldwide solicitation are presented. Following each of these public-invited readings the play is given a verbal and written critique by the audience as an aid to the playwrighting process. We also hold a monthly Scene Night, with a more intimate atmosphere for reading scenes and works-in-progress by members and nonmembers.

PLAYWRIGHT'S WORKSHOP MONTREAL
www.playwrightsworkshop.org/

A professional theatre center dedicated to new playwrights and new plays for the Canadian stage, *Playwrights' Workshop Montreal* believes in individual approaches geared to the playwright's particular needs:

> From dramaturgical consultation through public readings, we offer a unique passage for each play, our belief being that each project defines its

own needs. We are a national member based organization with writing, student and supporting members.

The site also offers access to plays, playwrights' portfolios, descriptions of how plays are workshopped, and links to other Canadian theatre sites.

THE SUNDANCE INSTITUTE
www.sundance.org/

Since it began in 1981, Robert Redford's *Sundance Institute* has become an American Cannes film festival that attracts worldwide attention to the Utah mountain retreat. Less well known is the Sundance Theatre Laboratory, a summer workshop for playwrights, directors, choreographers, composers, and solo performers. As the site explains, the focus is on the script, not production techniques:

> The physical resources at Sundance include four rehearsal rooms, a writing room, a music room, and literally thousands of acres of magnificent mountain scenery. Projects rehearse every other day to give playwrights adequate time for rewrites. Actors are usually double cast. There is no physically controllable space, such as a black box. Although no lighting or scenic production values are available to assist in project development, designers often participate as part of the development of text.

A long list of writers have participated in the theatrical program:

> Among the theatre artists who have developed work with the assistance of Sundance are: writers Carol Burnett, Nilo Cruz, Michael Feingold, Jessica Hagedorn, Carrie Hamilton, David Hancock, Israel Horovitz, Tony Kushner, Emily Mann, Carlos Murillo, Terry O'Reilly, Dael Orlandersmith, Sybille Pearson, Sapphire, David Schulner, Paul Selig, Julie Taymor, Regina Taylor, Terry Tempest Williams, and Charlayne Woodard.

For more information about submitting your play, click on Theatre Program on the site's home page.

EUGENE O'NEILL THEATRE CENTER
http://camel.conncoll.edu/NTI/oneill.html

The O'Neill, one of America's longest-established playwriting centers, sponsors conferences and workshops for students and theatre professionals to learn and develop their craft free of what it calls "the pressures of the marketplace." Each summer the O'Neill sponsors a conference that focuses on talented playwrights. Around 1,600 manuscripts are entered; 12 are selected. The National Theater Institute also offers an intense conservatory-based 14-week program twice a year for acting, directing, playwriting, movement, voice, and design. The home

page calls your attention to the various programs at the O'Neill, and time spent browsing
them can give you ideas of possible ways to
develop your art and craft.

THE CONTEMPORARY AMERICAN
THEATER FESTIVAL

www.catf.org/

Located on the campus of Shepherd College in Shepherdstown, West Virginia, CATF
operates with Equity performers and is
dedicated to developing new American theatre. It presents four plays in repertory during the summer.

THE AMERICAN ASSOCIATION OF
COMMUNITY THEATRE

www.aact.org/

At the AACT site you will find information
about playwriting contests and theatres
seeking new plays. Scroll down until you
see Play Contests on the left menu (or go
there directly with this address:
<*www.aact.org/cgi-bin/webdata_contests.pl
?cgifunction=Search*>). Sponsoring theatres
and deadlines are posted, and there also
are posts by play publishers. Each organization can be accessed for full details.

**More Information About
Theatre Programs and
Playwriting Links**

A search of the sites
described in Chapter 3 will
help you locate additional
theatre programs that support playwrights and focus
on new plays. For one example, *Theatre Central* (<*www*1
*.playbill.com/cgi-bin/plb/central
_res?cmd=show&code=2020*>)
lists theatres in a number of
cities. *Artslynx* has a sizable
group of Theatre Company
Listings (<*www.artslynx.org
/theatre/theatres.htm*>). Also see
The Dramatists Sourcebook,
described in this chapter.
Playwrights in Cyberspace gives
playwrights information
about using the Net
(<*www.teleport.com/~cdeemer
/guild-demo/home.html*>).

AMERICAN THEATRE WEB

www.americantheaterweb.com/

Clicking on Callboards takes you to two forums you can explore. Call for
Scripts also contains contest announcements. A second invites you to post
your script.

E-CLASSES, SEMINARS, AND ONLINE WORKSHOPS

Both free and pay-to-learn workshops and seminars are available to playwrights, along with forums and other guides that are designed to help you
advance your playwriting skills.

Free Sites

Run by people willing to contribute freely of their time and energy, the free
sites often offer helpful advice. Do check to see when the page was last

updated before accepting advice about current contests, theatres looking for new plays, or other time-limited information.

SCREENWRITERS & PLAYWRIGHTS HOME PAGE

www.teleport.com/~cdeemer/scrwriter.html

AUTHOR'S CHOICE   Charles Deemer operates this site and updates it regularly. The first thing you see on his home page is his three golden rules of playwriting, which include "American movies are about what happens next" and "The chainsaw is your friend."

There is a valuable search engine through a drop-down menu of almost 40 various aspects of playwriting categories, including Dramatic Structure, Story Treatment, Pitching, Directory of Producers and Agents, Contests, and more.

Especially helpful is Writing for Actors and Internet for Writers, which offers a "self-help six-week guided tour" that answers everything you wanted to know about getting around the Net but didn't know how to ask. Use this page's search engine to find other information. See, too, Playwrights in Cyberspace, which he calls "a guide to resources and strategies."

THE PLAYWRITING SEMINARS

www.vcu.edu/artweb/playwriting/

AUTHOR'S CHOICE   Richard Toscan calls his 230-page site "An Opinionated Web Companion on the Art & Craft of Playwriting," and his seminars reflect strong opinions. Better that, say I, than no convictions. He divides his approach into six basic areas: Content: Story and Themes; Characters and Dialogue; Film: The Screenwriting Craft vs. Playwriting; Structure: The -wright of The Playwright's Craft; Working: Writing Techniques, Rewriting and Editing; Format: For Manuscripts and More Interesting Things; and Business: Submitting Scripts, Copyright, Royalties, and Resources. His seminars are enriched by quotes from playwrights and recommended plays to read.

ESSAYS ON THE ART OF DRAMATIC WRITING

www.teleport.com/~bjscript/index.htm

Webmaster Bill Johnson, author of A *Story Is a Promise*, offers essays he says will help you write a dramatic screenplay, novel, or play. Scrolling down to The Craft of Writing for the Stage leads to reviews of four plays, and the descriptions may help playwrights see how to organize and develop their plays—providing they know the plays well. The discussion of Marsha Norman's *'night, Mother* appears most helpful.

WRITER'S RESOURCE CENTER

www.poewar.com/

John Hewitt's site is designed for all writers, and the home page offers Articles, such as Overcoming Writer's Isolation. You also can enter Exercises for Writers, The Beginner's Guide to Freelance Writing, and other units. There are a number of offerings under Topics, including Stage and Screen, where you'll find valuable connections to writing links, software for scriptwriters, and Hollywood studios.

DRAMA WORKSHOP
http://chdramaworkshop.homestead.com/Home.html

This is a subdivision of *Coffeehouse for Writers* (*<www.coffeehouse4writers.com>*) and says it is "the nuts and bolts of dramatic writing." Dramatic Structure gives quite brief descriptions of plays in one, two, three, and five acts, as well as short-short 10-minute plays, and musicals. Its links to radio plays, monologues, and screenplays were empty when I visited last.

There also is a Weekend Workshop (*<http://chdramaworkshop.homestead.com/weekendplaywright.html>*) that may sound simplistic, but it is worth a look. Through a series of exercises (mostly drawn from writing texts), you'll get a start on writing. The Toolbox leads to Aristotelian concepts (unfortunately it repeats an old erroneous concept about his three unities).

Pay-to-Learn Sites

A site requiring payment should give you more than a free one. The operative word is *should*. If you are paying, you expect consistent training, insightful comments, and attentive care from a trained and experienced writer-teacher. Before you send your fee, ask questions. Who will be my instructor? What are his or her credentials? What projects will I be assigned? Am I guaranteed the same person for the entire course, and can I shift instructors if one seems to misunderstand my goals? What are my recourses if the instructor doesn't give me comments on schedule?

As always on the Net, a little paranoia can be a good thing. Check carefully to be sure online payment is secure.

E-SCRIPT—The Internet's Scriptwriting Workshop
www.singlelane.com/escript/

Online workshops on playwriting and screenwriting that take place over five or ten weeks promise to help you polish your dramatic writing skills, get started on a play or screenplay, or finish the one you've got going. Costs range from $135 to $250, depending on the length of the session.

What it calls its good stuff (*<http://www.singlelane.com/escript/bwqa1.htm>*) can be valuable. E-script Miscellany has articles and interviews, The Virtual Q&A has professionals answering questions, and there are message boards for screenwriters and playwrights.

WRITERS.COM—Writers on the Net
www.writers.com/

Published writers and experienced writing teachers offer online classes for virtually all writers, including playwrights and screenwriters. Costs range from

$190 to $240 for eight- or ten-week sessions. Tutoring and editing is available for $36 an hour. The site also offers free writing group chat sessions and has a number of links to other areas of interest to writers.

SCREENWRITERS ONLINE

www.screenwriter.com/

Although this book focuses on theatre, not film, this site may serve those wondering about screenwriting. It offers frequent Master Class sessions, Screenwriter Chats and Seminars, and screenplay analysis. You'll be impressed with the credentials of the professional screenwriters who've led such classes or participated in question-answer meetings. It also has an Insider's Report written by professionals. Class fee is $89.

REFERENCE BOOKS FOR PLAYWRIGHTS

There are a number of valuable books every playwright should have, but two deserve special mention. First, if you are looking for producers, directors, grants and fellowships, contests, and theatres interested in new plays, *Theatre Communications Group* (<www.tcg.org/>) publishes *The Dramatists Sourcebook* around August every year, which means the information is continually updated. This valuable guide contains an impressive amount of information. The second TCG reference book is the *Stage Writers Handbook: A Complete Business Guide for Playwrights, Composers, Lyricists and Librettists*, by Dana Singer. Both deserve a place in the playwright's personal library. You can order them through TCG or a major online bookstore such as *Amazon* or *Barnes and Noble*.

THE WRITERS STORE

http://writerscomputer.com/cgi-bin/SoftCart.exe/store/playwriting_books.htm?E+writers

Playwrights searching for books may want to visit *The Writers Store*. This page lists recommended playwriting books, and along the left menu you'll find writing materials in other categories, such as Script Writing, Film, and Production; and Writing in Genres. Prose Writing, Non-Fiction, and Reference offers links to areas that may interest you, such as Nurturing the Creative Process; Doing Business as a Writer; and Writers Conferences, Workshops, and Other Programs. At the top of the page is Books of the Month Specials—writing-related books on sale.

To find playwriting books, on the opening page scroll down to Books,

Audio, and Video Tapes on Creating, Producing, and Selling Your Work. On the next page, click Playwriting (or go there directly with <*http://writerscomputer.com/cgi bin/SoftCart .exe/store/playwriting_books.htm?E+writers*>). Although it lists few books for playwrights, you're bound to find one or more that can help you develop your craft and start or polish your plays. The left menu lists books for other writing genres.

There are other good links tucked away in that left menu, such as Nurturing the Creative Process, which leads to recommendations for quite fine books about writing in general, including Dorothea Brande's *Becoming a Writer*; Anne Lamott's *Bird by Bird—Some Instructions on Writing and Life*; William Zinsser's excellent book for students and nonfiction writers, *On Writing Well*; Natalie Goldberg's *Writing Down the Bones*; Ray Bradbury's *Zen in the Art of Writing*; and more.

E-PUBLICATION

The Internet is raising interesting questions about the nature of "publication." In the past, playwrights or play readers only had one source—printed books—but now the Internet is providing a new and different form: *e-publication*. With it comes questions. Will books disappear in some near future, replaced by Net sites? (I vote a loud no. For me, a monitor will never replace the printed page or the joy of packing a couple of books to the beach, and the mind boggles at the thought of actors carrying little e-readers when rehearsing.)

More Information About Books for Playwrights

You may want to visit my personal website (<*http:// faculty.wm.edu/lecatr*>), where you'll find suggested books for theatre, websites for writers, opinionated statements about stage directions, copyright information, and other informational materials for theatre folk. Lewis Heniford, the author of *Small-Cast One-Act Guide Online*, suggests books for beginning or advanced playwrights. The list reflects his considerable experience (<*www.heniford .net/1234/writebib.htm*>). Additionally, this site contains useful information about playwrights.

Also check out the list of books that Charles Deemer, who runs a major playwriting/screenwriting site, recommends (<*www.teleport.com /~cdeemer/BooksP.html*>). Other recommendations are at <*www.geocities.com/Broadway /Alley/8578/books.htm*> and <*www.geocities.com/Broadway /Stage/5048/DramaBooks.html*>.

For authors, too, e-publication brings other questions. What about copyright? Does publication on the Net convey a free quality? What happens if a director or producer elects to produce one of these plays without even informing the author? Such thorny questions come with the popularity of e-publication. Still, there are also major opportunities waiting for us.

ELAC THEATRE ARTS WRITERS WORKSHOP
www.perspicacity.com/elactheatre/workshop/workshop.htm

Sponsored by the drama department of East Los Angeles College, this bouncy and cheerful site is designed for you to publish your own play or read those by others. It points out that several scripts were discovered on these pages and enjoyed productions.

DRAMATIC EXCHANGE
www.dramex.org/

While short stories and essays are appearing on the Net, there are fewer sites for playscripts. *Dramatic Exchange* is one. As the site explains:

> The Dramatic Exchange is a Web resource for playwrights, producers, and anybody interested in plays. We aim to provide a place where playwrights can make their plays available, and where producers and readers can look to find plays uploaded here by the playwrights.

The Index of Plays is arranged in subdivisions such as comedies, dramas, tragedies, children's theatre, musicals, and one-acts. Playwrights find the site attractive: in the one-acts file I found almost 200 scripts.

IUNIVERSE.COM
www.iuniverse.com/

iUniverse.com likes to think of itself as a new kind of book publisher that establishes a partnership relationship with authors. This print-on-demand publisher offers writers a variety of business arrangements, which are described when you click on New Manuscript from the home page. To investigate options, click on each of the units on the menu at the top of the first page. Additionally, *iUniverse* has pay-to-learn online classes, how-to information, chat rooms, newsletters, and message boards.

XLIBRIS
www.xlibris.com/

"Log on as a Writer, Log off as an Author," the site says. It's an attractive concept that avoids the risks of the vanity publishing gimmickry. *Xlibris* offers on-demand publishing, which means books are printed only when ordered, and they say their publications are listed with *Amazon* and comparable vendors. You supply the manuscript in accepted format on a disk, and *Xlibris* translates it into a book. The cost? Click on Publishing Services and you'll find that the core service is free (yup, no charge). Advanced, professional, and premium services are $300, $600, and $1,200 respectively. The FAQs should address most of your questions, but be patient—it is crabby about opening. *Xlibris* offers to send you a sample copy of a book it published. I received one and was impressed with its quality.

WRITER ONLINE

www.novalearn.com/wol

They pay, but so far they seek nonfiction and poetry, not plays. You might want to send them your very best short-short script to convince them to open their policy. The articles on writing have a nice flair and are designed to inspire and inform.

REFERENCE SITES FOR WRITERS

There are a number of well-designed sites that offer fine lists of references for writers in general. Some discuss significant aspects of the business of writing, and others give you access to research materials you can use to give your play an informed flair.

PREDITORS AND EDITORS—Literary Agents

www.sfwa.org/prededitors/pubagent.htm

Although less geared toward the playwright, this site has a large number of links any writer can use. You'll find a long list of Agents (including some the site helpfully marks as "not recommended"). Resources is remarkably detailed and is worth investigating, and Definitions likely can answer almost every question you have about the writing business, from "advance" to "vanity publisher." Click on Warnings to find businesses the site suggests you avoid.

ABSOLUTE WRITE

www.absolutewrite.com

Geared toward freelance writers ("screenwriting, playwriting, writing novels, nonfiction, comic book writing, greeting cards, poetry, or—well, you get the idea—"), *Absolute Write* is a breezy place with Interviews, Articles, and Columns that have how-to advice for writers. They sponsor a writing contest and ask for volunteers to lead chats.

Along the left menu you'll find categories such as News, Novels and Non-Fiction, a Writer's Directory for your Website, and Classifieds for you to post

More Information About E-publication

Also check out *Writer's Guild of America* (<*www.wga.org/*>), especially *First Internet Contract for Writers* (<*www.wga.org/index .html*>). *E-writers.net* also offers valuable information for writers venturing into e-publication (<*http://e-writers.net*>).

Additional Information on Playwriting Guides

You can also find playwriting guides at Dramatic Writing in ELAC *Theatre* (<*www.perspicacity .com/elactheatre/library/links.htm*>). Also try the playwright section under Theatre (<*http: //wwar.com/categories/Theater /Playwright_Related*>) at *World Wide Arts Resources* for individual playwright's sites and regional happenings. In addition, you can find playwriting listed on the sites discussed in Chapter 3. For example, *Theatre Central* has a site for playwrights (<*www1.playbill .com/cgi-bin/plb/central _res?cmd=show&code=2020*>).

your ad. There is a Play/Screenwriting section that's more heavily loaded toward screenwriting, but it contains tips and advice that playwrights can use, too.

WRITER'S TOOLBOX—Internet Resources for Writers
www.writerstoolbox.com/

The Drama section is unfortunately sparce, but the valuable part of this tool-box is the Research section where you can find a number of sites to help you find materials.

BLACK ON WHITE
www.blackonwhite.on.ca/

Writer's block—argh! What's the solution? Simple: *write*. This friendly site intends to help anyone overcome the procrastination syndrome. The organization is a bit unclear, so you'll need click around to take full advantage of the place.

INTERNET GUIDEBOOK FOR WRITERS
www.horsburgh.com/h_writer2.html

Although a bit wordy, this site offers valuable help for writers starting with recommended computers (both PC and Mac) plus a few words about Internet Service Providers (ISP) and search engines. It then gets to more valuable information. It suggests sites by topics and tells you where to find specific information on the Net. Helpful are lists of sites by the writer's specialization, such as Romance, Mystery, History, Science Fiction, Playwriting, and more. It concludes with brief comments about marketing.

URLS FOR A RAINY DAY
www.purefiction.com/pages/res2.htm

AUTHOR'S CHOICE Your play about business has characters arguing about average, mean, and median. Check for accuracy by clicking on Statistics Every Writer Should Know. Or one of your characters has traveled to an exotic location and you want her to glibly mention details of the place. Click on Association of National Tourist Offices or Virtual Tourist, and use these guide to worldwide websites to find what you need.

URLs *for a Rainy Day* is neatly named because you can spend hours surfing interesting facts and opening intriguing sites, or you can search directly for topics you need to ensure that your play contains accurate details. There is an amazing quantity of info.

INDISPENSABLE WRITING RESOURCES
www.quintcareers.com/writing

The site says it has a Complete Collection of Writing Essentials, and certainly there are well-organized categories of links. Reference Materials can give you ideas for your personal library, and Internet Reference Resources has descriptions of links to a variety of reference materials available on the Net. Valuable, too, are Writing-Related Web Sites and Writing References Sites.

BEAUCOUP! REFERENCE WORKS
www.beaucoup.com/1refeng.html

Information here is not directly related to writing per se, but the general information can be valuable to enrich and enhance your play. For example, you can locate more than 1,000 (!) dictionaries, go to a slang dictionary, investigate mythology, look up roots of names in European countries, or find major classical and medieval literary works.

COOL WRITING RESOURCES
www.teleport.com/~burrell/writing.phtml

The idea is cool—describe writing sites on the Web and rate them with a star system—but too few are listed. Drama Writing has but two. General Writing has about four times as many. I list it with hopes it will blossom.

THE WRITER'S SEARCH INDEX
www.writers-search.com/

A detailed index awaits you at this site. You can find Agents and Managers, Contests, Writing for the Theatre, Writing for Television, Screen Writing, and even Writing Greeting Cards. Expect to spend a bit of time experimenting with the radio buttons and search engine, though.

PLAYWRITING—NETSCAPE
http://directory.Netscape.com/Arts/Writers_Resources/Playwrighting

Although the organization is haphazard—maybe nonexistent is more accurate—here you find a substantial number of links to contests, awards, theatres interested in new plays, and writing organizations. Using the list, you may find theatres in your region that you can contact regarding your play. When I last looked, it listed theatres in regions from Austin to Washington.

SCRIPTSEEKER.COM
www.scriptseeker.com/

Saying it is "the most comprehensive listing resource for new plays and screenplays on the Web," *Scriptseeker.com* seeks to link playwrights and screenwriters with producers. You can browse its catalog by genre, author, or title. Along the left menu are links you may want to explore such as Script Tips, Evaluator, and Callboard. You'll also see Register a Script, which monthly fees ranging from $9.95 to $29.95, depending on which level of service you choose.

ABOUT.COM
http://home.about.com/index.htm

This index reminds me of the novel *The Never-Ending Story* because it doesn't seem to have a stop. You can find interesting information about the various interior sites. Clicking on Arts and Humanities can lead you to materials for writers, such as the three subsites listed next.

WRITER'S EXCHANGE
http://writerexchange.about.com/arts/writerexchange/gi/dynamic/offsite.htm?site =http://www.writers%2Dexchange.com

The left margin has entries for Chat Forums, Contests, Critique Groups, and MFA Programs, among others.

WRITER'S RESOURCES
http://writerexchange.about.com/arts/writerexchange/msubresrc.htm

More interesting places to surf.

THE WRITER'S INDEX
http://writerexchange.about.com/arts/writerexchange/library/howto/blhow2index.htm

Topics include how to find story ideas, beat the writer's block, or locate an agent.

More Information About Reference Sites

Playwrights in Cyberspace gives you information about using the Net (<*www.teleport.com /~cdeemer/guild-demo/home .html*>). *Crafty Screenwriting* offers a series of informational essays about many aspects of writing for film (<*www.craftyscreenwriting.com/*>). You also may wish to visit *Fade In Magazine—The First Word in Film* (<*www.fadeinmag .com/FrontPage.htm*>). Another excellent site with numerous resources is HollywoodNet (<*www.hollywoodnet.com /indexmain.html*>).

FORUMS FOR WRITERS

Writing is a popular forum topic, although overall you find less focus on the playwright and more on poets and fiction writers. Forums allow writers to rub elbows with other writers, to share experiences, to ask questions, to celebrate and, yes, to commiserate.

SCREENWRITERS AND PLAYWRIGHTS' DISCUSSION FORUM
http://writers-bbs.com/inkspot/threads .cgi?forum =screen

AUTHOR'S CHOICE Inkspot, a highly popular site for all writers (<*www .inkspot.com*>), has a number of services to assist poets, novelists, and more. It also offers various Community Forums. This one for playwrights and screenwriters is co-moderated by Charles Deemer and Gabrielle Sara Prendergast. You may encounter professional playwrights as well as those seeking first production. Although some overly authoritative answers occasionally creep in, the overall tone of comments is helpful and constructive. It is free of backbiting, ignorant shallow replies, and wisecracks, which can't be said about all writing sites.

INTERNATIONAL CENTRE FOR WOMEN PLAYWRIGHTS
www.cadvision.com/sdempsey/icwphmpg.htm

Meet a writer. Member Pages and Member Plays by Genre may be the first links that interest you at this international site designed for "communication and contact among the sister community of the world's women dramatists." The Awards, Productions, and Publications page lists a calendar of members' achievements, and also gives you ideas of theatres that may consider your plays. Links is a good collection of other sites.

LONELY BLUE COYOTE
www.lbcoyote.com/Writersgroups/world_find_wg.html

Writers often seek a live writing group near them. This site offers lists of organizations in America, Canada, and a few other countries, although you may have to click around to find one convenient for you. The same location also lists various virtual writing groups. If you're looking for personal website construction and maintenance, the Coyote says it specializes in helping writers make their own e-presence.

WRITERS' RESOURCES ON THE WEB
http://heartcorps.com/dramatica/writers_links.htm

Awkward page divisions require patient scrolling horizontally and vertically, but you can learn about the Dramatica Story System, a software program for writers. The left menu lists a large number of sites you may wish to explore.

THE PLAYWRIGHTS NOTICEBOARD—Playwrights on the Web
www.stageplays.com/markets.htm

Information about contests and production and publishing opportunities is listed here. Each entry describes rules, notes specifies deadlines, and gives you the organization's contact details. The site appears to be frequently updated, which should ensure that you find the latest materials.

BACKSTAGE.COM
http://backstage.com/

Although much of *Backstage* focuses on actors (and I discuss it in more detail in Chapter 6), there is a Callboard for writers. It appears active and lively.

WRITERS WRITE—The Write Resource
www.writerswrite.com/

The Author Website Directory includes many well-known writers, the Internet Writing Journal offers interesting interviews with authors, and there are Jobs and Markets for Writers.

THE RIGHT WRITER
http://nimbus.ocis.temple.edu/~cforrest/Lit/Right.htm

There are links to various sites. Where Everyone Knows Your Name, for example, leads you to links to the Writers Guild of America, International Women's Writer Guild, and Writer's Groups. Contests takes you to hookups for Writing Contests Links and Inkspot: Writing Contests.

THE WRITERS BBS
http://writersbbs.com/home.shtml

Once haunted by heavy-handed vitriol and personal attacks, new management did major housecleaning and threw out garbage. As a result, writers now feel comfortable looking through its various discussion forums dealing with writing book reviews, fiction, essays, poetry, science fiction, romance, and more.

A distinctly special value of this site is that several highly experienced professional and friendly writers hang out in the General, Publication, and Marketing forums, generously contributing their insight and answering questions. The Screenwriting and Playwriting forum typically has only a few stalwart participants, who clearly would welcome newbies.

YOUR PERSONAL WEBSITE

You may want to consider constructing your own personal website to showcase your writing. While they often are difficult to build "just right," many theatre artists enjoy having an e-presence. It's nice to say, of course just ever-so casually, ". . . and you can check my personal page." There's always a chance some producer or director may find you on the Web and contact you about your work. Too, a website allows you to keep your résumé up to date, whereas that material you sent out last year will lack valuable information.

A personal page reflects you, which means there's no single or best approach. I list a few playwright's pages here in hopes you'll find ideas you can steal, er, borrow. You'll notice each differs a great deal. You also can see which are on a site that offers free Web page hosting, and as you open them you can judge how efficient the hosts are.

THE FANTASY NOVELS OF VICTORIA STRAUSS
www.sff.net/people/victoriastrauss/

AUTHOR'S CHOICE   Content here will be valuable for everyone—writer or not—considering establishing an e-presence. In her site about her writing, Strauss adds excellent materials about personal sites, and clearly she has carefully researched the advantages of a personal site and available resources.

From her home page you can access Building a Writers Website (<*www.sff .net/people/victoriastrauss/victoria%20strauss%20whywebsite.html*>), which starts with reasons you should have your own page and gives well-thought-out tips about design. On the next page (*<www.sff.net/people/victoriastrauss /victoria%20strauss%20whywebsite2.html>*), you'll find a well-organized and thorough list of sites for Design, Servers, Webpage Authoring, Free Stuff, Publishing Your Site, Publicizing Your Site, and more.

KAREN MUELLER

www.homestead.com/karenmueller

Karen Mueller, a playwright and actress in Calgary, Alberta, starts with her photo, then lists her plays that have been produced throughout the United States. She offers links to her résumé, plays, photographs, and publications.

KEVIN O'MORRISON

http://kevin-omorrison.com/

Calling his page "The Place of The Winged Foot," Kevin O'Morrison's site lists plays, critics' reviews, agents, and his monologues.

DAVID J. AGANS

http://main.tellink.Net/~dagans

This playwright and lyricist gives brief bio notes and then describes his works.

More Information About Personal Websites

Find more sites at *Playwrights on The Web—International Playwrights and Their Plays* (*<www .stageplays.com/writers.htm>*). Also think about linking your website to a Web ring such as *La Ronde—The Playwright's Ring* (*<www.pipeline.com /%7Ejude/AboutLaRonde.htm>*). Its home page has a link that gives you information on how to join.

T03434l

5

Sites for Directing, Choreography, Dramaturgy, and Research

Directors, choreographers, dramaturgs, and researchers all share similar significant concerns. For example, directors and choreographers are focused on creating an artistic transformation from the page to the stage; directors and dramaturgs collaborate especially closely during the planning stages for productions. Directors, dramaturgs, and theatrical scholars research the play and playwright, examine the historical environment of the play and playwright's time, and study the playwright's other works—all leading to an interpretation and then a vision of the production. The dramaturg has research interests like those of the theatrical scholar, who in turn is aware that scholarship, however much it looks into arcane matters hidden in musty corners, ultimately has to do with the play and the production. Each of these four types of artists will find that the Internet has valuable aids.

PLAY DIRECTING AND CHOREOGRAPHY

The Net's coverage of theatre lacks balance. There are more sites for actors than for other theatre workers. Designers and technical theatre people have more e-homes than do playwrights, and playwriting sites in turn outnumber those for dramaturgs. Directors and choreographers have the fewest (although coverage of theatrical management also is skimpy). Shall we pause while the actors smile and say that indicates relative importance of each?

Not surprisingly, there are no how-to sites for play directors and choreographers. E-communication has yet to develop to the point that we go to the Net to observe the choreographer-dancer interplay or director-actor and director-designer collaboration. Nor does the Net allow us to watch director-choreographer techniques with actors and dancers during rehearsals. Live hands-on theatrical experience still has the edge, and theatre remains a human activity not subject to e-whims. As one who relishes theatre's human touch, I wouldn't want it any other way.

Organizations for Directors and Choreographers

There are notably few organizations designed for theatrical directors and choreographers. I list significant ones below.

SOCIETY OF STAGE DIRECTORS AND CHOREOGRAPHERS
www.ssdc.org/

SSDC is a national labor union that represents stage directors and choreographers. For full membership, a director or choreographer must have professional credits working on productions with union affiliations; associate membership is open to those starting their careers, college and university professionals, and community theatre directors and choreographers. One primary distinction between full and associate membership has to do with benefits such as health care and insurance.

In affiliation with the *Theatre Communications Group*, SSDC publishes *The Stage Directors Handbook* (at its home page click on Publications or go there directly with this address: *<www.ssdc.org/foundation/publications.html>*). This resource book contains valuable information about development programs, grants, fellowships, agents, and opportunities for theatrical directors.

Honoring one of the SSDC founders, the organization offers the Shepard and Mildred Traube Fellowship. Described on the site, it grants stipends for young directors and choreographers so that they may be economically free to observe veteran directors and choreographers during rehearsals and previews of Broadway shows.

At the opening page you can click on The Stage Directors and Choreographers Foundation (or go here directly: *<www.ssdc.org/foundation/index.html>*) for information. The site says:

> The Foundation is the only national organization dedicated exclusively to supporting and developing the professional director and choreographer. Based in New York City—and serving as a hub for events and networking for greater NYC directors and choreographers—SDCF offers services to artists throughout the country, with active groups and programs in the Bay Area, Chicago, Los Angeles, and the Puget Sound Area.

CANADIAN ACTORS' EQUITY ASSOCIATION
www.caea.com/

Despite the name, Equity membership in Canada is not limited to actors. This professional association includes directors, choreographers, and stage managers. The site contains audition notices, job opportunities, lists of theatre companies, and more. It recently initiated a program to mail members audition notices. It offers access to members' websites, although that service isn't mentioned on the home page. (To get there, click on Members Forum and at the bottom of the page you'll see a connection.) At my last visit I found an unfortunately large number of dead sites.

Career Development for Directors

The following sites focus on prestigious programs designed for directors' career development.

DRAMA LEAGUE

www.dramaleague.org/

Home of the Director's Project, which has made a significant impact on professional theatre by encouraging young directors, Drama League seeks to strengthen and enrich the American theatre by fostering the development of the art and craft of directing. To that end, it sponsors programs that offer practical information, directing experience, and professional exposure. The Project's success is proven by its track record. It says that since it started in 1984, more than 145 young stage directors have gone on to professional theatres as artistic or associate artistic directors, and many have won, or been nominated for, major theatrical awards and fellowships.

Further Information About Apprenticeships

If you're interested in an apprenticeship in film and television directing, you may wish to look at Assistant Directors Training Program (<*www.dgptp.org/*>).

THEATRE COMMUNICATIONS GROUP— Career Development Program for Directors

www.tcg.org/

TCG is one of American theatre's best assets, actively making a number of significant contributions to the art. For talented directors early in their career, TCG administers the NEA/TCG Career Development Program. Six directors receive financial support (currently $17,500) for six months, working with senior artists in theatre companies. There is a companion program for designers. Access information from its home page by clicking on Programs and Services. Once there, click on NEA/TCG Career Development for Directors and Designers.

Helpful Resources for Directors, Choreographers, and Dramaturgs

Directors, choreographers, and dramaturgs are required to have such a broad knowledge of theatre that they should visit all sites about theatre and dance. A good place to start would be the basic sites described in Chapter 3. Here I've selected two that deserve special mention.

MUSIC THEATRE INTERNATIONAL

www.mtishows.com/

Most of us know that MTI has scripts and materials for popular musicals. We may not be aware that it also offers a wide range of resources such as study guides, cast recordings, promo logos, production slides, and recordings. Directors and choreographers will want to investigate its RehearScores, which allows rehearsal accompaniment on an interactive computer program. Of special interest to directors and dramaturgs are MTI's Video Conversation Pieces, 30- to 60-minute videos that put you in touch with Broadway directors, lyricists, composers, and writers.

NON-TRADITIONAL CASTING PROJECT
www.ntcp.org/

An advocacy organization, NTCP directs attention to exclusion practices in theatre, film, and television. *Non-Traditional Casting* intends to open doors for wider participation by artists of color, females, and those with disabilities. Directors and choreographers will want to look at the New Traditions Compendium: Forums and Commentaries for interesting articles by actors, directors, and playwrights. NTCP gives producers, directors, and casting directors access to Artist Files Online, a collection of approximately 2,500 actors of color, with additional résumés of directors, designers, choreographers, stage managers, and playwrights. There is no fee to use or to be listed in the Files.

THE THEATRE RESOURCE
www.theatre-resource.com/

For a definition of *ambition*, see *Theatre Resource's* statement of goals. Webmaster Darleen Viloria says, "This is an attempt to put you in touch with virtually every theatre person and organization with a presence on the Internet." Whew. She hasn't achieved her goal—at least not yet—but her site is a rich resource, with categories such as Theatre Organizations, Theatre Training, For Actors, Directors, Playwrights, Jobs, and much more.

Sites for Choreographers

Choreographers will want to visit the various dance sites described in the next chapter. Here I mention websites that are more directly involved with choreography than dance.

DANCE NOTATION BUREAU
www.dancenotation.org/

Modern choreography notation took a leap forward in 1928 when Rudolf Laban published his *Labanotation* system, which uses symbols to record the choreographic work. Notation is to dance what the musical score is to music, and the system is a permanent and thorough record that allows dance to be shared around the world, now and in the

> **Additional Information About Directing**
>
> Look for Directing at the conglomerate sites listed in Chapter 3. A good source is the *Yahoo!* site (<*http://sg.yahoo.com/arts/performing_arts/theatre/directing*>). For information about directing for film and television, see *The Official Website of the Directors Guild of America* (<*www.dga.org/*>) and the *Director's Guild of Canada* (<*www.dgc.ca/*>).

future. The record includes the particular steps plus imagery, motivation, and characterization the choreographer gives dancers.

The DNB site is well organized and clear, and its opening design cleverly uses the basic notation system. You can click on Notation Basics to see diagrams of the system, Notated Theatrical Dances Catalogue (you'll need Adobe Acrobat to access them; a free connection is on the site), Bibliographies, Links, and more. The Theory Discussion Bulletin Board contains materials by serious contributors.

More Information About Notation

Check out the Encarta Encyclopedia entry <http://encarta.msn.com/find/Concise.asp?z=1&pg=2&ti=761552195&MSID=d74bed5c490811d498880008c7d9e3db>). The article traces dance notation from the ancient Egyptians to the work of Rudolf von Laban, known for his Labanotation, which consists of abstract symbols for direction, rhythm, and movement.

CYBER DANCE
www.cyberdance.org/

AUTHOR'S CHOICE   This very valuable mega-site guides you to a collection of more than 3,500 links to classical ballet and modern dance resources on the Internet. From the home page you can access nine categories such as Companies, Colleges, Schools, People and Organizations, Goods and Services, and Dance Websites and Return Links.

SOCIETY OF DANCE HISTORY SCHOLARS
www.sdhs.org/

An attractive series of electric line drawings of dancers enhance the visual aspects of this site. SDHS takes a broad view of dance history, pointing out that the moment dance is performed, it becomes part of the past. It examines the tradition of Western theatrical dance from Renaissance and Baroque court entertainments to postmodern dance theatre.

In addition, the site has valuable links of Dance Organizations, Related Organizations, Funding Sources, Libraries and Research Institutions, and Booksellers and Publishers.

DANCE EDUCATION—Choreography Case Studies
http://come.to/theballet

The opening page is The College of Choreography, and three doors take you to divisions. Book Store offers well-thought-out brief reviews of recommended books. Backstage gives insight into the overall artistic collaborative process. Main, the largest, leads you to a valuable long list of Links.

Copyright for Choreography

In Chapter 13 I discuss copyright for playwrights and directors. Choreography, too, is eligible for copyright protection. The idea is not even two decades old, but a number of choreographers have copyrighted their works, and one case charging infringement has reached federal courts. The following sites can start you thinking about copyrighting your choreography.

COPYRIGHT OF CHOREOGRAPHIC WORKS
www.csulb.edu/~jvancamp/copyrigh.html

Julie C. Van Camp is author of a scholarly and detailed examination of choreographic copyright. She examines problems of defining dance and originality, and her discussion of recording the choreographer's work is thorough.

> **More Information About Dance and Choreography**
> See the detailed listing for dance at *Artslynx* (*<www.artslynx.org/dance>*). *Encarta Encyclopedia* offers articles on choreography (*<http://encarta.msn.com/find/Concise.asp?ti=0670B000&MSID=d74be92b490811d498880008c7d9e3db>*).

HOW CHOREOGRAPHY CAN BE RECORDED IN FIXED FORM
http://edie.cprost.sfu.ca/~jacsen7/janedancerecord.html

This site describes, albeit briefly, how choreographers can seek the legal protection afforded them by copyright.

DRAMATURGY

A dramaturg? If you've wondered about the meaning of this admittedly funny-looking word, here you'll find answers. (A tip: Don't allow the final syllable—*turg*—to make you think of turgid, leading you to call your friendly local dramaturg swollen or puffy. Bad idea.) Although dramaturgy tends to have various meanings to different folks, a good start is to think of the dramaturg as an active link between playwright and production. (*Dramaturgy Northwest* offers interesting, often conflicting, opinions about dramaturgy: *<www.ups.edu/professionalorgs/dramaturgy/nwquotes.htm>*.)

Dramaturgs research facts about the playwright and the play's historical place in time and space. They discover the mores of the play's time period, look up unusual words, and are alert to literary references. One typical function is to write notes for the program that's given to audiences or perhaps to speak to audiences before or after a production. Whether or not a person specifically called a dramaturg is assigned the task, *someone* in theatre process must select, research, and prepare plays for production. Modern theatre practice increasingly uses the dramaturg.

A dramaturg's training should include such theatre courses as playwriting, theatre history and dramatic literature, directing, theory, and design, as well as comparative literature and broad history courses. Philosophy would be helpful—there is a strong argument that students of philosophy study playwrights as well as works by recognized philosophers—and for the same reason history, religion, literature, and sociology could be part of the dramaturg's education. And those likely are only the beginning of the ideal course of study.

A key book for dramaturgs is *Dramaturgy in American Theatre: A Source Book*, by Susan Jonas, Geoffrey S. Proehl, and Michael Lupu (Harcourt Brace College Publishers). Its 50 chapters and 600 pages contain excellent guides. Online booksellers like *Amazon* and *Barnes and Noble* will offer discount prices. See also the booksellers listed in An E-Shopping Spree (Chapter 12).

As you'll see in the sites listed here, various college and university libraries offer valuable bibliographic lists for the dramaturg, and they are well worth searching out. There also are sites specifically designed for dramaturgy.

DRAMATURGY NORTHWEST

www.ups.edu/professionalorgs/dramaturgy/

AUTHOR'S CHOICE   Don't let the apparent geographic limitation of the Northwest lend you to conclude that this site is only for one section of the country. On the contrary, this is a primary home for dramaturgy. Certainly it has a high level of expertise. *Dramaturgy Northwest* says it is an ongoing project of the Northwest region of literary managers and dramaturgs of the Americas (LMDA), the Association for Theatre in Higher Education (ATHE), and the University of Puget Sound. Here you'll find information about training and employment, along with insightful discussions by professional dramaturgs.

THE DRAMATURGY PAGES

www.dramaturgy.net/dramaturgy/

This address sometimes acts flaky; if you can't connect with it, you can go to a master page (*<www.dramaturgy.net>*) and from there click on *The Dramaturgy Pages*.

Working dramaturgs are here to give you information and insight. You'll also find links to affiliated research and books. Given the various definitions of the term, you'll want to glance at What is a Dramaturg? Resources for Dramaturgy is a rich collection, with strong historical emphasis as well as information about finding specific plays. Dramaturgical Work is unfortunately skimpy.

THE PLAYWRIGHT'S WORKSHOP

www.playwrightsworkshop.org/

For discussion of the dramaturg's functions, scroll down the home page. On the right margin you'll see the chance to "Find out all about the meaning of that elusive word—Dramaturgy!" Alternatively, you can go there directly (*<www.playwrightsworkshop.org/drama.html>*). What is their definition? They think of the dramaturg as a play-revision-expert: "A dramaturg . . . is to a playwright as an editor is to a novelist."

THE EARLY CAREER DRAMATURG GROUP
www.ups.edu/professionalorgs/dramaturgy/early.htm

This program offers services to dramaturgs and literary managers beginning their careers. To be eligible, you must be a member of Literary Managers and Dramaturgs of the Americas. A special strength of the offer is that services appear to be rather like a mentor relationship.

DRAMAURGY.NET
www.dramaturgy.net/

Although currently there are but a few entries, the site promises to grow.

LITERARY MANAGERS AND DRAMATURGS OF THE AMERICAS
www.lmda.org/

A central clearinghouse for literary managers and dramaturgs, this voluntary membership organization seeks to promote specific standards and goals. One hopes this site is still a-bornin' because when I last visited it, there were formatting errors and but few entries.

> **More Information About Dramaturgy**
> *National Theatre Resources Online* has lists of other dramaturgy sites. The Association for Theatre in Higher Education has a focus group on dramaturgy (<*www.ups.edu/professionalorgs /dramaturgy/focusgrp.htm*>) and offers you an opportunity to join its listserv.

RESEARCH TOOLS

Sites listed in Chapter 3 are excellent sources for theatrical research, whether into scholarly/historical areas or focused on more recent theatrical activities. Indeed, research topics can be so varied that you likely will find helpful sites throughout this book. You also will want to look in the various encyclopedic sources.

Encyclopedia for Initial Information

There are more than 100 encyclopedia sites on the Net. Some are specialized for a particular area of study—philosophy or health, for example—but the general sites can give you good basic, authoritative materials to serve as a foundation for more research. And that's the way a good researcher should think of an encyclopedia: a starter motor, not your main engine.

BRITANNICA.COM
www.britannica.com

AUTHOR'S CHOICE   You'll recall I described *Britannica* in Chapter 3, so here I'll briefly remind you that this site includes the complete *Britannica* encyclopedia. That's quite enough in itself, but the *Brit* folk also give you a searchable guide to the Web's best sites, articles from top magazines, editorials, and news. I'd suggest you make it your first encyclopedia search.

ENCARTA ONLINE
www.encarta.msn.com/

AUTHOR'S CHOICE *Encarta* is a reference site with interesting media effects, and—providing your computer has the appropriate bells and whistles—you can hear audio excerpts.

Scrolling down the home page leads you to Performing Arts, where you'll find folders for Dance, Music, and Theatre. Each will lead you to a number of excellent sites, including some multimedia. A few are marked with a star, which indicates that they are only for subscribers. After you've explored Performing Arts, go back to the home page to click on Art, Language, and Literature. Here you'll find playwrights listed alphabetically along with poets, novelists, and other authors. Most listings give you brief descriptions of the dramatist's basic facts and also suggest other sites you can click to enrich your study.

ENCYCLOPEDIA.COM
www.encyclopedia.com/

The Concise Columbia Electronic Encyclopedia offers more than 14,000 articles, many with extensive cross-references. There's an online Question and Answer facility that offers a chance to "Get real answers from real people by asking one of the thousands of experts in our database." Answers I received were of mixed value. Still, you might want to take it for a trial e-drive.

INFORMATION PLEASE—On-Line Dictionary,
Internet Encyclopedia, and Almanac
www.infoplease.com/

Information Please is described as the world's largest reference site. Perhaps. But it is ample. Using the search engine for choreography opened sites of significant dance troupes. Looking for theatre directing and dramaturgy was less profitable. However, skipping the search engine and opening Arts and Entertainment and then Performing Arts showed interesting sites such as Performing Arts Timeline, brief chronological developmental stages of our arts. This site is worth using for basic facts.

ENCYCLOPEDIA.COM
www.encyclopedia.com/

Although search engines that rank sites by popularity give this site high marks, it has a pop focus more than a scholarly in-depth approach. It may help you if you are looking for brief reference materials. The search engine is effective, albeit a bit pokey. Entertainment refers to modern celebrities. Reference takes you to a Library Tracker that promises to e-mail you some headlines; a search engine for books, magazines, newspapers, and radio-television interviews; and a Library Q&A that is an online ask-the-expert sort of site with, they say, thousands of experts in their database. (When I last visited, as an example of their expertise, the place listed a Divorce Specialist with these credentials: "I have been divorced four times and know general divorce law as well as specific divorce law for the state of WA.") Getting around in the site is considerably hampered by drop-in Company Sleuth ads. Overall, it seems to have a star fetish—it likes to look up stars more than facts.

Theatre- and Dance-Oriented Sites

THEATREPEDIA—ELAC Theatre Internet Library
www.perspicacity.com/elactheatre/library/library.htm

This rich website of the Theatre Arts Department of East Los Angeles College leads you to the *Theatrepedia Internet Theatre Library*, which is a research-helpful site of links. Included are directories for plays, history, periodicals, and other materials. If you're looking for information about notable workers in theatre's history, try Theatre People at this site (or go there directly at <*www.perspicacity.com/elactheatre/library/people.htm*>).

The left menu contains items the webmaster categorizes as pertinent to Research. You'll find Playwrights, Plays by Author, Plays by Title, Play Texts, Theatre People, Theatre Terms, Theatre Characters, Internet Tools, and Greek Theatre. A Recent Additions entry directs you to new materials.

Plays by Author lists a large number of playwrights' works. An added bonus is that the site directs you to sites containing the text of selected early playwrights, especially the classical Greeks, such as Euripides and Aristophanes, as well as those by Gilbert and Sullivan (now *there's* a mix for you!). Theatre Characters helps you find selected characters, and in some cases there are interesting descriptions.

The right menu is for Careers. Here you can access a Writers Workshop, Writing (Dramatic), Acting, Directing, Stagecraft, and Writing (Academic). There's also a Newsgroup List.

Basic Reference Sites

In one sense, the Net itself is a vast reference site. Judicious searching can uncover a wealth of information. Here I've selected certain sites that can help the theatrical researcher.

THE INTERNET PUBLIC LIBRARY RESEARCH CENTER
www.ipl.org/ref/

AUTHOR'S CHOICE   This excellent site takes you to numerous locations for research. The divisions include Reference, Arts and Humanities, Business and Economics, Computers and Internet, Education, Entertainment and Leisure, Health and Medical Sciences, Law, Government, and Political Science, Sciences and Technology, Social Sciences, and Associations. Each has rich materials.

Theatre is listed within several categories. One is Arts and Humanities, but the link reference is missing. Use the search engine. The search is worth it, for there is a fine collection of theatrical materials, most of which will lead you to additional locations. Arts and Humanities also offers Drama and Performance references, but again the link is missing so you'll want to use the searcher.

Entertainment and Leisure has a theatre section that currently has five entries that range from musicals to the Federal Theatre Project.

PERFORMING ARTS LINKS

www.theatrelibrary.org/links/ActorsHistory.html#theatre

This rich collection of sites will help you find detailed information about theatrical history, from ancient times to modern. Many links here lead to more links. For example, there is the broad-based *Jack Wolcott's Theatre History Home-Page*, with online resources for theatre history; *The Internet Classics Archive*, which has more than 400 works of classical literature by 59 different authors; *The Development of Scenic Spectacle* on the Renaissance and Baroque stage; *Elizabethan Costuming Page*; *Renaissance Dance*; *American Variety Stage Vaudeville and Popular Entertainment, 1870–1920*; *Theatre History Researches* from the Department of Theatre, University of Minnesota Duluth; and much more.

AMERICAN THEATER WEB

www.americantheaterweb.com/

What's the latest theatre news? What are critical responses to recent productions of new or older plays and musicals? When my schedule permits, I like to visit this site each morning to get a daily fix of theatre events (with some dance and ballet) from around the country. You'll find a wide number of newspapers, usually from metropolitan areas, with reports and reviews. The site is faithfully updated.

The home page has a convenient index and an effective search engine that allows you to search by region, theatre, or name of show. Still, you don't get a full idea of the depth of coverage until you visit articles. Often you'll find a menu of links to theatre happenings.

You'll also find a callboard, bookshop, and facility for your e-mail home. The feature called Take Center Stage with ATW allows you to post your theatre's website or your own.

NEW YORK TIMES ON THE WEB

www.nytimes.com/

The New York Times is recognized as a powerful—perhaps the single most powerful—voice in critical reviewing. You can look at Broadway and off-Broadway play reviews here. The index on the left will lead you to Arts and Theatre. Although you have to register, access is free.

THE LAWRENCE AND LEE THEATRE RESEARCH INSTITUTE
www.lib.ohio-state.edu/OSU_profile/triweb

Ohio State University's Lawrence and Lee Institute honors Jerome Lawrence and Robert E. Lee, who collaborated to create significant plays and musicals such as *Inherit the Wind*, *The Night Thoreau Spent in Jail*, and *Auntie Mame*. The Institute collects research materials pertaining to performing arts, with a primary emphasis on live performance. The archives are valuable for research scholars as well as for playwrights and performers.

AMERICAN THEATRE HISTORY
www.georgetown.edu/murphy/netsearch/american.html

College professor Donn B. Murphy of Georgetown University maintains this page of links about American theatre. The sites deal primarily with places, movements, and events. In some you can see posters and handbills.

There is an interesting assortment of material. African-American Theatre. Vaudeville. *Uncle Tom's Cabin*. Wild West Shows. Movie Palaces, which once housed variety shows and vaudeville. Actress Adah Isaacs Menken. The Astor Place Riot. The Chestnut Street Theatre. Archives of the famed Shubert Theatre. Chicago's Steppenwolf Theatre Company. Theatre History Links. And more.

THEATER CONNECTIONS—Comprehensive Research Guide
http://libweb.uncc.edu/ref-arts/theater

Many of the subjects listed on the left menu will be directly helpful. Research Tips leads you to Drama Criticism, a list you'll want to take to your library. General Sites and Links suggest various large theatre homes, and Electronic Journals directs you to potential research materials.

WWW VIRTUAL LIBRARY—Theatre and Drama
http://vl-theatre.com/

A good-sized site with richly diverse materials, the WWW *Virtual Library* has a variety of resources that you aren't likely to find elsewhere. A brief list illustrates the wide variety of topics, countries, genres, and time periods: Cornish Medieval Drama; Medieval European Drama in Translation; Native American Women's Playwrights Archive; International Brecht Society; Dion Boucicault Theater Collection; Max Reinhardt Archives; Shakespeare Oxford Society, which is based on the premise that the Earl of Oxford wrote Shakespeare; American Variety Stage, which has materials about vaudeville and popular entertainment between 1870 and 1920; British Women Playwrights around 1800; and SCENIS—Stage of Central Europe and Newly Independent States Database of Performing Arts, which has websites from such countries as Albania, Armenia, Azerbaijan, Belarus, Bosnia and Herzegovina, Bulgaria, Croatia, Czech Republic, Estonia, Georgia, Hungary, Kazakhstan, Kyrgyzstan, Latvia, and Lithuania.

The site is divided into four classifications—Bibliographies and Databases; Libraries, Museums and Archives; Scholarly Organizations; and Articles and

General Resources—but those titles don't accurately reflect content, and you're better advised to scroll down the page while looking at the sites.

MEDIEVAL DRAMA LINKS

http://collectorspost.com/Catalogue/medramalinks.htm

All of us who've tried to find particular links can easily empathize with Sidney Higgins, this site's webmaster, who says, "I have wasted countless hours chasing after alleged medieval drama links on the World Wide Web that turned out to be either non-existent or of little value." Countless hours? You bet. If we counted time expended, we'd have to admit time wasted.

> **More Information About Medieval Drama**
>
> HotBox/Lycos *Directory* lists a number of sites worth exploring, especially if you're searching for scripts (*<http://dir.hotbot.lycos.com/Arts /Literature/Drama/Medieval>*).

We can benefit from Higgins' search. He has a carefully organized series of categories of medieval resources . . . er, resources about medieval drama. One major folder takes you to Texts, where you find the Towneley Plays, York Plays, and *Everyman*. There also are folders for Articles and Books, Bibliographies, and Publications.

His site isn't merely theory. He includes such categories as Performance and Set Design, Props and Makeup, and Costume, which is subdivided into General, Women, Men, and Armour. You'll also find Medieval Drama Manuscripts, Medieval Paintings and Sculpture, and Medieval Music. There are links and more.

FRENCH THEATRE

www.discoverfrance.net/France/Theatre/DF_theatre.shtml

An overview of the history of theatre in France, this site offers links to significant playwrights, such as Pierre Corneille, Jean Anouilh, Samuel Beckett, Alexandre Dumas père and fils, Jean Genet, Jean Giradoux, Victor Hugo, Eugène Ionesco, Pierre de Marivaux, Molière, Jean Racine, and Edmond Rostand. There also are links to the Comédie-Française, Sarah Bernhardt, and more.

THE MOSCOW ART THEATRE

www.theatre.ru/mhat/eindex.html

One of modern theatre's most exciting developments was the revolutionary Moscow Art Theatre, which ushered in vibrant new concepts of theatre practice. Here you find detailed information about its origin.

The cover page has a photograph of the theatre and links to History of Moscow Art Theatre (in English) plus the Moscow Art Theatre page (in Russian). There is also a link to 100 years of the theatre's growth, starting with the famous meeting of Stanislavsky and Nemirovich-Danchenko at the Slavyansky Bazaar restaurant in Moscow, which began the Moscow Art Theatre and, more significantly, a new movement in modern theatre. That site has excerpts from the men's journal records of their discussions.

ARTSLYNX
www.artslynx.org

I've mentioned *Artslynx* before, but here I point out that it has numerous sites the dramaturg or researcher may wish to explore. From its homepage click on Theatre and select a category to investigate. Dramaturgy leads you to Playwrights (or go there directly with <*www.artslynx.org/theatre/authors.htm*>), where you'll find sites for playwrights and composers. Some have detailed materials.

AMERICAN SOCIETY FOR THEATRE RESEARCH
*www.inform.umd.edu/*THET/Personnel/CSchuler/ASTR

Established in 1956, ASTR focuses on theatre as a field for serious scholars. You won't be surprised, then, to find that its site offers an International Bibliography of Theatre, Awards, Prizes and Grants, Publications and Directories, and Conference Information. Its Resources on the World Wide Web is designed for researchers and students looking for theatre locations in the Internet, WWW, and beyond. This no-frills site is efficient and quick to load.

FEDERAL THEATRE PROJECT COLLECTION
http://memory.loc.gov/ammem/fedtp/fthome.html

Why doesn't the American government support the arts, like theatre, the way so many other countries do? That question provides a popular topic among theatre managers and others concerned about keeping the arts healthy. In fact, however, there was a major governmental effort to support theatre. Part of President Franklin Delano Roosevelt's New Deal to help the U. S. recover from the Great Depression, it was called the Federal Theatre Project, one of five arts-related projects established during Roosevelt's first term under the WPA (Works Progress Administration).

This site is devoted to that project. Part of the American Memory Collection at the Library of Congress, it contains more than 13,000 images on everything from stage and costume design to the script for the Orson Welles production of *The Tragical History of Dr. Faustus*. The Federal Theatre Project included remarkably innovative docudramas called the Living Newspaper—full-scale dramas dealing with significant new events and issues of the day, such as *One Third of a Nation*, a title suggested by President Roosevelt's 1933 inaugural address in which he said, "I see one third of the nation ill-housed, ill-clad, ill-nourished." The site has more than 3,000 images of another Living Newspaper production called *Power*, focused on electrical resources for impoverished areas. You can find 68 other playscripts (6,500 images) and 168 documents selected from the Federal Theatre Project Administrative Records (3,700 images).

THEATER AND PERFORMANCE STUDIES RESOURCES
www.nyu.edu/library/bobst/research/hum/perform

From New York University's Bobst Library comes this well-researched page for theatre and drama information. It is organized under categories such as General Information, Electronic Play Texts, Other Important Library Collections, E-Journals, Playwriting, Theater Awards, Theatrical Costumes, Theater Reviews, and Professional Organizations.

Lists of Individual Theatres and Theatre Companies

Often a dramaturg researches activities of other theatre organizations. To find companies and individual theatres, look in *The Drama Guild* (*<www.dramaguild.com/>*) and from its opening page scroll down the left margin and click on Links. For a list of theatres by states, go to *American Theatre Resources* (*<www.theatre-resources.net>*).

Finding Individual Plays and Playwrights

Often we need to locate details about a given play or dramatist. While many of the sites discussed in this chapter can help you locate that information, there are Web pages that focus on that topic.

INTER-PLAY—An Online Index to Plays in Collections, Anthologies and Periodicals
www.library.yale.edu/pubstation/databases/interplay.html

If part of your job requires you to find copies of a play, try this site. Most of us searching for a play are used to visiting the library to look in standard reference books like *Ottemiller's Index to Plays in Collections* or H. W. Wilson's *Play Index*. This site goes beyond those indices and can help you find additional authors. From the title page, go to the Start Searching button at the bottom.

INDIVIDUAL PLAYWRIGHTS
http://dir.yahoo.com/Arts/Humanities/Literature/Authors/Playwrights/

I wish I had known of this site earlier, because it contains materials that I needed for a recent writing project (*The Power of One*). Almost 80 individual playwrights are listed, modern and ancient, all with linking sites.

Individuality reigns on writers' personal sites, and they are fun. For example, the first entry on solo performer Eric Bogosian's home page (*<www.ericbogosian.com>*) is "CAUTION: This page contains pure unadulterated filth" (i.e., quotes from the press on *Wake Up and Smell the Coffee*), which is his way of showing what he thinks about a letter someone wrote to an editor complaining about his work. So, too, playwright Beth Campbell Stemple's home page (*<http://hot.uconect.net/~bstemple>*) reflects a bouncy and comic personality, taking the visitor through a bit of a funhouse maze to get to her.

Other sites here are about, not by, the playwright. Most are essays or articles. For Tennessee Williams, for example, there are 11 entries, most about A

Streetcar Named Desire. Not surprisingly, Shakespeare has the most entries—almost 250—including a number that tackle that popular question, Did Shakespeare write Shakespeare's plays?

PLAYWRIGHTS AND PLAYWRITING
www.georgetown.edu/murphy/netsearch/playwrit.html
Donn B. Murphy hosts this no-nonsense, no-opening-page-frills site full of playwrights, ancient and modern, from Aeschylus to George C. Wolfe. Playwrights are listed by individual name or in categories such as African-American Dramatists or African-American Female Playwrights. For most authors, there are no scripts.

It is an eclectic place. A number of different countries are represented. There are also Festivals, like the Actors Theatre of Louisville; Essays on Playwriting; sites like Inkwell for Writers; and other assorted entries.

The site isn't complete. For example, for Medieval author Hroswitha of Gandershein and for Spain's great poetic dramatist Federico García Lorca, there is a "need links" note. Contemporary authors' references have information that needs updating, as is the case for A. R. Gurney, which lacks a mention of his *Sylvia*. Strangely, for Clare Booth Luce, author of *The Women*, the biography does not mention her playwriting. Unfortunately, some links are dead, as in the case of Beth Henley's *Miss Firecracker Contest.* These nits aside, the site can give you basic information on many authors.

ANCIENT GREEK THEATRE
http://users.groovy.gr/~ekar/index.html
The writing style and some spelling errors suggest this is a translation from Greek. Still, despite some awkward sentence structure, the site offers a good insight into the ancient Greek theatre that formed the foundation of Western theatre. The home page gives you options so you may select only areas that interest you (I found I went first to The Form of the Play, Machines Used in Ancient Theatre, and discussions of several playwrights) or decide to go step by step through the development of that Greek theatrical experience.

More Research Sites
StudyWeb (<*www.studyweb.com*>) appears to be designed for primary grade school students, but the sites listed under Theatre—which appears under Arts on the home page—are more advanced, and a search of sites may help you discover materials you can use. Links at *The Society of Dance History Scholars* (<*www.sdhs.org/*>) can lead to valuable research sites, including the American Vaudeville Museum, The Eserver, and more.

Also valuable for research is a site I mentioned in Chapter 3: *McCoy's Guide to Theatre and Performance Studies* (<*www.stetson.edu/departments/csata/thr_guid.html*>).

ENGLISH VERSE DRAMA, 1300–1900
http://etext.lib.virginia.edu/evd.html

Hosted by the Electronic Text Center at the University of Virginia, the database collection comes from Chadwyck-Healey Ltd. It contains more than 2,200 works, from the Shrewsbury Fragments of the late 13th century through the unparalleled output of the Elizabethan and Jacobean period to the end of the 19th century. To access it, you'll need to consult your college library for linkage.

PERFORMING ARTS LINKS—Plays and Playwrights
www.theatrelibrary.org/links/PlaysPlaywrights.html#Playwriting

Performing Arts Links is a mega-site with folders for various aspects of theatre, dance, and the like. Its theatre folder is a well-organized grouping of costume, lighting, acting, and more—including playwriting. A subdivision of playwriting is this list of sites for individual playwrights. More than 40 dramatists are included, classical and modern, from Aeschylus to Voltaire, with (as you'd expect) a large section of Shakespeare.

PLAYWRIGHTS AND PLAYWRITING
www.georgetown.edu/murphy/netsearch/playwrit.html

If you're searching for plays and playwrights, a wealth of information waits for you here. Plays, playwrights, list of dramatic characters, playwriting contests—and, unfortunately, a number of dead sites.

SMALL CAST ONE-ACT GUIDE ONLINE
www.heniford.net/1234/

Here's an example of a writer's labor of love. Webmaster Lewis W. Heniford is so dedicated to the one-act form that he has compiled an amazingly detailed and extensive list of short plays, valuable for directors searching for short plays to present as well as for playwrights seeking examples of the one-act form. Among the helpful materials is an author index and cast size/gender index. Many entries give you a great deal of information on the playwrights. He also lists books for playwrights.

THE WWW VIRTUAL LIBRARY—Theatre and Drama
http://vl-theatre.com/

The library has a number of resources you may want to explore. One highlight is an excellent Plays in Print. Opening that takes you to two sets of alphabets, one for Plays in Print and the second for Theatre Books in Print. The former, despite its title, is also an index for Playwrights in Print because mixed in with the plays are authors. There's a broad mix of plays and playwrights, from classic to modern.

GOLDSMITH'S PLAY LIST

www.gold.ac.uk/%7Etgp/index.html

You first must register—it's free—to search this London college's database of plays and musicals that have been overlooked by publishers. You won't find the big hits, but expect instead to see new plays or plays that faded out of sight after initial production.

WOMEN OF COLOR, WOMEN OF WORDS—AFRICAN AMERICAN WOMEN PLAYWRIGHTS

www.scils.rutgers.edu/~cybers/home.html

Focused on African American female playwrights, the site is still growing and is frequently updated. On the home page scroll down to the bottom for a menu that

> **Trying to Find a Particular Playwright?**
> Try the *Dramatists Guild of America* (<*www.dramaguild .com/*>) for Find A Member's Agent.

includes Writers, where you'll find links to individual playwrights; Plays, which includes titles and playwrights; and a Reading Nook of plays with links to *Amazon*. Critical Resources is a richly detailed bibliography, and Dissertations lists scholarly examinations of individual playwrights.

Library Bibliographies

Not everything is on the Net. For the serious researcher, library investigation is essential. Thanks to dedicated librarians, the bibliographical sites included here give you excellent lists of significant texts that you'll want to consult. The lists may appear to be dependent on a given library, but you'll have little difficulty translating the call numbers to your own.

BIBLIOGRAPHY—Dramaturgy

http://dizzy.library.arizona.edu/users/btravers/tar445.htm

If you're a dramaturg who needs research advice for a play, start here. A rich source for research materials dealing with plays and playwrights, this library guide lists many references that can help you find materials. It is organized with a librarian's thoroughness. You can scroll through its categories, such as General, Finding Play Texts, Reviews of Texts and Performances, Biography, Visual Imagery/Art, Dramatic Criticism, International Drama, Journals, and The World Wide Web. Most of the books will be in a well-stocked library. Because directors often ask dramaturgs to research the play in a particular time and place, especially valuable is this site's Visual Imagery and Art.

LITERARY RESOURCES—Theatre and Drama

http://andromeda.rutgers.edu/~jlynch/Lit/theatre.html

Part of a larger Literary Resources collection maintained by Jack Lynch, this site is a handy guide to e-research links.

BOBST LIBRARY, NYU—Theater and Performance Studies Resources
www.nyu.edu/library/bobst/research/hum/perform/rg34.htm
I mentioned this library's collection earlier. Here is a different site. Although like other librarians' bibliographic lists this resource information refers specifically to a particular library, you'll have little difficulty using it in your library. It is worth the effort. This excellent list of resources is organized into such categories as Directories, Guides, Handbooks, Encyclopedias, Dictionaries, Histories, Bibliographies, Indices, Biographical Information, and Reviews—Reprints of Complete Articles.

THE NEW YORK PUBLIC LIBRARY FOR THE PERFORMING ARTS
www.nypl.org/research/lpa/lpa.html
A primary research collection awaits the visitor. As the library says of itself:

> The New York Public Library for the Performing Arts houses the world's most extensive combination of circulating, reference, and rare archival collections in its field. These materials are available free of charge, along with a wide range of special programs, including exhibitions, seminars, and performances. An essential resource for everyone with an interest in the arts—whether professional or amateur—the Library is known particularly for its prodigious collections of non-book materials such as historic recordings, videotapes, autograph manuscripts, correspondence, sheet music, stage designs, press clippings, programs, posters and photographs.

The research collections include Music Division, Dance Collection, The Rodgers and Hammerstein Archives of Recorded Sound, and The Billy Rose Theatre Collection. Clicking any of those leads you to archives and, in some instances, helpful Net sources.

FINE ARTS—General Reference Sources
www.lib.virginia.edu/fine-arts/guides.html#artguides
Theatre exists within a panoply of arts. The University of Virginia's library provides a mega-site of resource materials, and surfing through the various categories will help you increase depth of understanding of the topic you're researching.

WORLD WIDE ARTS RESOURCES—Theatre and Performing Arts
http://wwar.com
This mega-site offers a searchable inventory of sites for theatre, opera, and dance. On the opening page, scroll down a bit. In the left menu you'll see Performing Arts, which is subdivided into Dance Arts and Theatre Arts. Each leads you to a collection of sites. There also is a Chat Forum and Arts Forum, but you'll need explore to get to them.

THEATER CONNECTIONS
http://libweb.uncc.edu/ref-arts/theater

Use the menu on the left side of the home page and click on Research Tips. You'll be taken to a page where you'll see Drama Criticism, which leads to a detailed list of sources you can use at your local library. Check, too, Local Resources, which takes you to Drama Criticism: Print Resources. Note that on the opening page there are other possible areas you may want to explore, such as Shakespeare, Electronic Journals, and Plays and Playwriting. Actors and Acting takes you to biographies.

6

Acting, Stage Combat, Mime,
Improvisation, and Dance

Advice for actors is easy to find. Actress Glenda Jackson, for example, tells us how she approaches performing: "Acting is not very hard. The most important things are to be able to laugh and cry. If I have to cry, I think of my sex life. And if I have to laugh, well, I think of my sex life." Or consider this: "The most important thing in acting is sincerity," we're told George Burns said. "If you can fake that, you've got it made."

If Burns is right, then we might as well end this chapter here and instead go search for sites that tell us how to be a timeshare salesperson.

But Burns' deliberate humor may not be too far off, after all. Sincerity in acting involves nebulous qualities we call *honesty, believability, credibility, plausibility.* Combined, they contribute to that big T word—*Truth.* "Play well, or play badly, but play truly," Stanislavsky tells actors, seeking to shift the actor's attention from "good" and "bad" acting to focus instead on authenticity. Can the Net help you learn believability, authenticity—"good" acting? Can it show you ways to improve your dance? Can it help you get training, locate auditions, find an agent? Try these sites and see.

UNIONS

Various unions represent professional performers—actors, dancers, stage managers, musicians, directors, choreographers—depending on their performance specialization. (In later chapters I talk about unions for designers and technicians.) The unions make an alphabet soup of acronyms. For example, Actors Equity Association (AEA) represents theatre performers as well as stage managers. The American Guild of Musical Artists (AGMA) represents live music and variety performers. For film and television performers, there is the Screen Actors Guild (SAG), and in some instances, the American Federation of Television and Radio Artists (AFTRA). Self-explanatory are the American Guild of Musical Artists (AGMA), the American Guild of Variety Artists (AGVA), the Italian Actors Union (IAU), Society of Stage Directors and Choreographers (SSDC), and the Hebrew Actors Union (HAU). All are branches of a master organization—the Associated Actors and Artistes of America (4As), the umbrella organization directly affiliated with the American Federation of Labor-Congress of Industrial Organizations (AFL-CIO). Whew. Puts a new meaning on show *business*, doesn't it?

ACTORS' EQUITY ASSOCIATION

www.actorsequity.org/home.html

Founded in 1913, Actors' Equity Association is a union that represents actors—dancers are included in that definition—and stage managers in the legitimate theatre throughout the United States. You become eligible for Equity after 50 weeks of work at accredited theatres. Following an $800 initiation fee, annual dues are $78 plus 2 percent of your working income.

For its 40,000 members Equity negotiates minimum wages, focuses on contracts and working conditions, and makes agreements with theatrical employers. Its site offers information about Equity. From its home page you can click to helpful links.

Casting Call leads to Audition Hotlines of contacts in theatrical cities and to Audition Codes and Procedures that govern Equity Principal or Chorus Calls. There, too, you'll find a morale-building long list of Audition Notices that are neatly organized with pull-down menus by state, type of contract, and type of job. A convenient New Postings calls your attention to notices placed in the last five days.

Theatre News not only deals with New York theatrical events but also takes you to other cities when you click on Cross Country. The page also includes brief reports on ShowBuzz of gossipy tidbits about performers and shows, and a Council Feature about members of Equity's council.

Resource Center is a support group. You can click on FAQs, find related websites, and study the constitution and bylaws. Services for You, similar to the Resource Center's supportive nature, gives you valuable information such as Contracts, Pensions and Health Funds, Unemployment Compensation, Income Tax Assistance, Talent Agents, and Interviews/Auditions/Casting.

CANADIAN ACTORS' EQUITY ASSOCIATION

www.caea.com/index.htm

The Canadian Actors' Equity Association is a professional association of performers, directors, stage managers, and choreographers working in live performance in English. It protects members, promotes the arts in Canada, and attends to contracts, working conditions, and fees. It thinks of itself as an artists' association because it seeks to encourage the growth and development of professional theatre in Canada as well as theatre artists in Canada and abroad.

This friendly and well-organized site takes you to informational areas. Auditions lists job openings and allows members to sign up for regular e-mail

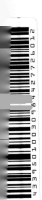

announcements of forthcoming auditions. Opportunities leads to a broadly diverse number of workshops, competitions, and announcements. InfoCulture takes you to national announcements about Theatre, Dance, and Opera. A Members' Forum encourages both venting and congratulations.

SCREEN ACTORS GUILD
www.sag.com/

The *Screen Actors Guild* is the collective bargaining representative for members' wages and working conditions. SAG began with a small group of character actors in the 1930s who struggled to overcome hostile studio opposition. It has grown to become a powerful voice for performers.

From its home page you can click on Beginning Actors, which takes you to So, Ya Wanna Be an Actor? The opening is decorated with a photo from a Marx Brothers film, but the tone shifts to less-than-comic discussions about actors' average wages, hard work, and employment statistics. It then offers you a chance to click on Basic Information, which has valuable advice for those considering a professional acting career.

The Member Area offers a SAG Directory, Residual Department, and information about Contracts, Wages, and Working Conditions. Agency Department leads you to SAG Franchised Talent Agency List and Agent Commission on Residuals, which is interestingly complex, making you imagine the negotiations that led to a final agreement.

Time exploring the site can lead to valuable information. For example, fascinating is SAG History, which has a number of short quotations from early members who started the Guild, and if you're an old movie buff you'll recognize many of their faces. Hidden away down toward the bottom of Basic Information, you can find Young Performers Handbook, Terminology of the Craft, Links, and recommended Books.

RESOURCES FOR ACTORS

"What's a LORT?" "Can someone give me tips for auditioning?" "How do I find out when there'll be auditions in my area?" "What should I know about headshots?" "What is U/RTA?" You can find sites that answer these and other questions for amateur and professional actors.

In this section you'll find sites with audition information. Perhaps this is a good time to urge you to avoid "the Broadway mentality" syndrome. Yes, certainly, seeing your name in lights on a Broadway theatre's marquee is an attractive idea. But Broadway is not the only place for exciting theatre. Across the country are numerous excellent theatres. The Mark Taper in California. The Actors Theatre of Louisville. The Arena in Washington. The Guthrie in Minneapolis. There are some 300-such resident, not-for-profit professional regional theatres around the U.S., and each deserves your attention. In addition, summer festivals—such as the ones in Alabama and

Colorado, which focus on Shakespeare—can provide you excellent performance opportunities.

My suggestion: Be flexible, keep auditioning, take classes, continue studying, and keep honing your art and craft with every performance you can—no matter where it is. Theatre is a small city. What you do at one theatre will be known at other theatres across the country.

General Resources

As is typical with Net sites, most individual locations offer a variety of services and links. Internet resources from performers range from thorough sites to lightweight vanity sites. I'll try to skip the latter type.

ARTSLYNX
www.artslynx.org/

AUTHOR'S CHOICE You'll recall that I've mentioned this site before. It deserves our attention again. Click on Alphabet Soup at the bottom of the home page and you'll find the meanings of those letters you hear others discuss so glibly. Many have a Web presence awaiting your click. For example, there's LORT (League of Resident Theatres, but unfortunately no website), USITT (United States Institute for Theatre Technology), NEA and NEH (National Endowment for the Arts and National Endowment for the Humanities), even SL (but you knew that meant Stage Left) and SOL (which means . . . oh, look it up)—about 370 different entries to flavor the soup. While you're there, you'll find that other parts of *Artslynx* are worth exploring, too.

UNIVERSITY/RESIDENT THEATRE ASSOCIATION
www.urta.com/

For those seeking training in professional theatre work, the *University/Resident Theatre Association* is a coalition of prestigious professional theatre training programs and theatres. Although most are universities, U/RTA—pronounced as one word, Urr*Tuh*—also includes theatre companies and summer festivals. Each winter U/RTA sponsors unified auditions in three selected areas. A large group of actors arrive to audition and find representative directors from the universities and theatrical organizations.

From their home page you can find what universities and theatres participate by clicking on Who We Are. What We Do describes the audition process and tells you dates and cities. Clicking on Auditions leads to another page where you're to click on a box marked NUAI (National Unified Auditions/ Interviews), which describes the process.

Audition Informational Sites—Paid Membership

Some sites offer information about auditions for a fee. Before signing up for a year's membership, it makes sense to first take it for a trial drive. You should be able to get a one-month trial membership for something under $10.

Personally, I object to sites that charge to give you information about auditions. Charge for other things? Okay. But not for audition information. Theatre folk should be helpful and contribute to theatre folk. However, that's only one person's opinion, and I'm not facing the bills and time expenditure attendant on keeping a website up and running.

CASTING NETWORK.COM

www.thecastingnetwork.com/

Developed by actors for actors, *Casting Network.com* is a membership site that provides online databank resources for casting directors and talent agents. It claims to have more auditions in its databank than any other site, and it offers you a chance to try out the site by paying the first month's dues ($9.95) and looking around for 48 hours. If you're disappointed you can ask for a refund within those 48 hours. To find its Membership Agreement, click on Join, then scroll down to the bottom of the form. A Message Board is free; it had eight entries when I visited.

THE CASTING NETWORK

www.castingnetwork.net/

Although it sounds like the previous site, this is a different organization. Based in Studio City, California, TCN says it is dedicated to providing "top quality cold reading and prepared scene showcases for professional performers who meet our standards and are committed to career advancement." It requires actors to audition for entry and thereafter encourages them to attend various workshops with casting directors. Workshops usually cost $30.

There are six buttons to click on the home page, including New Members, Policies, Online Reservations, and Pricing and Discounts. When I visited, the Calendar had an encouragingly sizable number of forthcoming workshops with casting directors who, the site says, prefer to cast actors from TCN. The Studio Store offered a few videos and CDs that seemed irrelevant for casting.

Audition Informational Sites—Free

You've seen audition information in the sites I mentioned at the beginning of this chapter. Now I'll add more. In earlier chapters I've discussed the first four of these sites in some detail, so here I'll list them with little discussion.

THEATRE CENTRAL/PLAYBILL ON-LINE

www1.playbill.com/cgi-bin/plb/central?cmd=start

For professional theatre notices, *Theatre Central/Playbill on-Line* has rich materials. On the opening page, click on Casting and Jobs. To access Job Openings you need to sign up for a membership—it is free—in The Playbill Club. Once you're a member, on the opening page scroll down to Job Search on the left menu. Clicking that, you find categories such as Performer, Technical, Design, Administrative, Academic, and Other.

ELAC

www.perspicacity.com/elactheatre/library/links.htm#Employment

I discussed other aspects of ELAC earlier. This address takes you directly to Employment links. Frequently updated, they are informational and worth investigating regularly.

ARTSLYNX

www.artslynx.org/

From the home page click on Theatre, then examine the large number of links. Theatre Employment Resources has about a dozen listings. Theatre Company Listings will lead you to sites where you can find details of particular theatres.

SCOTT'S THEATRE-LINK.COM

www.theatre-link.com/

On the home page scroll down to Casting and Contract Services Link (or go there directly with <*www.theatre-link.com/casting.html*>) and you're led to Casting and Contact Services, which offers a wide variety of links. Valuable, too, is Actors' Pages, which you can examine to compare and evaluate your own website.

BACKSTAGE.COM

www.backstage.com/backstage/index.jsp

Backstage.com is an excellent resource for actors, and because of its contents I would have labeled it AUTHOR'S CHOICE. Unfortunately, however, sometimes it has been quite slow to load, and—worse—on occasion it has paralyzed my browser to the point where I had to leave the Net to cleanse my computer's memory, apparently due to obnoxious pop-up ads. Those problems aside, it contains valuable information.

The site mixes free service and paid membership. Free is its audition information, which you can access by clicking Casting from the left-hand menu (or go there directly with <*www.backstage.com/backstage/index.jsp*>). Once there, you'll find casting information from Chicago, Florida, and the East and West coasts. The Performing Arts Service Directory—also free, thank you—is divided into geographic regions, each with valuable practical sites like Voice Overs, Temp Services (the performer's traditional employment while waiting to be cast), and Dance. Scrolling down the home page shows you articles and information about theatre as well as reviews of productions.

You may elect to become a member, thus obtaining yet more details. Membership costs $9.95 monthly or $114.90 annually. It offers advance casting notices and articles. Members may post their résumés and headshot pictures. Additionally, you receive your own Web page.

OPEN CASTING

www.opencasting.com/

This bulletin board—free both to those seeking information and those announcing auditions—contains casting notices, auditions, crew calls, and other information and links. It seeks to be a full service Web resource for the entertainment community.

EPERFORMER.COM
www.eperformer.com/

You'll find valuable information at *eperformer.com*. From the front page click on Auditions and you'll be taken to information about auditions divided into Theatre, Music, Dance, Film and TV, Other, and Tech. Alternatively, you can click on Monthly Listing Calendars for audition schedules over two months. The site lists a number of auditions around the country.

While there, look at other pages. Resources, for example, lists Agents, Acting Resources, Dance Resources, Voice Overs, and others. Links leads you to performing arts locations by either state or subject. Of special value is the Regional Theatre Sites.

THEATRE SERVICES GUIDE
www.theaterservicesguide.com/

Obviously updated frequently, this guide offers a number of services. If you're seeking job information, you have several choices. On the bottom of the left menu click on Call Board and you'll find notices for actors, stage managers, technicians, and others. Also from that left menu you can open Message Boards, which includes Auditions/Crew Calls.

ACTOR SITE
www.actorsite.com/

AUTHOR'S CHOICE Scrolling down the left menu leads you to Equity Casting Call. A click and you find Audition Hotlines of phone numbers in selected cities, Audition Codes and Procedures that dictate Equity systems, and Audition Notices with announcements of auditions around the country. They show up inside a small frame that requires busywork scrolling horizontally and vertically. The site has numerous other categories, such as free websites, forums, headshot photographers and guidelines, and industry headlines.

DIRECTORY OF SUMMER THEATER IN THE UNITED STATES
www.summertheater.com/

Summer theatres provide numerous opportunities for actors and dancers. Some are full-fledged operations while others are smaller. This site allows you to search by geographic region or by alphabetized listings. It would be more valuable if each theatre's website were there for you to click to find additional information.

Hollywood Dreams

This book is about theatre, not film, but many actors dream of "what if" and practice the speech they'll make with Oscar firmly in hand. For them, I show a possibility.

MOVING TO HOLLYWOOD

www.io.com/MovingToHollywoodGuideForActors/
Preparing For Hollywood. What To Expect. Sexual Exploitation And Acting. Actor/Writer Advice. Scams In Hollywood. Personal stories make up this site. It is chatty, insightful, and probably often wise. Don't expect formally written essays or hard-core specific facts, but the stories ring with truth. The site also wants you to buy its video for about $30.

ONLINE WORKSHOPS AND PROGRAMS

Yes, acting is real-life and not virtual reality. Can the Internet nonetheless help you improve your acting abilities and hone your talent? There are sites that answer "yes!" After all, one major portion of your learning process comes from books, so why not from Net sites? Most of those listed here are led by actors whose experience helps them know what advice is valuable.

ACTING WORKSHOP ON LINE—AWOL

www.redbirdstudio.com/AWOL/acting2.html
AWOL is for actors who seek to learn more about their art and want information about breaking into the business. This strong site has "hundreds of great acting links," which means a number of theatres are represented in one locale—regional auditions for summer stock, festivals, theme parks, and college-university programs. Here you can find out about auditions by SETC, URTA, LORT, and others. There are links to the major professional unions.

More Information About Auditions

Check for audition information at the union sites, described at the beginning of the chapter, especially *Actors Equity* and *Canadian Actors Equity*. See also *ActorSource*, Buzz/NYC/LA, *Acting Workshop on Line*, and *ONStage —The Actor's Resource*, which are described later in this chapter. See, too, *CastingNotice.com* (*<www.castingnotices.com>*).

Listings for Regional Theatres

To my surprise and frustration, I could not find a complete list of all nonprofit regional theatres in the U. S. Even TCG doesn't have an online listing (I e-mailed them to be sure). If there is a site for such info, I couldn't find it. Perhaps few of those organizations have an online presence, although that's hard to believe. *Eperformer* lists some regionals (*<www.eperformer.com /links/links_regionals.htm>*).

Additionally, AWOL offers "lessons," primarily geared for newbies, which are available for you to enter from the opening page. Although the attempts at chatty humor gets strained, you'll find advice about audition techniques, memorization, and well-thought-out recommendations of books for beginning or advanced actors.

ACTING ON THE WEB
www.actingontheweb.com/

AOW's premise is that using videotapes means you can learn acting at a distance. Lesson One (the first one is free) starts teaching you acting by giving you a monologue to perform. Tape it, send it to AOW, and you'll receive comments designed to help you improve. That helps you decide if you wish to continue (for a fee). You can click on The Director to find who leads AOW.

There also is an e-mail address inviting you to send in questions about AOW or acting in general. The Actors Call Sheet at the bottom of the page had only a few entries when I last visited—and one of them was a cooking recipe.

ACTING SCHOOLS, COURSES, AND TRAINING CLASSES
http://pages.prodigy.net/kenstock/schools.htm

Although far from being an all-inclusive list, here you'll find links to significant acting schools.

ACTORSOURCE
www.actorsource.com/

AUTHOR'S CHOICE The home page declares this is "the most extensive acting related homepage on the Internet" that can be "used by anyone from the beginning actor to the seasoned veteran." It certainly has a rich menu. Webmaster Christopher Brian Barrette is an actor who seeks to help steer others through the maze of the profession. He apparently updates the site frequently; when I visited, the last date was only a couple of weeks old.

With a working actor's awareness of the pragmatic needs of the trade, he includes information for Voice Over Studios and Classes, Mailing Labels and Résumé Services, and—for those needing headshots—Photographers and Reproduction Studios. He includes How To Get Into Show Business, Monologues, Common Questions and Answers About Agents, and a Step By Step Guide on How to Get Started In Acting.

You'll find Auditions, Casting Calls, College and Universities, and addresses of Talent Agents and Casting Directors. There are addresses, too, for Television Network Offices and Studios, Dramatic Serials, and Comedy Club and Bookers.

THE COMPLETE GUIDE TO THE ALEXANDER TECHNIQUE
www.alexandertechnique.com/

Fans of the Alexander Technique are quick to point out that it is valuable not only for actors but also for a healthy everyday life. F. M. Alexander (1869–1955) was an actor who discovered that muscular tensions created personal vocal problems. He believed that reducing neck tension stops the head from compressing the spine, allowing it to lengthen. The core of the Alexander Technique is a method that encourages all the body's processes to work more efficiently.

This "complete guide" site is neatly organized. You click on questions to find detailed answers. It also gives you directions for additional resources.

DIRECTION—A Journal on the Alexander Technique
http://directionjournal.com/index.htm
Over a decade old, the *Direction Journal* is distributed to some 40 different countries. The journal contains articles by expert Alexander Technique teachers. The site also offers links to Teachers, Organizations, and Freemail News.

> **More Information on the Alexander Technique**
> Also check out the *Alexander Technique Center of Washington* for The Insiders Guide to the Alexander Technique (<*www.alexandercenter.com/*>).

ONSTAGE—The Actor's Resource
www.onstage.org/
Designed for professional stage and screen actors, this site has helpful guides. An Auditions section covers numerous cities, although unfortunately some services charge for what should be free information. There also is a Services category for professional needs such as photographers, résumé designers, and answering services. A neatly organized Theatre division lists companies by states, allowing you to visit individual theatre's Web pages.

THE TONGUE TWISTER DATABASE
www.geocities.com/Athens/8136/tonguetwisters.html
Actors' warm-up exercises typically include tongue twisters, which are designed to make lips and tongue more limber. Often they are pure fun. One of my favorites is "Hi. I'm a pheasant plucker. I pluck mother pheasants. I'm a pleasant mother pheasant plucker." A leader says each sentence and the group repeats it, increasingly rapidly. In that same playful spirit, this site contains a pageful of tongue twisters, more than I cared to count.

IMPROVISATIONAL THEATRE

A healthy movement for creative theatre experiences, improv is popular in many communities and especially on college campuses. There are two basic forms of improv. One is the exercise used in acting classes to encourage creativity and in rehearsals to help actors explore characterization. The second form is a performance. No script is used—although an improv troupe may have a rough scenario or some set approaches—and the performers spontaneously create dialog and action while the audience is present. Highly popular is "spot improv," a particularly freewheeling performance in which the actors ask the audience for suggestions and quickly develop them into scenes.

For me, Chicago's Second City has been the major headquarters of improvisational theatre, and many of its scenes are firmly in my memory banks.

**More Information
on Improv**
You can put yourself on an improv mailing list by clicking *listserv@netcom.com* and entering *subscribe* in the subject line.

Longtime fans of Second City still talk about the amazing improvs of Mike Nichols and Elaine May.

College and university improv groups often are innovative, with high standards that guarantee warm audience support. For example, on my campus—The College of William and Mary—our Improvisational Theatre has earned widespread respect, and the troupe's performances draw large crowds.

The following sites can help you establish or improve your own group to create equally memorable experiences. At these sites you also can locate troupes around the country.

THE SPOLIN CENTER

www.spolin.com/

Here you find details about Viola Spolin, a key creator of modern improvisational theatre. Clicking on The Spolin Players will lead you to another place to click—Spolin Games—which gives you a good idea of improv performance ingredients. The site also features newsletters and workshops.

IMPROV ACROSS AMERICA

www.improvamerica.com/

If you're looking to find improvisational activity, this state-by-state breakdown of Improv Troupes gives quick information on companies. Some have websites.

IMPROVISATIONAL GAMES

*http://americantheater.about.com/musicperform/americantheater/gi/dynamic/offsite.htm?site
=http://www.accessone.com/%7Eup/playbook/type/Game.html*

This address is flaky at times. If it doesn't work for you, try accessing the *American Theatre* home page (<*http://americantheater.about.com/musicperform
/americantheater/?once=true&*>). Once there, click on Improv on the left menu, then Games.

If you're looking for improv games for an audience, you're bound to find what you want here. This site has so many, I gave up counting them. Listed alphabetically, there are sure to be some inspirational materials here to spark your creativity.

MIME

Say *mime* and most people immediately have an image of Marcel Marceau, the great French master of mime for more than fifty years. (Said one reviewer, "The man has the most expressive hands since Michelangelo.") He set a high standard for all who follow him. A favorite for generations, Marceau and his loveable everyman alterego, Bip, raised the public's consciousness—and mime artists—to what mime can be. For more about him, you might want to visit the Marcel Marceau Foundation for the Art of Mime (<*www.marceau.org*>), although it contains less about him than you might wish.

THE WORLD OF MIME THEATRE

www.geocities.com/Broadway/5222/

The opening graphic is attractive: a body and a set of tragedy-comedy masks morph into a symbol of the mime. It tends to load slowly, so avoid scrolling down until you see the effect. This excellent site seems to have everything you might wish except video clips and photographs.

The World of Mime Theatre promotes mime as a serious theatrical art. Created by Lorin Eric Salm, this is a genuinely international site, with references to many countries and links to just about everything you seek regarding mime. It provides education, exchange of information, and a way to connect those who are interested in mime. Links invite you to browse a Library and Information and Resources. A Performance page deals with the "who and where of Mime performance around the world." Theatre Links takes you to a list of other locales you may wish to visit.

Additional Information About Mime
See Artslynx, Physical Theatre and Mime Links: <*www.artslynx.org/theatre/physical.htm*>).

Materials seem to be up to date. For example, Calendar has a number of worldwide mime shows, festivals, and events, and all were current when I visited the site. Information and Resources also has new materials, along with older classics, and you'll find such sites as Mime Training and Workshops, Bookstore, Publications, Film and Video, and websites related to mime. Organizations is a rich international listing of mime groups.

THE GOLDSTON MIME FOUNDATION—School for Mime

www.goldmime.com/

Founded in 1980 by Nick Johnson and Gregg Goldston, the *Goldston Mime Foundation* holds annual summer workshops and seminars at Kenyon College (Gambier, Ohio). It has hosted five summer seminars with Marcel Marceau, Artistic Advisor to the school, who has said that "Gregg Goldston is a solo performer who has developed a unique and powerful style of mime. His work is among the best I have seen in my long career of performing throughout the world."

STAGE COMBAT

When movie actor and movie-swordsman Errol Flynn Jr. died, part of the eulogy was a reported interview in which he was asked whether he was as good a swashbuckler as his father, who also had made many sword movies. The younger Flynn supposedly replied thoughtfully that his father was better at swashing but he thought he excelled at buckling. (If the term *swashbuckling* confuses you, perhaps you might enjoy looking at an excellent book describing stage combat: *Swashbuckling: A Step-By-Step Guide to the Art of Stage Combat and Theatrical Swordplay*, by Richard J. Lane. Lane is Executive Director at The Academy of the Sword in San Francisco—<*www.academyofthesword.org*>.)

No doubt you've seen many movies full of swordplay, full of slash, parry, and foot stomps, and of course you remember the motion pictures' barroom brawls that broke tables, chairs, and jaws (but, curiously, the guy who was clobbered and then smashed over the head with a huge barrel would spit out a tooth and return to the fray). Stage Combat today may have inherited some of that spirit, but now the concern is first for safety and then credibility.

Stage Combat Schools, Workshops, Teachers, and Leaders

You might want to look over these sites for more information about stage combat.

The Academy of the Sword. San Francisco, California: <*http://home.flash.net/~rjlane*>

The Academy of Theatrical Combat. Los Angeles, California: <*www.catalog.com/academy*>

Los Angeles Fight Academy (LAFA). Los Angeles, California: <*www.4lafa.org*>

Ring of Steel. University of Michigan, Ann Arbor: <*www.deathstar.org/groups/ros/*>

THE SOCIETY OF AMERICAN FIGHT DIRECTORS

www.safd.org/

The Society of American Fight Directors is dedicated to training and promoting safety, and committed to excellence in the art of directing staged combat/theatrical violence. Founded in 1977, SAFD certifies teachers of stage combat and is considered the primary authorizing organization. It also sponsors summer workshops in Las Vegas and South Paris, Maine.

NETSWORD—Stage Combat 101

www.netsword.com/stagecombat.html

The Internet Medieval Weapons Discussion Group, NetSword here presents e-lessons on stage combat. Your teacher, Winston Glen Kyle, first warns you that live practice is better than reading, and then guides you through the selected basics. Helpful diagrams illustrate his points. The lessons also contain practical advice. About stage blood, for example, there is this tip: "The best mixture I've found for washout-ability, cost effectiveness, appearance, and tasty goodness is Karo Corn Syrup with red food dye." He concludes with suggestions for further education—books, movies, and online resources.

RING OF STEEL

http://maniac.deathstar.org/groups/ros

This theatrical combat and stunt group has put together an excellent page of stage combat materials. You'll find information and articles about weapons, groups, fight choreographers, and weapons for rent. Located in Ann Arbor, Michigan, they also teach classes and workshops, choreograph shows, and perform. The Web Links can be especially valuable if you are searching for suppliers of combat equipment or troupes and individuals involved in stage combat.

More Information About Performances

Look in AltaVista (*<http://dir.altavista.com/Top/Arts /Performing_Arts?o=10>*). From this directory, you can click on Acting, Mime, Performance Arts, or Theatre. Of the four, the latter has the most riches.

DANCE

Just as actors can find valuable Net locations, so can dancers. But why aren't there sites that treat acting and dance as one entity? Probably because so many of us separate the two. That's a shame. The ideal dancer is an actor, using characterization techniques as does an actor. The ideal actor has had dance and movement training to be able to physicalize roles, along with lessons in Alexander Technique. For musical theatre, dancing and acting (and, of course, singing) are essentials.

Directories of Directories

A substantial number of sites list groups of dance-related categories that lead to homes you can visit. They are far more complete than theatre informational sites, and I'd guess there isn't a significant dance group, person, company, or service that you can't find through these directories.

CYBER DANCE—Ballet on the Net

www.cyberdance.org/

AUTHOR'S CHOICE   Mega-site certainly applies to *Cyber Dance*, which says it has more than 3,500 links to resources for modern dance and classical ballet. After searching through the site, I'd guess there may be twice that number. They are organized under nine basic categories: Companies, Colleges, Schools, Summer Programs, News and Information, People and Organizations, International, Goods and Services, and Dance Web Sites.

Each contains a wealth of information, neatly organized, and they are so complete it is difficult to think that there are any omissions. People, for example, leads you to a lengthy alphabetical list, which is followed by an index of lists such as List of Ballet Choreographers, List of Choreographers, Bolshoi Ballet Dancers, and more. Goods and Services has links to such groupings as Dancewear, Dance Jewelry, and Accessories; Dance Books, Videos, Audio

Tapes and CDs; and Other Dance Goods and Services. Companies is a detailed alphabetical list that you can scroll through or, alternatively, search by letter of the alphabet.

DANCE PAGES.COM—Resources for Dance Teachers
www.dancepages.com/
A bit brief but with interesting sites, *Dance Pages* has both chatty and informational links. In the former group, It's a Living deals with one person's experiences. Ballet Central fits the latter category with an involved and detailed dictionary and pedagogical techniques.

DANCE DIRECTORY
www.sapphireswan.com/dance
A mega-guide to dance resources, the *Sapphire Swan Dance Directory* organizes materials according to more than 30 dance styles, such as ballet, ballroom, belly, clogging, modern, zydeco, and more, all listed on the left menu. Each leads to other sites. For example, Tap Dance offers you 11 sites. At the bottom of that left menu is More Styles, which gives you about a dozen additional sites.

Other Dance Links at the top of the page puts a new menu on the left side. You'll see sites for schools, books, supplies, links, and other directories.

@URL INTERNET ARTS RESOURCES
http://url.co.nz/arts/dance.html
This New Zealand mega-site has a well-organized and detailed list of sites worth investigating. As it says, "This hotlist makes links to a representative sample of dance resources on the World Wide Web. The megasites listed below are the places where you'll find links to ALL the dance resources that are known." It keeps its dance resources section current—A Dance is Worth 10,000 Words (<*http://url.co.nz/arts/dance.html*>) had been updated within a month when I last visited.

You'll find such categories as Mega Dance Resources, Cyber Dance Resources, Ballet Resources, Software for Dance, Contemporary Dance Resources, Scholarly Resources and Archives, Dance Publications, and more. Many have a strong international presence.

BALLET/DANCE
http://balletdance.miningco.com/musicperform/balletdance
The center of the page brings new events In the Spotlight. Along the left menu are some 30 categories, including unusual ones like Art, which leads to dance-related homes such as Noguchi, Isamu, a Japanese sculptor responsible for stage designs for many of Martha Graham's ballets; and Big Star Video Store, where you can order more than 30 dance-related videos. Other categories include Articles, Reviews, Health Care, Photography, and History (not quite limited to historical subjects).

EDANCING—Eating Disorders in Dance

www.danceart.com/edancing

Carol Baines, a registered clinical psychologist and former ballet student, brings to this site a focus seldom found: eating disorders, a problem that unfortunately flourishes among dancers. The opening page asks, "Have you ever met someone who is overly concerned with their food intake, who sometimes starves themselves while other times overeats, or who abuses medication in order to stay slim? These are all symptoms of serious eating disorders." The valuable site has an explanatory column with recommended reading plus various links on the topic.

ANSWERS FOR DANCERS

www.answers4dancers.com

AUTHOR'S CHOICE This is a breezy, cheerful site, sponsored by *Dance* magazine and hosted by Grover Dale, whose extensive professional musical theatre experience makes him a good person to serve as Answer Man. The front page has an article dealing with an aspect of dance and a menu along the left. You may want to look at Auditions and Dancers first.

Along the left menu you see a long list of selections, and you probably will want to look at Questions/Answers of the Month and the Hall of Fame Q&A sections, where the advice is thorough and complete. For example, this is one part of the advice to a New York–based dancer: "Take classes, hang out, and witness the action at the Broadway Dance Center where five floors of classes are filled with working dancers and choreographers." Another answer includes advice about finding information for auditions: "Open calls in N.Y. are listed in *Backstage* and *ShowBusiness* (it comes out on newsstands every Thursday). Ditto for L.A., except the paper is called *Backstage West.*"

Also on that menu are thought-provoking entries like College versus the Biz, Financial Challenges, and Training Counts. How Do I Start? has sensible encouragement. Professional Audition Workshop discusses special workshops in California.

Presenters, Festivals, and Workshops

For dancers, festivals and workshops provide excellent experience and training. I list here a few of the more significant ones.

CANADIAN ALLIANCE OF DANCE ARTIST

www.mcsquared.com/cada

Formed because of the status of the Artist Legislation in Canada that would have allowed only one bargaining unit organization for all types of dance (commercial, ballet, modern etc.), CADA is developing a national Basic Dance Agreement that responds to funding of the arts in Canada. Relating to that premise, it offers links such as Self Employed Artists, Independent

Contracting, and Copyright and Dance. There also is a Dance Links. When I last visited the site, I noticed that its last update was well over a year ago.

DANCE ON LINE
www.danceonline.com

"New dance from around the world," the site says, and to that end it has Dance News, Features, Reviews, and Previews and Listings for New York City. Other features include Services and Links. Multiple episodes of the Chronicles of Dancer "X" take you into the world of dancers as seen through her eyes.

The Photo Exhibit looked promising but turned out to be skimpy and presented in an unfortunate blue overcast. More interesting are the chat boards, which focus on three basic topics: Open Forum—General Talk About Dance; Dancer's/Choreographer's Opportunities; and Research Forum for Dance Scholars.

WORLD WIDE WEB VIRTUAL LIBRARY—DANCE
www.artswire.org/Artswire/www/dance/dance.html

The *World Wide Web Virtual Library*, which you've seen listed elsewhere for theatre, operates this dance page, and it is co-maintained by Arts Wire and DanceUSA. They seek a comprehensive coverage of dance-related information, and invite contributions. Pages are updated every two months.

The opening page has a bare-bones design and immediately invites you to browse the Dance Library. Clicking that takes you to another simple page with four choices: an Alphabetical List; Dance Schools: College and University Dance Programs; Dance Pages Organized by Type; and Dance Resources.

Whichever you select, the pages fill. The alphabetical list is long. You'll find individuals, organizations, schools, ensembles, and workshops. Countries include America, Canada, Britain, and Japan. There are also types of dance, including those seldom listed elsewhere, like clogging and flamenco. The pages organized by Type appear to present the same information. Dance Resources has a rather short entry list, with such files as Advocacy, Competitions, Calendars, Funding Resources, and Library/Research Collections.

AMERICAN DANCE FESTIVAL
www.americandancefestival.org

ADF is a multifaceted organization. One focus is on performances, and the site points out that "since its founding 66 years ago, ADF has been the scene of more than 480 premieres by artists" who are innovative leaders in the art. A second focus is on classes and workshops for young dancers and professionals. It holds auditions around the country, starting at the beginning of the year, and scholarships are available.

DANCE THEATER WORKSHOP
www.dtw.org

Located in New York, DTW has a professional program. Indeed, several of their people recently won Obies—Annie B. Parson and Paul Lazar's *Big Dance Theater* won a 1999–2000 Obie, as did Cynthia Hopkins for her performance in *Another Telepathic Thing*. The site lists DTW's calendar, programs, and staff. It also has Artist Services, How to Get Produced, and Other Links.

CONTACT IMPROVISATION
www.contactimprov.net

The page, frequently updated, seeks to inform people interested in Contact Improvisation about jams, workshops, and classes. But what *is* "contact improvisation"? Because it is *improvisation*, it doesn't lend itself to easy definitions. I venture a suggestion that it is for dancers as improv is for actors—an exercise, a challenge for the creative spirit, or a free-spirited public performance. The site's definition shrugs a bit:

> I've never seen a definition of Contact that I really liked. For some people, it's a post-modern folk dance. For others, it's a process for finding new choreographic ideas. Some people perform it, others do it as a practice or discipline. Some people look at it and see gymnastics, or wrestling, or swing dance. What are the "mere facts" about it? It's usually done as a duet (but sometimes solo or in larger groups), it's usually in silence; and it's improvised. Dancers are as likely to be on the floor as standing, and sometimes they're flying on someone else's shoulders.

The site recommends more definitions at *Bibliography of Contact Improvisation* (*<http://users.lanminds.com/~contact/ci25/biblio.html>*).

Other Dance Resources

The Net offers you dance scholarship, history, and a wide variety of materials. The first site listed here is a scholarly organization. The next has numerous links you may wish to investigate.

SOCIETY OF DANCE HISTORY SCHOLARS
www.sdhs.org

A scholarly organization, SDHS promotes "study, research, discussion, performance, and publication in dance history and related fields." As it says, it defines "dance history" broadly:

> The field encompasses the tradition of Western theatrical dance from Renaissance and Baroque court entertainments to postmodern dance theater; the dance traditions of non-Western cultures; and a range of theatrical and participatory dance forms constitutive of popular culture—from country dancing and the waltz to the tango and MTV.

SDHS publishes a newsletter twice yearly and the periodical *Studies in Dance History*. It also holds an annual convention, usually in June. Annual

More Information for Dance
See these two excellent mega-sites: *Performing Arts Online* (<*www.PerformingArts.net/Links/i-nlinks.html*>) and *Performing Arts Links-Index* (<*www.theatrelibrary.org/links/index.html*>). The *World Wide Arts Resources—Visual Arts, Performing Arts, and Resources* offers links to Dance if you click on Performing Arts (<*http://wwar.com*>). You may also want to look at the dance sites listed on *Yahoo!* (<*http://dir.yahoo.com/Arts/ Performing_Arts/Dance*>) and *Netscape* (<*http://directory.netscape.com/Arts/Performing_Arts/Dance/Modern*>). Valuable, too, are the sites on AltaVista (<*http://dir.altavista.com/Top/Arts/Performing_Arts/Dance*>). For information regarding cultural events—including dance events around the country—try *CultureFinder.com* (<*www.culturefinder.com*>).

membership fees range from $30 for students to $65 for regular members. Some members teach dance and theory in university or college dance or theatre departments. Others are performers, arts administrators, independent scholars, or dance critics.

DANCE LINKS
www.dancer.com/dance-links
Compiled by Amy Reusch with the assistance of James White for newsgroup *alt.arts.ballet*, *Dance Links* offers opportunities for surfing. Although the home page looks brief, with only a dozen categories, clicking on each leads to long lists of sites. You can investigate entries for such divisions as Ballet Companies, Modern Dance Companies, Dance Presenters, Dance Organizations, University Dance, and Dance Schools. Funding Resources offers a number of excellent choices. Miscellaneous Resources leads to a variety of materials, such as Dancewear Suppliers (a long list), Employment (again a long list), Choreography and Labanotation Software, Health and Medicine, and more.

PERSONAL WEB PAGES FOR ACTORS AND DANCERS

Why have a Web page? It gives you more space than you're permitted on the résumé (although that's also a potential negative if you get too involved on the website in talking about your hobby of collecting antique lint). You can list it on your résumé, and you can mention it to any directors, casting directors, or choreographers you meet. Because you can work on your website easily, it's a great place to update the info attached to the headshot you gave directors last year. Furthermore, there's always the chance that surfing directors will find you and want to hire you immediately. (Hey, it is *possible*, right?)

Sample Web Pages

What should your Web page look like? You'll want it to open easily and quickly (which means limiting animations and graphics at least on the first page); it should get directly to the point that you're available (versus stuff about your hobby of iris propagation); it ought be attractive; and, most of all, it should reflect your personality (or maybe the image you're trying to project). It is a personal decision. Here are some samples to help you design your own.

KEN STOCK, ACTOR

http://pages.prodigy.net/kenstock/index.htm

This personal website is more than just a professional's "hire me" page, although it does have the appropriate headshots and credits. It goes past that, however, and also displays the owner's personality. The image is one of a professional attitude based on accumulated knowledge and experience. For example, Actor's Links is a long and valuable compilation of sites, indicating that Stock does his homework carefully. While you're there, also click on Other Actors and Friends to find a list of personal Web pages you can examine.

JILL SCHACKNER

www.geocities.com/JillSchackner

This home page illustrates a working professional's site. Jill Schackner is familiar to the legions of Les Misérables fans—she played Young Cosette and Young Eponine in the Broadway production. Audiences at Disney's Out of the Box will also remember this young star. As you'd expect, her site has a résumé and pictures, both headshots and photographs from production. Less common but typical of more advanced sites, it also has Sounds, allowing you to hear the young actress sing brief extracts from several songs.

OPEN CASTING

www.opencasting.com/HSAnnounce.htm

I mentioned Open Casting earlier in this chapter. Here I draw your attention to its offer to let you post your headshot on its site.

Other sites will help you get an e-presence. For example, see Performing Arts Network (<*www.webmentors.com/Auditions/index.asp*>), which says it is in the business of providing inexpensive website development and hosting for the performing arts, and Actor Site (<*www.actorsite.com*>), which offers free websites.

Newsgroups for Dance
uiuc.org.dance
ucla.dance
FAQ—rec.arts.dance
rec.arts.dance
ba.dance
alt.arts.ballet
rec.folk-dancing

Finding an Actor's Website
You can search out individual actors and look at their websites by clicking on Actors at *American Theatre*'s site: <*http://americantheater.about.com/musicperform/americantheater/?once=true&*>.

7

Introduction to Design
and Technical Theatre on the Net

Certain sites apply to all theatre technicians and designers of costume, lighting, scenery, sound, props, and makeup. In this chapter, we'll start by looking at those basic pages. In following chapters we'll examine sites for specific tech and design areas.

SHOP SAFETY—REQUIRED READING

ARTS HAZARD MENU
http://artsnet.heinz.cmu.edu:70/1/csa/arthazards

AUTHOR'S CHOICE   This safety-oriented site from Carnegie Mellon should be required reading in all theatre shops. Everything here deserves attention, but you can start by clicking into Performing Arts Hazards Files and Art Hazards News Issues, where you'll find such valuable information as Theater Health and Safety Self-Evaluation Checklist, Smoke and Fog Hazards in Theater and Film, and Fire Retardants for Theater.

Firearms Safety relates tragedies with *blank* pistols:

> There have been many accidents involving blank ammunition, one of the most infamous being the 1984 fatal shooting of Jon Eric-Hexum during the filming of the TV series *Cover-Up*. He pointed the gun at his head and pulled the trigger, not realizing that blank bullets can cause death. The 1993 death of Brandon Lee while filming *The Crow* also shows the danger of dummy bullets.

The entry also discusses state and federal firearm regulations and makes recommendations for safe operations.

Fire Safety discusses the problems and has a check-off list for you to use while examining your theatre space. There also are entries regarding noise damage to ears.

The entry for Shared Makeup for Actors has a stern warning. There you'll discover that

one problem with shared makeup is the fact that some types of cosmetics can possibly be vehicles for biological transmission of disease. Bacterial infections, such as staphylococcus, impetigo, and streptococcus can be passed from one individual to another. However, most current concern and questions surround the possibility of transmission of AIDS, herpes simplex, and hepatitis B. . . . According to theatrical makeup manufacturers, preservatives used in makeups do not in any way protect against transmission of infection. These additives only increase the shelf-life of the product.

After looking at Performing Arts Hazards Files that pertain directly to theatre, you'll want to look at other safety issues available on this site. General Arts Hazards and Visual Arts Hazards, for example, contain materials related to theatre.

ARTS, CRAFTS, AND THEATER SAFETY
www.caseweb.com/acts/index.html

More Information About Safety

The IATSE site (discussed later in this chapter) has a number of discussions regarding safety (<*www.iatse .lm.com/safety.html*>). See also the Center for Safety in the Arts (<*http://artswire.org*:70/1 /csa>). Visit *United Scenic Artists* (<*http://frontpage1.shadow .net/~usa829fl/*>) and click on Health and Safety for valuable discussions and links to safety issues such as Urethane Resin Systems, Solvents, Artist's Paints, Ventilation, and more. The *Western Australia Academy* has a link to a substantial number of safety sites (<*http:// waapa.cowan.edu.au/lx*>). The University of Wisconsin offers a mega-directory of health and safety concerns (<*www.uwm.edu/Dept/EHSRM /EHSLINKS*>).

AUTHOR'S CHOICE A nonprofit corporation, ACTS specializes in health and safety services to the arts. Clicking on Publications on its home page takes you to a list of safety materials. It provides a series of significant safety data sheets at reasonable cost and describes books about safeguarding artists. A special advantage of the ACTS site is its promise that questions and requests for service will be answered.

Links include The U. S. Occupational Safety & Health Administration (OSHA), The U. S. Environmental Protection Agency (EPA), and The Material Safety Data Sheet (MSDS) Search Page.

ORGANIZATIONS FOR DESIGNERS (LIGHTS, SCENERY, SOUND, MAKEUP), TECHNICAL DIRECTORS, PROPERTIES, STAGE MANAGERS, AND TECHNICIANS

Among the advantages of unions is their concern for members' working conditions, salaries, employment security, health, and pensions. If the worker is an independent contractor—not a regular employee of one particular company but instead apt to be a transient working for hire—such concerns take on added significance. For professional designers and technicians, the IATSE can be a significant aid. Other organizations, such as USITT and CITTI, provide services, publications, and annual conventions.

THE INTERNATIONAL ALLIANCE OF THEATRICAL STAGE EMPLOYEES
www.iatse.lm.com

The full name of this union is The International Alliance of Theatrical Stage Employees, Moving Picture Technicians, Artists and Allied Crafts of the United States, Its Territories and Canada, AFL-CIO, CLC. The labor union "representing technicians, artisans and craftspersons in the entertainment industry, including live theatre, film and television production," IATSE has more than 100,000 members in the United States and Canada who work in such areas as Stage Technicians; Costume Design/Set Design; Wardrobe; Hair and Makeup; Treasurers and Ticket Sellers; and Publicists, Press Agents, and Managers. Founded in 1893, IATSE has taken an interesting path through vaudeville, burlesque, the "white rats," talkies, and more, all shown in The History of the IATSE.

From the home page, Crafts of the IATSE leads to information about the crafts represented and links regarding training and education materials. For information about membership benefits, click on An Introduction To The IATSE, and on the next page open Membership Services. Of Interest to Members has links to a number of Safety issues.

UNITED SCENIC ARTISTS
http://frontpage.shadow.net/usa829fl/

For "Designers and Artists for the Entertainment Industry," United Scenic Artists is a union for professionals. If you're interested in becoming a professional designer, look in its Designer Apprentice Program. Its Heath and Safety page offers excellent advice for shop managers. Internet Links takes you to selected sites for theatre and film.

ASSOCIATED DESIGNERS OF CANADA
www.ffa.ucalgary.ca//

ADC is a national, nonprofit, professional association that promotes and protects the interests and needs of set, costume, lighting, and sound designers working within Canadian theatre. Professional Membership is open to those who have a minimum of three professional productions; Apprentice Members need have had one. The former receive insurance and retirement benefits as well as certain legal support. The site has a Virtual Resource Centre with links to "general information about the performing arts industry and self-employment practices for cultural workers (including information on finances, taxes, human resources, agents, etc.)," a statement regarding standards and working practices, and comparable industry information.

UNITED STATES INSTITUTE FOR THEATRE TECHNOLOGY

www.culturenet.ca/usitt/

A major association of theatrical design, production, and technology professionals and educators in performing arts and entertainment, the *United States Institute for Theatre Technology* seeks to enhance knowledge and skills of members. Started in 1960, USITT has grown to international stature, and its board members include Canadian theatre professionals. It sponsors exhibits of design, conventions, symposia, and advocates safe and ethical practices. Its conferences are must-do events for those in the field (especially for jobseekers in any of these areas; the conventions offer employer-employee meetings).

Members come from both the United States and Canada and include technical directors; sound, set, costume, makeup, properties, and special effects craftspeople; stage managers; architects; lighting designers and technicians; production managers; allied distributors; manufacturers and suppliers; and academic staff and students. Membership costs vary from $51 for students, $68 for seniors, and $85 for individuals. Members receive the quarterly TD&T—*Theatre Design and Technology* and 10 issues of *Sightlines*, USITT's newsletter, as well as discounts and other benefits. USITT sponsors summer costume symposiums that attract designers from around the nation.

The left menu on its home page allows you to click on Future Conferences, Publications, and Classified Ads of job openings. Grants and Fellowships leads you to information about USITT's financial support to help members improve knowledge and skills. Valuable is WOW!—Wading on the Web—with a number of sites submitted by members.

THEATRE COMMUNICATIONS GROUP

www.tcg.org

AUTHOR'S CHOICE   TCG is one of American theatre's major service organizations, existing to strengthen, nurture, and promote the not-for-profit American theatre. For jobseekers, its bimonthly ArtSEARCH is a major resource, and it says it annually lists more than 6,000 positions in theatres, performing arts centers, colleges and universities, dance and opera companies, and more. It publishes the highly regarded *American Theatre*, a lively and informative examination of productions, people, theatrical organizations, and events. For playwrights, its annual *Dramatists Sourcebook* is an essential tool to find producers, contests, grants, and theatres interested in new plays. There are bulletin boards you may wish to explore; one for members only, and the other open for everyone. TCG also has a powerful Career Development Program for Designers, which I describe later in this chapter.

THE CANADIAN INSTITUTE FOR THEATRE TECHNOLOGY
www.citt.org/frames.htm

The CITT mission is to actively promote the professional development of its members and to work for the betterment of the Canadian live performance community. It has ties to USITT, and members receive publications and other aspects of its American relative.

Members include architects, designers, educators, manufacturers and suppliers, props workers, scenic carpenters and painters, technicians, technical directors, wardrobe personnel, and more. Membership fees range from $30 for students, $60 for individuals, and $120 for professionals.

Its home page has links to various CITT programs. Advocacy points out its record for safety, and Workshops lists its activities for members. Conferences describe its annual meeting, where members meet to exchange ideas, socialize, and attend workshops that illuminate aspects of the discipline.

BASIC SITES FOR DESIGNERS AND TECHNICIANS

The following sites contain general basic materials valuable for designers and technicians.

THEATRE COMMUNICATIONS GROUP—
Career Development Program for Designers
www.tcg.org

For talented designers early in their career, TCG administers the NEA/TCG Career Development Program. Six designers receive financial support (currently $17,500) for six months, working with senior artists in theatre companies. There is a companion program for directors. Applicants cannot be enrolled in, or on leave from, university training programs. Directors must have directed a minimum of three fully staged professional productions; designers must have designed professionally for at least two, and no more than five, years.

For information, at the home page click on Programs and Services. Next, enter Artistic Programs. To download the guidelines and applications, you'll need the Adobe Acrobat Reader program—a nice freebie—which you can pick up at the TCG site.

ARTSLYNX—Theatre Design and Technical Resources
www.artslynx.org/theatre/design.htm

If you've persevered through this book, you've already noted *Artslynx*, an excellent site worth repeating. The above address takes you to one subdivision: Theatre Design and Technology. This area contains links about design—costume, lighting, scenery, sound, makeup, and masks—plus stage management, overall theatre engineering, and architecture. There also is a link for jobseekers.

ELAC THEATRE LIBRARY—Theatre Links

www.perspicacity.com/elactheatre/library/links.htm#Costume&Design

ELAC, which I've mentioned in earlier chapters, has a short list of Designers, References, and Suppliers. The Newsgroups and ListServs make ELAC especially helpful if you want to talk online with others involved in design and technical theatre.

THE INTERNATIONAL THEATRE DESIGN ARCHIVE

www.siue.edu/ITDA

Do you want to see Tony Award designs from the 1940s through the 1990s? Or are you interested in the work of a certain designer or the design for a particular play? You may find that here, now or soon. Formerly known as Project 2000, this *United States Institute for Theatre Technology* site plans to provide links to 2,000 scenic, costume, and lighting designs. Already this well-planned site has rich visuals with designs for scenery, costumes, and lighting, all conveniently organized by play title, playwright, designer, and producer.

DESIGN IMAGE ONLINE

www.performance-design.com/dol/desimage.html

You can access websites of designers, divided into Lighting Design; Scenic Design; Costume Design; Sound Design; Computer Graphics, Rendering, and CAD; and Scenic Technology. Each has a substantial number of individual pages, although unfortunately some are dead. Why are these particular designers included and others excluded? The site doesn't say. Still, browsing through the various design pages can provide interesting insight into design practices, and designers considering creating their own Web pages will find useful ideas here.

THEATRE CENTRAL—Stagecraft Sites

www1.playbill.com/cgi-bin/plb/central_res?cmd=show&code=2059&subcode=2062

Theatre Central offers more than 70 links to costumes, stagecraft, lighting and electrics, theatre suppliers, stage management, scenic design, technical theatre, computers for stagecraft, wigs, and more.

GLOSSARY OF TECHNICAL THEATRE TERMS

www.theatrecrafts.com/glossary/glossary.html

Why do people talk about the "smell of greasepaint"? What's a "ghost light"? What theatre workers are called "casuals"? (No, it doesn't refer to the lazy ones who just hang around.) Just why is the "greenroom" called the "greenroom"?

Find answers to those questions and theatre jargon here on the "biggest Theatre Glossary on the Web"—its self-description. This U. K. *Glossary* defines more than 800 terms. For efficiency, it is divided alphabetically, and a click-menu lets you select clumps of about eight letters at a time. Alternatively, you

More Information for Stage Managers

Stage managers may want to visit their professional union, *Actors' Equity Association*, described in discussions about acting (<*www.actorsequity.org*>).

can use your browser to search for particular terms (on Netscape, click on Edit and then Find).

THEATRE SERVICES GUIDE

www.theaterservicesguide.com

Primarily for access to commercial suppliers, this mega-site has a mega-front page that can mega-confuse, and it is so full that downloading often is mega-slow. Despite the handicaps using this *Guide*, however, it has piles of information.

Placing your cursor over the colorful headlines pulls up descriptions of the various internal sites. Clicking Theatre Services Guide takes you to another crammed page, where you can select from various supplier Categories, including Costumes, Props, Scenery, and Lighting. Also from the front page you can click on Product Directory, which takes you to an alphabetized list of products and services. Again, be prepared for a sluggish download.

Tony Awards and Oscars for Scenery, Costumes, Lighting, Makeup, and Sound

For a list of the American Theatre Wing's Tony Awards —more formally, Antoinette Perry Awards—for nominees and winners of Broadway's annual Bests for Scenic, Costume, and Lighting Design (plus all other categories), go to the official Tony site (<*www.tonys.org/*>).

For a list of Oscar Awards for Costumes, Makeup, and Sound (as well as all awards), see this chart with connective links (<*http://us.imdb.com /Sections/Awards/Academy_Awards _USA/Best_Costume_Design*>).

THE STAGE TECHNICIAN'S PAGE

www.geocities.com/Broadway/3738

Although experienced theatre folk may find that this site contains familiar information, it is a strong page for newbies. Nicely organized, it has links to Lighting, Sound, Special Effects, The Stage Crew, Stage Jargon, and Theatre Links, with lists of vendors, rings, and personal pages.

ART HISTORY RESOURCES ON THE WEB

http://witcombe.sbc.edu/ARTHLinks.html

Compiled by art historian Christopher Witcombe at Sweet Briar College, here is a mega-site of art history that, while not directly related to theatrical design, can give designers historical authenticity and inspiration. There's thorough coverage of Prehistoric Art, Ancient Art, Art of the Middle Ages, Renaissance Art, Baroque, and 18th, 19th, and 20th centuries. Each has subdivisions. Research Resources has a large number of sites.

ART RESOURCES ON THE INTERNET

www.newschool.edu/library/artres.htm

Like the site above, *Art Resources* isn't directly related to theatre (although there is a short section on Fashion and Costumes). That said, however, it does offer insightful access to various museums, photo collections, art references, and art collections, all of which can be useful to designers.

CLASSES FOR THOSE WHO WORK BACKSTAGE

In a real sense, much of the Net is genuinely educational. Here, however, are a few special sites for those who work backstage.

STUDYWEB—Theatre Behind the Scenes

www.studyweb.com/links/5032.html

Designed for classes—and with sites rated by grades, like Grade Level 6–9+—*Study Web* may interest teachers seeking to make Web assignments. This particular section of the site focuses on backstage; the pulldown menu at the top left indicates other study areas. Entering *theatre* in the search engine pulls up 10 other sites, such as theatre history and production techniques as well as a Costuming link that shows how to make your own *Cats* costume, costumes for dance, and more.

More Information on Design

For a design bibliography, *Encyclopaedia Britannica* has a rich list of books for stage, lighting, makeup, and costume design (<*www.britannica.com /bcom/eb/article/1/0,576,121371 +1+110173,00.html*>). For lists of companies that offer theatrical supplies, see *Scott's Theatre-Links.Com* (<*www .theatrelink.com/commerc.html*>), which includes about 90 listings of suppliers of such items as Carpentry, Costumes, Makeup, Design and Consultation Services, Gifts, Lighting, Sound, Acoustics, and Software. *Yahoo!* also has some stagecraft sites you may wish to explore (<*http://dir.yahoo.com/Arts /Design_Arts/Stagecraft*>).

CAREERS IN TECHNICAL THEATRE

www.abtt.org.uk/train/workin.html

"So you want to work backstage?" the site asks. It describes the various functions and responsibilities of backstage workers—all of them. (The only theatre job *not* covered in this document is that of the performer.) Organized from the first steps and initial planning to final productions, descriptions are succinct but adequate and will help new techies find the home that fits them best in theatre. Although this is a U. K. site, theatre work is theatre work no matter where it is done.

From the home page you can go to the Green Room, which has a number of discussion areas such as CAD Forum, Sound and Technology, Safety Forum, and a Green Forum for other things technical. Info has a number of files, including Organisations and links to theatres.

JOBS IN DESIGN AND TECHNICAL THEATRE

Searching for a theatrical job takes patience, endurance, and persistence. There's no single source that lists all available openings, so you'll want to develop a series of bookmarks you can use regularly. The sites listed here can help you.

Also consider creating a personal website so you can steer prospective employers to follow your career on the Internet. One major advantage of your personal site is that you can continually update it, so you can revise any materials you gave an employer during an interview. Some sites—*Scotts Theatre Link*, for one—encourage you to post your page (<*www.theatre-link.com/*>).

THE THEATRE DESIGN AND TECHNICAL JOBS PAGE
www.backstagejobs.com

This is a freebie, designed "to help the 'behind-the-scenes' people in the live entertainment industry find work, and to help entertainment groups fill their job openings." Neatly organized and designed with users in mind, this site lists jobs available. It is regularly updated, and each entry indicates the date the job opening was posted and when it will expire.

Material is presented in tables for categories such as Design, Management and Administration, and Everything Else. Each has detailed subdivisions. In the Design box, for example, there are links to openings for Designers, Electricians, Costumes, Rigging, Carpenter, Properties, Sound, Scenic Painters, Special FX, and Assorted Tech. These aren't idle. For example, when I visited the sites, I saw 24 openings for carpenters and 18 for electricians. All were new; there were no old, out-of-date listings.

Despite the title, it also lists jobs for choreographers, directors and musical directors, management, box office, casting calls for actors, and "everything else."

BACKSTAGE.COM
www.backstage.com/backstage/casting/index.jsp

From the front page click on Casting. Even though that sounds like it implies jobs for actors, the listings include Staff and Tech. You'll be taken to a map of the United States, and you can click on the region that interests you.

BACKSTAGE WORLD
www.backstageworld.com

Backstage World needs to oil its URLs because it always has opened very slowly for me. Once it has opened, you scroll down past a number of clever globes representing different countries to find links to new lighting and audio products, used gear, and manuals and tips.

If you're hunting for a backstage job as designer or crew, click on Job List and then Job Opportunities. When I last visited, there were some 20 jobs posted. Indicative of *Backstage*'s international coverage, about one-third were in countries other than the U. S. If you want to post your résumé, click on Job List and then Jobs Wanted for instructions and examples. Interestingly, there were fewer "hire me" posts than "come work for us" ads.

ELAC THEATRE LIBRARY—
Theatre Links

www.perspicacity.com/elactheatre/library/links .htm#Employment

A rather small section invites you to visit links for theatre employment.

ARTSLYNX

www.artslynx.org/jobs.htm#Ttheatre

Again I mention *Artslynx*, this time to call your attention to its Theatre Employment Resources. At this subdivision there are several dozen links you can consider.

ENTERTAINMENT TECHNOLOGY
ONLINE

www.etecnyc.net/default.html

While you're here you may want to browse the site, but if you're looking specifically for employment possibilities and don't want to fritter, click on Classifieds.

THEATREJOBS.COM

www.theatrejobs.com

More Information About Theatre Jobs

See also USITT, and consider attending their annual convention (<*www.culturenet .ca/usitt/*>). Clicking Employers at *United Scenic Artists* (*http://frontpage.shadow.net /usa829fl/*) gives you valuable information that is regularly updated. That same site also describes a Designers Apprentice Program for those persons who have exhibited the basic skills, talent, and desire to become a fully developed working professional designer through a series of assistant relationships with 829 established members. *Theatre Communications Group*, discussed earlier in this chapter (<*www.tcg.org/*>), publishes ArtSEARCH, a bimonthly newsletter that is highly valuable for employers and jobseekers.

Be patient. Every time I've tried to access this membership site, it has been unfortunately pokey to open. Click on Guests to discover its services.

8

Technical Theatre, Costume, and Makeup

The previous chapter listed basic sites for design and technical theatre. Here we begin exploring sites for individual design, starting with technical theatre, costume, and makeup. The next chapter continues the discussion of design.

THE PROFESSIONAL UNION FOR TECHNICAL THEATRE, COSTUME, AND MAKEUP

In Chapter 7 I mentioned the labor union for many of the theatrical crafts. I list IATSE again here to remind you how it serves your professional needs.

THE INTERNATIONAL ALLIANCE OF THEATRICAL STAGE EMPLOYEES, MOVING PICTURE TECHNICIANS, ARTISTS AND ALLIED CRAFTS OF THE UNITED STATES, ITS TERRITORIES, AND CANADA, AFL-CIO, CLC
www.iatse.lm.com

IATSE is a union that represents a large number of professional theatrical folks, including those discussed in this chapter—hair and makeup, stage technicians, and costume designers and wardrobe personnel. It also represents nontech workers such as treasurers, ticket sellers, publicists, press agents and managers, as well as those in film and television production and animation.

Whether you're a member or not, you can visit its site for a great deal of information. In particular, try clicking on Crafts of the IATSE, then open your theatrical area to find information about your craft, including training and educational materials.

TECHNICAL THEATRE

Stagecraft lends itself to e-presentation of drawings, illustrations, and how-to pages. Although many tech theatre sites exist, I've selected several special homes for your exploration.

THE STAGE TECHNICIAN'S PAGE
www.geocities.com/Broadway/3738

For newbies, this serves as an introduction to stagecraft. It has basic materials on Lighting, Sound, Special Effects, The Stage Crew, and—perhaps most valuable—Stage Jargon (although many terms cry for visual illustrations). It's easy to imagine a high school or college beginning tech class assigning this site, and it also could be useful for theatres with consistent turnover in volunteer stage personnel.

CANADIAN INSTITUTE FOR THEATRE TECHNOLOGY
www.citt.org/frames.htm

Serving the "Canadian Live Performance Community," CITT says its "Mission is to actively promote the professional development of its members and to work for the betterment of the Canadian live performance community."

Not only does CITT seek to serve all of Canada, there also is an international flavor. CITT is the Canadian center for the International Organization of Scenographers, Theatre Architects and Technicians, a UNESCO-sponsored organization with centers in more than 40 counties.

CITT members receive *StageWorks*, a quarterly journal. It holds conferences and workshops. The Callboard (password required) is one key advantage for members, who can Network with other CITT members. CITT also makes awards, and recipients are listed (but unfortunately with neither details nor access to their home pages).

RIGGERS PAGE
www.rigging.net

Riggers Page has detailed technical information about stage rigging equipment from bolts to rigging formulas. Safety is emphasized, as this warning notice states: "Failure to read, understand, and follow manufacturer's instructions may cause death or serious injury." This is a straightforward instructional site with no frills.

Its special value is the thoroughness. For example, click on Bolts and you're lead to an illustrated chart that describes grade marking, material, proof load, and tensile strength. The same details are found in other categories such as Chains, Shackles, Wire Ropes, Wire Rope Clips, Rigging Formulas, Master Links, and more. Visitor's Notes contain comments and some questions (unfortunately, no answers show up). Riggers will find that the details make this a significant site.

Mega-Sites and Suppliers

Well-organized connections to links can guide you to a number of pages in given categories. The trick is to garner many sites without creating a mess. The following sites are clean and helpful.

TECH THEATRE LINKS
www.iwaynet.net/~phantom/theatrelinks/design.htm

The crowded menu on the left guides you to Lighting, Makeup, Costume, Construction, Sound, Rigging and Drapes, Special Effects, Intercoms, and broad-based theatrical information. Below those categories are Additional Services, primarily humor "services" with pages of 199 Uses for Gaffa Tape, Theatrical Calamities, and other techie jokes, quite often at the expense of actors and directors—and, hey, just what does *that* say about collaboration and mutual respect in the theatre?

Designers will find a number of links to CAD programs and other computer tools; sound designers may want to explore CyberJaz with "rare and hard to find recordings and music"; tech directors will want to visit the many pages for rigging and running the show; and costume and makeup designers will find a healthy list of suppliers.

TECHNICAL SOURCE GUIDE ONLINE
www.nwmissouri.edu/%7Epimmel/usitt/source_guide/index.htm

Having difficulty being sure everyone knows the configuration of lighting instruments? Use Velcro tabs for labels. Do you want to prevent damage to shapes made of foam? Try this two-part polyurethane coating. Do you need a quick and inexpensive way to build fluted columns and Corinthian capitals for a set? Here's a neat technique that uses corrugated roofing panels found in home supply stores.

These sorts of problem-solving suggestions are on *Technical Source Guide*. Because this site is sponsored by USITT, you know that the solutions to technical problems will be sensible and well thought out. More than 30 articles were listed when I last visited this site. All look tested; all are by experienced technical personnel.

BMI SUPPLY
www.bmisupply.com

BMI clearly wants to be helpful. It says it offers

> a multitude of services free of charge. These include: advice on what product will work for your particular application; comparative pricing among manufacturers to help you find the best price for what you need; advice on how to use products to your best advantage; basic troubleshooting; assistance in finding items we don't carry; and most importantly, friendly, courteous service.

From its offices in Queensbury, New York, and Greenville, South Carolina, BMI sells about every backstage item except makeup, and it typically has ongoing "special sales" of various items. Among its listings are hardware, ladders, rigging, lighting and electrics, sound, scenic materials, and paint. You can download its catalog, but you'll need Adobe Acrobat Reader (free at <*www.adobe.com/products/acrobat/readstep.html*>).

THEATRE EFFECTS
www.theatrefx.com

This supplier says it "stocks the largest variety of theatrical special effects equipment and supplies in the world." It has machines for fog, haze, snow, and bubbles, plus black lights, strobe lights, and a collection of stage lighting equipment and dimmers. A special advantage is the free special effects technical advice that is available from its staff. An Auction Area places selected equipment up for sale, and a Weekly Special has reduced prices. There is a monthly contest that gives away a prize for correct answers to questions drawn from their equipment list.

Five active Discussion Groups have questions and answers on special effects problems in such categories as Pyrotechnics, Aerotechnics, Lighting Technics, Balloon Technics, and Other. All seemed current, and replies to questions looked authoritative, such as a recipe for making breakaway glass, keeping fog close to the stage floor, making stair steps change colors, using flash paper without burning your hand, and more.

SETS/PROPS/COSTUMES/STUNTS/SPECIAL EFX
www.creativedir.com/html/18.html

The word *big* comes to mind when visiting this site. It is an extensive directory of theatrical suppliers. I counted almost 150 different companies when I last visited the place. They are listed alphabetically, although it would be helpful if they were gathered into categories. Not all have websites. There even are a number of places that supply animals—as one company puts it, "Tamed and trained from aardvark to zebra." When's the last time you wanted an aardvark in a show?

COSTUME

Of the hundreds of sites I visited preparing this book, one category stood out with the most attractive sites, clever content, rich detail, and often delightful humor—costumes. Not the organizational sites, which need more juice, but the sites by individuals who are clearly dedicated. Some of these personal costume sites are painstakingly prepared and lovingly maintained, and they could be models for other theatre homes.

Still, there's a bit of schizophrenic construction in some costume pages that rather uncomfortably straddle different missions. Are they for theatrical costume design, reenactments, or holidays like Halloween? There also is a strange omission: costumes for dance. Luckily, *The Costume Page* (<*http://members.aol.com/nebula5/costume.html*>) has a dance design section, and *Watercolour Dancewear* (<*www.watercolourdancewear.com/intro.html*>) offers quality costumes for dancers.

Organizations for Costume

Societies and guilds for costumers are found in numerous countries, and in the United States there are regional organizations. To locate those in your area, use a search engine. For example, key in *costume guild* on *AltaVista* (<*www.altavista.com*>) and you'll get some 20 pages of results, although not all will deal with that subject. Guilds promote the art and craft of costuming, offer special benefits to members such as publications and conventions, and provide a source for information.

COSTUME SOCIETY OF AMERICA

www.costumesocietyamerica.com/welcome/

CSA intends to "advance global understanding of all aspects of dress and appearance." It offers nine different levels of membership, with costs ranging from $40 for students to $350 for patrons. Members attend symposiums and receive publications, notably *Dress: The Journal of the Costume Society of America*. It also has a well-equipped bookstore. While there are member sites listed, it seems strange that CSA does not use its expertise to offer a page of selected links to costume sites.

INTERNATIONAL COSTUMERS' GUILD

www.costume.org/

A nonprofit and educational worldwide organization of costume professionals, the *International Costumers' Guild* seeks to "promote the educational, cultural, literary, artistic, and theatrical advancement of costume design and construction, and the influence of costume (clothing), fabrics, and design upon societies and cultures." It publishes *The Costumer's Quarterly* and sponsors conferences. You can find locations of chapters near you by clicking on Local International Costumers' Guild Chapters (or go there directly with <*www.costume.org/chapters.html*>).

COSTUME CONNECTIONS

www.costume-con.org/

Costume-Con holds annual show-'n-tell conventions with a focus on science fiction, fantasy, and historical costumers. Their site describes their birth and future plans. From their home page you can access Resources in the Northern Virginia-Baltimore-Washington area. Links takes you to a potpourri of pattern guides, organizations, museums and exhibits, historical sites, suppliers, and other resources.

General Sites for Costume

Typical costume sites make excellent use of the Net's ability to display color drawings and pictures. The disadvantage of visual illustrations is that they can make the site deadly slow, but judicious restraint overcomes that problem, as you'll see in the sites listed here.

COSTUME GALLERY
www.costumegallery.com/

AUTHOR'S CHOICE Start a contest for the "Most Attractive and Useful Theatrical Site on the Internet" and I'd nominate the *Gallery* for its tasteful decorations, excellent illustrations, and attractive color scheme. But it isn't merely a pretty face. On the contrary. Even without the neatly planned decorations, it would win for usefulness. With more than 800 Web pages and 2,500 images of fashion and costume, the *Costume Gallery* has a wealth of materials. It even will translate from one language to another, such as English to Spanish, French, German, Italian, or Portuguese, and vice versa. It is a genuine delight to find a site that glows with such excellence.

The owner, Penny E. Dunlap Ladnier, has divided the site into four main historical areas: Mesopotamia: The Cradle of Civilization; Medieval Fashion Research Section; 20th Century Fashion; and History of Hairstyles. Each category has a number of subdivisions. For example, in the 20th Century gallery there are links for each decade plus units for Designers, Film, Hairstyles, Celebrities and Royalty, Men, Women, and Children.

The Product Palace offers links to vendors. But instead of merely listing names, the webmaster places each vendor's link in a colorful and neatly decorated box. Study is for research. Here the links (again in those marvelous boxes) can take you to bookstores and video sites. The Courtyard is for fun, and you can see *Titanic* costumes or enjoy a cyber-ball with Cinderella—Ms. Ladnier's personal adventure, which echoes the typical Hollywood actress preparations for fancy dress galas.

I found myself admiring Ms. Ladnier's meticulous dedication to her website. No hastily thrown together effect, this. On the contrary, as any webmaster will recognize, she had to spend an amazing amount of time putting the combinations together. One hopes she'll keep revising and adding to it; it appears that it has been some time since she updated it.

THE COSTUMER'S MANIFESTO
www.costumes.org/

AUTHOR'S CHOICE Another winner. This richly detailed site, nicely organized with a flair for humor, belongs to Tara Maginnis, costume designer for Theatre UAF, the Theatre Department of the University of Alaska, Fairbanks. The site's title reflects the name of her online book, *The Costumer's Manifesto*, described as "the first 'self-help' manual for those artists who make clothes for imaginary people." It contains a number of highly informative chapters ranging from Costume Shop Safety to humorous Costume Shop Quotes to Things Nobody Tells You About Sewing Machines.

Manifesto is a major site. It indexes more than 1,000 costume- and makeup-related links, and there is information about costume history, excellent how-to advice, and leads to suppliers.

The Costume History Links by itself is worth the price of admission. The site also offers a Discussion Forum that contains exchanges between professionals, Costume Patterns, Costume Suppliers, How to Make Your Own Web Page, and more. I think you'll agree that it is an excellent site.

COSTUMES AND CLOTHING

www.geocities.com/Heartland/Acres/7631/costume.html

Annette Allen's opening page deserves a special nomination for innovation and, while we're at it, wry humor. She shows a male and female warrior dressed in "primitive clothing"—you know, the let's-show-as-much-skin-as-possible-of-those-improbably-shaped-models-who-are-glamorized-movie-versions-of-warriors—and asks, "Do you think that women really dressed like this? Or men really dressed like this?" She then says, "If you do, you either accessed this page accidentally or you are at the beginning of an education in historical clothing."

The site has rich information in historical categories such as Ancient, Classical, Medieval, Renaissance, 17th Century, 18th Century, 19th Century, 20th Century, and Non-Western. Her insightful discussions of Climate and Geography, Migration, and Fashion add meaning to the evolution of dress.

BISSONNETTE ON COSTUME

http://dept.kent.edu/museum/anne/costume/?table

Anne Bissonnette calls this "A Visual Dictionary of Fashion," and she has made it into a well-designed site, thorough, neatly organized. There is a Geographic Search and a Time Search divided into 18th, 19th, and 20th centuries. Subject Search takes you to Lingerie, Hats, Hairstyles, Footwear, Textiles, Accessories, Coats, Women's Wear, Men's Wear, and Children's Wear. Each shows you photographs of sample costumes.

THE HISTORY OF COSTUME

www.siue.edu/costumes/costume1_index.html

This history consists of attractive illustrations of costumes from ancient Egypt to the late 19th century, organized chronologically and geographically. While the drawings are fine, one wishes for insightful text to enhance them.

HISTORIC COSTUMING BBS

www.dnaco.net/~aleed/corsets/BBS

Got a question? Or maybe an answer? Drea Leed's *Historical Costume Bulletin Board* is an active place, with forums divided into General; For Sale/Wanted/Looking For; How Do I? questions and tips; costumes for favorite Films and Movies; and Costume for Specific Periods, which is divided into five periods from Medieval to Modern. All are active, and both questions and answers look substantial.

Mega-Sites for Costume

Directories of links—mega-sites—can be greatly helpful if they are well organized and regularly maintain their links by adding new ones and discarding sites that have died. The pages in this section fit those criteria.

THE COSTUME PAGE

http://members.aol.com/nebula5/costume.html

AUTHOR'S CHOICE   Go here first. It may be the last place you need to visit. More than 2,000 (!) unique links are listed on these pages, which are created and maintained by Julie Zetterberg. The breadth is outstanding and the outline organization is clean and clear. Webmasters of mega-sites for other aspects of theatre could stop here to find a model of the way these can be best put together.

You'll find divisions for The Study of Costume, such as reference works, historical, and ethnic. Sources are included, divided into supplies plus costumes and accessories.

Divisions have detailed subfolders. For example, under The Study of Costume—Costume History, there are entries for Ancient, Medieval Era, Renaissance, Elizabethan and Shakespearean Era, 17th and 18th Centuries, 19th Century—Regency and Victorian Era, and 20th Century Fashion and Couture (1901 to 2000).

More Places to Look suggests resource lists for General Costume; Historical Costume; Craft, Textile, and Fiber Arts; Theatre and Dance; Fashion; and Art and Design in such categories as Theatre and Opera, Dance, Circus, Figure Skating, Fantasy, Movie and Television, and more. If you're looking for a place to study costuming, the Schools and Instructions folder lists around 20 colleges and seminars.

The Costume Page is thorough. There is a Costuming Resources Online page (*<http://members.aol.com/nebula5/tcpinfo.html>*) that has Bibliographies, Book Lists and Dictionaries, Costume Books and Images On-Line, and Costume Exhibits & Images On-Line. Click on Museums and you'll go to lists exhibits.

COSTUME IMAGE DATABASE

www.lib.colum.edu/costwais.html

You can access costume images that are used in the study of fashion and costume at Columbia College Library. An index allows four methods of search. You can select from a search of keywords, individual fields, specific video frame number, or specific slide accession number. Obviously the last two require you to know details in advance, but the keyword search is quite flexible.

WORLD WIDE ART RESOURCES

http://wwar.com

On the home page scroll down until you see Theatre on the left menu. From the list you find, select Costume Related (or go there directly with

<http://wwar.com/categories/Theater/Costume_Related>), and you'll have more than two dozen choices. Unfortunately, it needs a better selection process because a few are but distantly related to costume.

COSTUME HISTORY RESOURCES
www.artslynx.org/theatre/costume.htm

If you've persevered through the various chapters of this book, you recognize Artslynx. This is its Costume History Resources page with museums and costume collections, master sites, costume history pages, and—for fun—some all-time favorites from the webmaster, including an organization that analyzes just what happens to missing socks in the laundry.

COSTUME SEWING RESOURCES
www.lyonslpgas.com/sewscape/costume.html

Sewing resources? Not really. Despite the site's name, this isn't just about sewing. There are valuable links to design and execution inside such categories as General Historical, Medieval and Renaissance, Elizabethan, Regency, Victorian, and Edwardian. There also is a section for Ethnic, National and Folk. This isn't merely a listing of sites. Instead, all have brief thumbnail descriptions.

Each category also has links for Pattern Resources and Books. There are sites that deal with broad design concepts and others with a distinct focus on specifics, such as How to Make an Elizabethan Chemise or a step-by-step guide to making a realistic animal tail. You also find valuable research materials, such as Godey's Lady's Book Online, and examples of designers' work, as in The Titanic Project, which includes details about Rose's costume.

SHAN'S COSTUME HISTORY AND THEATRE HISTORY
http://members.aol.com/msj1140/index.html

Music accompanies your journey through Shan's attractive site. You can go to ShanJen's Renderings of various shows such as Death of a Salesman or A Midsummer Night's Dream, visit Theatre History and Costume History pages, or look at shop craft information.

THE COSTUME SITE
http://milieux.com/costume

Small fonts may give you difficulty navigating this site, the left menu's buttons with illegible words can mystify, and the organization isn't easy to understand. That's unfortunate because it has valuable materials and a great deal of information, making this one of the most thorough sites for costuming.

For example, this is one of the rare sites to show Computerized Costume Designs-Images using Fractal Painter (on the home page, scroll down to Milieux Costume Images and you'll find the link). Interesting, too, are photographs of such stars as Sarah Bernhardt, Ellen Terry, and many more (filed under Theatrical as Actors of the Early American Theater, although there's no note that they are British performers). Sources/Supplies leads you to a healthy list, organized by Armor, Garb, and the like.

THE COSTUME RING
www.marquise.de/webring/costumering.html

A resource for people looking for a group of related sites, a ring consists of interconnected home pages. Most often you click on Next at the bottom of a site's page and you travel to the next ring in order. This *Costume Ring* is dedicated to noncommercial offerings (commercial sites must have informational value), and it leads you to carefully selected costume pages. See the associated *Garb'n Frock Ring* (<*www.geocities.com/Paris/4440/costuming.html*>) for suppliers.

PERFORMING ARTS LINKS
www.theatrelibrary.org/links/

Scroll down to Costume and Set Design (or go there directly with <*www.theatre library.org/links/Technologies.html#costume*>) to open a list of about 20 sites you may wish to visit.

TERESA'S PORTFOLIO
www.geocities.com/Broadway/Lobby/1357/portfolio.html

Teresa Doggett's colorful site can serve as a model for designers' personal Web pages and résumés. Designers will appreciate her comprehensive list of links, and the details of the Timelines section are extremely helpful.

ALTAVISTA
www.altavista.com

At the *AltaVista* home page you can enter Arts and Entertainment, click on Arts and Culture on the next page, and finally click on Theater. Using its search engine for such categories as *costumes* and *costume history* will lead you to resources.

HOTBOT/LYCOS
http://dir.hotbot.lycos.com/Arts/Performing_Arts/Theatre/Costuming

Several dozen costume sites are listed by historical periods.

LYCOS
http://dir.lycos.com/Arts/Performing_Arts/Theatre/Costuming

Perhaps 50 sites are listed, although some are at best tenuously related to costume.

YAHOO!
http://search.yahoo.com/bin/search?p=costume&y=n&e=2193&f=0%3A2766678%3A27 18086%3A1%3A7086%3A2193&r=Arts%02Performing+Arts%02Theater

You'll find around 40 sites here that have some relation to costumes.

Scholarly Information on Costuming
A good scholarly site is the *Encyclopedia Britannica*'s page of costume materials (*<http://search.britannica.com/search?query=costuming>*). For general searches, Netscape lists sites (*<http://directory.netscape.com/Arts /Performing_Arts/Theatre/Costuming>*) and shops (*<http://directory.netscape .com/Shopping/Clothing/Costumes>*). *Project 2000* currently has only a few costume designs in its archives (*<www.siue.edu/PROJECT2000/indexes /costdes.html#E>*). The *Gibson Library* (*<www.brocku.ca/library/research /drama/cost.htm>*) lists selected costume sites. *Yahoo!* has guides to a few dozen sites (*<http://dir.yahoo.com/arts/design_arts/stagecraft/costuming/>*). *Lycos* has a Fashion Guide—Costumes (*<www.lycos.com/wguide/wire /wire_969159_ 46855_3_1.html>*) with a large number of sites about construction and design.

Bibliographies for Costume

Some of the previous sites include books for costume. In addition, organized bibliographies such as those listed here can help you research your design project.

THEATRICAL COSTUME
www.fsu.edu/~library/guides/theatricalcostume.html

The library of Florida State University provides this list of books for costume research, organized into such categories as Bibliographies and Catalogs, Biographies, Chronologies and Histories, Research Guides and Directories, Periodicals, and more. You should have little difficulty translating this list to your own library.

COSTUME RESEARCH
www.glasscity.net/users/fkkannik/research.htm

If you seek texts for research for your costume design or to use to teach others, this Bibliography of Costume Books is an excellent source. The books are listed by historical periods, with additional texts on construction.

COSTUME AND FASHION DESIGN
www.nyu.edu/library/bobst/research/hum/art/cos.htm

Tom McNulty, a fine-arts librarian at New York University's Bobst Library, has compiled a short list of special sites valuable for researchers.

Commercial Sites and Suppliers

There are more suppliers than I can possibly list here, so the following sites serve more as samples than as an inclusive list.

THE COSTUME SOURCE

www.milieux.com/costume/source.html

AUTHOR'S CHOICE   In addition to providing a detailed list of online sources for Costumes, Materials, Accessories, Books, and more, the webmaster makes this site more valuable by highlighting "recommended" vendors. The sources are organized by Arms and Armor; Books, Video and Patterns; Footwear and Leather; Hats and Wigs; Metalwork and Findings; Notions, Trim and Fabric; Prosthetics; Masks and FX; Miscellany; and Costumes and Accessories.

TECH THEATRE LINKS

www.iwaynet.net/~phantom/theatrelinks/

This mega-site has folders for various aspects of theatre. Click on Costume from the left menu (or use this address: <*www.iwaynet.net/~phantom/theatrelinks /candm.htm*>), and you'll find a long list of costume vendors for wigs, costumes, and makeup as well as sites for research.

BOSTON COSTUME

www.bostoncostume.com/

Boston Costume says it has "thousands of clean professional costumes" for theatre and numerous other activities, as well as a "Complete Professional Make-Up Center for Every Level of Expertise." Like many costume sites, it offers costumes for events like Halloween, but unlike other shops, Boston Costume also sells coffins. Yup, *actual coffins.* Now you can be the first theatre shop in your neighborhood to own. . . .

THE GARB'N FROCK RING

www.geocities.com/Paris/4440/costuming.html

A Web ring links together sites that share mutual interest. This particular ring allows you to go to interrelated suppliers, custom costumers, and fabric shops. Each site has a place for you to click to go to the next or previous site.

TRACY THEATRE ORIGINALS

www.tracytheatreoriginals.com/

With a long history of service to the theatre community, the Tracy company was founded in 1890 as a music library for the Gilbert and Sullivan operettas. They now are designers and suppliers of theatrical garments, properties, and makeup. A special feature is Audrey II puppets for *Little Shop of Horrors.*

PIERRE'S MASCOT AND COSTUME SHOP

www.costumers.com/

"If we can't costume you, nobody can!" trumpets this Philadelphia shop. "We have been around long enough to have costumed just about every show in existence many times over, and can easily learn the new ones."

Ignore the mascot and party information and instead click on Theatrical at the top of the page. You're taken to a page where you can enter Theatre Services, Plot Services, or Theatrical Costume Sales. They offer a number of services of interest to designers, such as tailoring to measurement and free last-minute alternations.

AMERICAN COSTUME COMPANY
www.americancostume.com/

Located in Denver, *American Costume Company* says it has "10,000 exceptional costumes and accessories for all of your extra special occasions," and it "loves theatrical requests." Rentals start as low as $45 and average $65 to $70. As you scroll down the page, you'll see tempting thumbnail pictures of costumes for various plays and musicals.

BROADWAY COSTUMES
www.broadwaycostumes.com/

Located in Chicago (despite the name), this company began as a supplier of rental costumes for the masquerade balls held by Chicago society and a provider of costumes for opera productions. It then grew to a large theatrical operation. Clicking on Show Rentals takes you to Costume Plots, where you fill out a form to order costumes, and Show Photos, which illustrates a large number of productions—almost all musicals—they've costumed.

WATERCOLOUR DANCEWEAR
www.watercolourdancewear.com/intro.html

This California company has exploded in popularity, in just a few years growing to some 700 stores in the United States, Canada, Japan, Europe, and other countries. The costumes are attractive, with innovative design and colors. Owner Joanna McMillan says, "Our process of hand-painting fabric results in spontaneous and undefined bleeding of one color into another" with "fabrics that best complement dance—fabrics which have a 'soft hand' and which encapsulate movement and soften the flow of gestures."

The site shows some of their magical color combinations, and Styles has pictures of dancers in their costumes. If you're interested in seeing their materials at a local shop, click on Stores to go to a list organized by states.

THEATRE DEVELOPMENT FUND
www.tdf.org/tdf.html

We know of the *Theatre Development Fund* as a large nonprofit service organization for the performing arts, and especially for its discount Ticket Centres (TKTS) in New York at the World Trade Center and Times Square Theatre. It also offers a variety of other theatre services, including a Costume Collection, a rental company that serves not-for-profit theatres, opera and dance companies, universities, colleges, and schools. It says it has "more than 75,000 professional quality costumes, hats, shoes and accessories, which are available at discounted prices." You can access the Costume Collection from the left menu on the main page (or go there directly: <*www.tdf.org/programs/costume/index.html*>).

THE COSTUME LOFT
www.eviltwin.org/index.html

H'mm. Wonder what eviltwin means. Maybe it's better we don't know? From its home page, click on Theatre (<*www.eviltwin .org/theatre.html*>), where you'll see that they have "high quality theatrical costumes and accessories at an affordable rate." You can look in their Shows in Stock (of some two dozen shows), Pricing, Measuring, and Design Services.

ALTERYEARS—Your Online Costume Resource
www.alteryears.com/

Specializing in historical, ethnic dance, and specialty patterns, *AlterYears* also has a large collection of costume books and supplies.

More Information About Suppliers

CostumeCom lists suppliers (<*www.costume-con.org/links .shtml#supply*>). *The Costume Site*, discussed earlier, has an extensive and neatly organized Best Online Sources for Costumes, Materials, Accessories, Books, Etc. (<*www.milieux.com/costume /source.html*>).

In addition, *The Whole Costumer's Catalogue* is an excellent source of suppliers. In 224 pages it lists well over 1,000 companies that sell costume-related supplies. For more information or to buy the book, there is a online source (<*www .castleblood.com/wcc/wcc.html*>).

LARK BOOKS
www.larkbooks.com/

Although the first page may make you wonder why I've listed this site in the costume section, there is a Folkwear Patterns page you may wish to explore (*folkwear* here means *high glamour* and *sophisticated*, not *rural* or *rustic*). They offer a free catalog.

DRAGONFLY DESIGN STUDIO
http://DragonflyDesignStudio.com/

Dragonfly offers "historical, fantasy, and uniquely elegant accessories, costumes and gifts."

Sample Individual Costumer's Web Pages

Not everyone is yet comfortable with the idea of having a personal Web page. They demand a large amount of time and energy to design and create, and regular TLC to keep them up to date. But your own site allows you to contribute to costuming, and it helps prospective employers see your work. While there are many personal pages on the Net, I've selected a few costumer's pages to illustrate possibilities you can consider as models for your own site.

119

MELANIE SCHUESSLER
www.faucet.net/costume/

Her Design Portfolio shows costumes from such productions as *Twelfth Night* and *The Boy Friend*, among others. Each displays thumbnail photographs; clicking on them leads to an enlargement and her costume rendering. Although her résumé isn't linked on her home page, you can find it on the Design Portfolio page. There also are links to Research, where you see some of her papers, and a Links category with selected pages.

CHARLES E. MCCARRY
www.geocities.com/~mccarrynyc/

This design résumé and portfolio has an attractive front page set against a background of blueprint. It is an easily navigated site, with color renderings and photographs.

MAKEUP

Makeup artists paint, and sometimes sculpt, on living canvases. One major goal is to create the visual image of the character as well as the time period of the production, making each character different yet staying consistent with the overall tone of the show. A second is to enhance actors' facial features so they are not washed out by bright stage lights. Sometimes makeup seeks to hide blemishes or make the actor more attractive. Often a new look is demanded—Cyrano de Bergerac's nose, for example, as well as a wig to capture the time period—which requires building a new face and fashioning a wig that won't flop off during the dueling scenes. With all of that, makeup artists have yet another goal: Their work can't call attention to itself.

Organizations

For makeup, organizations may be a professional union or a nonprofit group that seeks to bring like-minded people together for mutually valuable education, training, and sharing. You'll recall that at the beginning of this chapter, we listed the union for many theatre workers—IATSE (<*www.iatse .lm.com*>). Here we point out that among those it represents are hair and makeup artists.

S.A.P.S.E.M.A.—Society of Amateur and Professional Special Effects Makeup Artists
www.geocities.com/Hollywood/Lot/4759/

This nonprofit worldwide organization is open to film and theatrical makeup and special effects artists and enthusiasts regardless of their degree of experience. Membership is free. Its purpose is to encourage communication, to teach, to share information. As the site says:

Being part of S.A.P.S.E.M.A. can put you "in-touch" with others like you who are interested in film or theatrical special makeup effects and who may possess the skills or who have made many of the mistakes you might make and from whom you can learn and improve in this craft. This homepage is being created to be a resource where you can get tips, ideas, e-mail help, resource links to companies, addresses of suppliers, interviews with many people from amateurs to semi-professionals to working professionals, notices of conventions or group activities and a whole world of other valuable things as you pursue your own path in this art form.

Among the links you'll find are Product Reviews, General Announcements, Lifecast Collection, an F/X Message and Chat Board, Bookshelf, and Tips and Techniques. There is special information regarding makeup artist and teacher Dick Smith and his course for makeup artists.

The Links page connects you to diverse sites such as latex masks, hair and wigs, organizations, and supply companies. When I visited the product review section, there was a lengthy and nicely detailed discussion of makeup cases.

Makeup Resources

Compared with other theatrical crafts, few makeup sites are on the Web. That seems surprising. The Net's ability to display pictures seems ideal for show-'n-tell techniques, and you'd think that makeup supply companies in particular would want to show how their products can be used.

MAKEUP FX.COM—Special Makeup Effects by Lars Carlsson
www.makeup-fx.com

This site is both something of a personal résumé and a detailed "how-to" school that lets you look over the shoulders of a makeup artist through a nicely detailed step-by-step process. To access it, click on the posterlike photograph on the opening page, and on the next page scroll down to such categories as Beauty Makeup, Character Makeup, Three Dimensional Makeup, False Teeth, Wig Making, and Makeup Pictures Gallery. The Making of a Wax Doll, although not directly related to makeup, is a fascinating look at Carlsson's process of making a wax doll of King Gustaf III.

There is a lengthy list of Links to Other Makeup Pages. The FAQs give suggestions to would-be makeup artists. For example, to the question about how to become a makeup artist, Carlsson's answer is blunt: "The best way is to go as an apprentice on a theatre for 3 years."

ACTRESSES IN CHARACTER
http://members.tripod.com/~llwyd/makeup./

Although for film, this is a marvelous site, updated almost weekly. There are more than 2,000 images that show makeup effects on Hollywood actresses. You can see the step-by-step process transforming actresses. Goldie Hawn becomes

Additional Information About Makeup

Netscape has entries for makeup (<*http://directory .netscape.com/Arts/Performing _Arts/Theatre/Special_Effects _Makeup*>). See, too, The Makeup Artist Network (<*www .makeupartistnetwork.com*>).

Jeff Dafys' Actresses in Character has a list of Oscar Awards for makeup artists (<*http: //members.tripod.com/~llwyd /makeup/oscars.htm*>) as well as Emmy Awards for makeup artists (<*http://members.tripod .com/~llwyd/makeup/emmys .htm*>). If you're interested in knowing who the makeup artists were for specific movies—as well as others involved in the films —try scrolling through The Internet Movie Database (<*www .imdb .com*>). Just be patient; the site's organization is baffling.

a plump-cheeked matron in Death Becomes Her. Glenda Jackson turns into the stern (and bald) Elizabeth R. Cicily Tyson ages amazingly for Autobiography of Miss Jane Pittman. Kim Hunter morphs into an ape for Planet of the Apes. For each actress, there are photo essays showing the transformation in progress.

THE MAKE-UP ARTIST WEBRING

www.geocities.com/Hollywood/Hills/5829 /myring.html

This is the central page for a "ring" of people involved with makeup. The ring consists of member websites that band together to form linked circles, allowing visitors to contact them. Here are a hundred links to that ring, and a box invites you to move through the ring at random. Most folks, I suspect, will instead go to the list of sites so they can chose ring sites that interest them.

MAKE-UP ARTIST MAGAZINE

www.makeupmag.com

Started in 1996 by makeup artist Michael Key, winner of an Emmy Award, Make-up Artist Magazine calls itself the "premiere magazine for make-up artists and movie enthusiasts." Clicking on About Us and then Testimonials leads to what can only be called rave notices from significant industry leaders, many of them winners of an Emmy or Oscar. Much of the focus is on motion pictures.

Of course, the site encourages you to subscribe (six issues annually at $24.95), but it also offers Make-up News, details from the magazine; In This Issue; information on the International Make-up Trade Show; a Calendar of Events, such as trade shows and schedules of awards; and access to Makeup.com, which is an online source of makeup books and videos. There also is a Message Board, which looked active with questions and messages from makeup artists.

ENCYCLOPAEDIA BRITANNICA

www.britannica.com

The Brit offers a scholarly examination of the history of makeup, starting with Thespis and coming to modern practices (<*www.britannica.com/bcom/eb/article /0/0,5716,118830+8+110173,00.html*>).

Suppliers

If you want to compare prices or order makeup supplies, the Net's makeup suppliers are ready to help you. Most of the sites are pretty bare-bones affairs without much pizzazz—they include words, not illustrative pictures of the products—which seems to me to be an unfortunate missed opportunity.

MEHRON
www.mehron.com/

Maker of such products as StarBlend Cake, CreamBlend Stick, Original Mask Cover, and Celebre Professional Cream, Mehron says it is the "oldest family owned professional cosmetic company in the United States. This longevity is due to the secure feeling professional makeup artists have in using Mehron products."

From its home page you can access Applications Instructions for (all-too-brief) suggestions. Studio and Stage takes you first to professional endorsements, and at the bottom of that page you can click on View Products for a series of pages about products. Also from the home page you can open Educational Theatre, where you'll find an endorsement in a leading book on makeup about the company's student makeup kits:

> In the fourth edition [of] *Stage Makeup*, the celebrated makeup artist and author Richard Corson describes Mehron's Student Kit as the best available student kit.

Should you wish to purchase products, the site has a secure online ordering system.

BEN NYE
www.wyb.com/makeup.html

When you open this no-frills site, you immediately are in the product area for Ben Nye, one of the well-known suppliers of makeup. Scroll down the page to find the many various categories, a complete line of makeup and supplies. At the bottom of the page, Would You Believe? leads you to announcements about specials.

DAN READ COSMETICS
www.danreadcosmetics.com/

It is easy to overlook the small numbered radio buttons in the upper left-hand corner, but if you place your cursor over them you'll find that they will then flash a sign about other sections of this site. The line features natural, breathable professional cosmetics that also can be used as street makeup. Products (the second of those radio buttons) takes you to a list of available makeup products.

MOTION PICTURE FX COMPANY

www.makeupkits.com/

Despite the title, this site offers supplies for any production. Their makeup kits are recommended on chat boards—highly and frequently recommended, as a matter of fact. To look at kits, on the left menu click on Cases and you'll find a variety of cases and prices. Before ordering, you'll want to be certain you know if the case comes with equipment or is sold as a case only. From this site, also check the Links for other makeup sites.

STEINS THEATRICAL AND DANCE SUPPLY—Makeup

www.steins-theatrical.com/makeup1.htm

An attractive home page marks this Virginia company's site. From it you can access the various brands it supplies—M. Stein, Ben Nye, Bob Kelly, and Kryolan. You can view each brand, but it does not offer online purchasing.

SCHENZ THEATRICAL SUPPLY

www.schenz.com/hmpg.html

Scroll down to the bottom of the home page, where you'll find Theatrical Makeup, and Wigs, Beards, and Mustaches, along with various costume supplies. The makeup page offers products by Mehron and Ben Nye. Also on the bottom of the page is a link to the company's How To section, helpful online tutorials with new topics introduced every six weeks or so.

PB THEATRICAL MAKEUP SUPPLY

www.bwsolutions.com/pbmakeup/index.shtml

When you enter you find a colorful first page with eight pictures of people in show makeup. You can click on the pictures to see where they'll take you, or scroll down to the bottom of the page and see the eight categories: Beauty, Fantasy, Magic, Style, Masquerade, Imagine, Effects, and Details. Apparently this is a relatively small company, and this seems a good place for me to confess that, given a chance, I prefer to patronize the smaller businesses instead of the Goliaths.

MAKEUP ARTISTS NETWORK CHATROOM

www.makeupartistnetwork.com/messageboard/messageboard.html

Intended for both early-career and experienced makeup artists, this chat room invites you to place your résumé here to attract attention of production personnel—and maybe to get you hired for their next project. The board also has lively questions and answers to exchange insight and information, and on my visits I found experienced experts were generously willing to share their knowledge.

Bibliography for Makeup

No matter how potent Net sites may be, books still have the edge with photographs, drawings, and clear organization. Some sites give you access to books. Remember, there are discount e-book stores. You might wish to check prices at Amazon (<www.amazon.com>), Barnes and Noble (<www.barnesandnoble.com>), or Borders (<www.borders.com>). You can go to ByPath.Com (<http://buypath.com>) for a comparison of prices from almost 20 e-book vendors. Perhaps the newest book available is Theatrical FX Makeup, by John Pivovarnick and David Sartor, published by Heinemann and available from the publisher (<www.heinemanndrama.com>).

SPECIAL EFFECT SUPPLY

www.fxsupply.com/

Within the list of assorted materials are various makeup items, such as Dermacolor Color Makeup, which is designed to correct skin disfigurements or discolorations; Makeup for Film and Theatre; Makeup Prosthetics, which includes a video to help you through foam processing; Makeup Case; and Mask Making Basics.

This large company, which supplies several FX materials, also lists a number of makeup books that deserve your attention (go there directly with this link: <www.fxsupply.com/books/books.html>). You can order them from the company.

MASK MAKING

www.norcostco.com/mask.htm

Norcostco, a major theatrical supplier, has books and videos relating to making masks. You can choose from Ben Nye or Bob Kelly instructional videos, or books by authors such as Thurston James. The page also has brief instructions about aspects of making masks, such as Positive Casting, Ready Made Masks Forms, and Prosthetic Style Masks.

NIGHTMARE FACTORY

www.nightmarefactory.com/rvideos.html

Although the site name suggests an orientation toward Halloween, Nightmare Factory has a nice collection of instructional reference videos that theatrical makeup artists and instructors of makeup classes may find helpful. For example, there is a two-video makeup course taught by Bob Kelly, Lee Baugan, and Jay Pearlman ($65), a Rob Burman Beginner's Guide ($39), and a number of other videos for special effects.

Jobs and Career Advice for Makeup Artists

To judge by what you find on the Net, there are many more potential jobs in television and film than in live theatre. I'd like to think that's just a fluke of the Net.

MAKEUP ARTISTS

www.make-upartists.com

To makeup artists this site says, "We're going to make this the best place on the Web to display your talents and advertise your services to the world." It limits membership to 400. Annual leases range from $99 for the basic category to $499 for front page listings in the Gallery. Free, however, is Industry News, a compilation of Hollywood events.

More Information About Jobs

I mentioned this site in Chapter 7, but it's worth repeating: BackstageJobs.com (*www.backstagejobs.com*), formerly known as *The Theatre Design and Technical Jobs Page*, is a valuable site for theatre jobseekers.

SPECIAL EFFECT SUPPLY

www.fxsupply.com

I mentioned this company earlier in the discussion of makeup books. The site also offers career advice for those interested in special effects. One page (<*www.fxsupply.com /features/careers.html#top*>) deals with career preparation and techniques. There's a chatty and informational letter to a mythical someone seeking a job, advising preparation—education and experience—and presentation, which includes insight into an effective portfolio and résumé. The letter concludes with "the big secret," which starts with the premise that "the secret of success is to do one thing better than anyone else, period," and gives illustrations.

Also on the site is Job Opportunities in the Entertainment Industry, which includes notices from employers for specific jobs (<*www.fxsupply.com/features/jobs .html*>). When I visited last, there were some 12 listings for special effects experts for television and film.

JUDITH DENNY MAKEUP SERVICES

www.execpc.com/%7Ecp/faq.html

The list of FAQs explores the reasons why professionally trained makeup artists are important, in contrast to amateur or—apparently worse in Ms. Denny's opinion—do-it-yourselfers. For makeup artists, these can be significant points to promote your services.

9

Scenery, Lighting, Sound, and Properties

You'd expect theatrical design and the Web would make a comfortable marriage. After all, the Web excels at visual displays, making it almost as good as photographic books—almost, that is, but not yet of the quality of high-grade print.

A fair expectation, but that marriage hasn't happened yet. Although sound has a number of fine sites, those who design scenery, lighting, and props find that sites in their areas are disappointing. They do not glow with the perfection or radiate the depth of coverage so often found in costume design sites, and none has the richness that results when a dedicated professional shares hard-earned knowledge, like we see in certain playwriting and acting home pages.

Perhaps we might view the current sites as works-in-progress, because so far they don't fulfill technology's promises. Still in the future are video displays to show theatrical designers in progress as they make artistic and pragmatic choices, and we cannot yet see design's dynamic changes during productions. Even commercial sites of theatrical supply companies seem tame when we think of what can be.

Nonetheless, those reservations aside, you can call up numerous sites for scenery, costume, sound, properties, and lighting design. I list some here. Remember that the best sites in Chapter 3 also will have links to valuable sites for all design.

Before I start the listings, a short preface is in order if you're looking for designers' unions or associations. Chapter 7 discussed *The International Alliance of Theatrical Stage Employees* (<*www.iatse.lm.com*>) and *United Scenic Artists* (<*http://frontpage.shadow.net/usa829fl*>). That same chapter also has information about *United States Institute for Theatre Technology* (<*www.culturenet.ca/usitt*>) if you're interested in the major association for scenic, lighting personnel, sound, and properties people. If you're looking for a tech job, see Chapter 7 for *BackstageJobs.com* (<*www.backstagejobs.com*>).

Note that there's considerable overlap and that sites listed under one category may contain information for other categories. *Electrics Land* (<*www*

.geocities.com/Broadway/2736/index3.html>), for example, is filed here under Lighting Design, but it also contains information for Sound Design.

SCENIC DESIGN

The Net treats scene designers unfairly. Although its ability to show visuals leads us to expect many pages of designs, renderings, and models, there are few sites for scenic design. Even individual résumé pages, opportunities for artists to show their work to prospective employers, lack punch. The Net is a fluid e-organism, however, and no doubt improvements will come. You may be the one to lead the advance.

SCENIC COLLECTION

www.vpa.niu.edu/theater/Aweb1.htm

This site will inspire you to take a research trip to Northern Illinois University to see the historical exhibit, and quite likely it will make you hunt for funding to purchase the slide collection. Lavish in execution and awesome in size, the *Northern Illinois University/Lyric Opera of Chicago Historical Scenic Collection* has elements from the settings of almost 90 operas that were staged between 1889 and 1932.

Housed at NIU, the collection has five million square feet of painted surfaces, with approximately 900 backdrops and borders and more than 2,200 framed scenic units that were designed and painted by a variety of artists. The site lists the "Russians Anisfeld and Roerich; painters from La Scala such as Santoni and Rovescalli; from Vienna, the painters Burghart, Kautsky, and Rottonara; Dove and Schroeder from Berlin; and the Americans Norman Bel Geddes and Robert Edmond Jones."

The variety of styles is impressive. The site points out that the designs reflect "the influence of Realism, Romanticism, Impressionism, Modernism and Art Nouveau in scene painting."

Unfortunately, there are but few illustrations of the collection. Still, the site tempts us with details of arches from *Parsifal* (1914) and a magnificent 66' x 36' drop from *The Magic Flute* (1915). Looking at them can make us wish we had a time machine to experience those productions.

Slides are for sale, with prices ranging from $500 for a sample set to $3,750 for a complete collection of 3105 slides.

PARTRIDGE DESIGNS

www.adayat.com/designs

A pair of scene designers—Allen and Mary Partridge—have created this page, which shows their work and that of their students. At the same time it gives scene designers insight into design processes. Clicking on Portfolio leads to Creating the Digital Design Portfolio and Scene Design at Graceland. Be patient: *Partridge* loads slowly.

YEOMAN DATA CDS

http://user.ausnetwork.com.au/~yeoman

A book on disk—*Scenery Design and Construction for Schools and Community Theatres*—is based on David Waterhouse's "50 years of experience designing sets for the theatre in England and Australia." Its 12 chapters cover all aspects of both design and construction. At his site you can view Background, which explains how the book came about; Contents, which provides chapter titles, although no other descriptions; Reviews, which are done by theatre professionals; and, of course, How to Order.

CRAWFORD INTERNATIONAL THEATRICAL COMPANY

www.citcfx.com

Based in Lynnwood, Washington, CITC creates special stage effects machines to make haze, fog, bubbles, snow, wind, and the like. Their site points out that they are safety-conscious and are working with study groups to be sure the effects present no health hazards. You can access their reviews, credits, product information, and new releases.

GERRIETS INTERNATIONAL

www.ushwy1.com/gerriets

Specialists in stage curtains, this North American affiliate of the German company manufactures a projection cyclorama (PROCYC), rear screen projections, theatre curtains, and muslin up to 41 feet wide. They offer a variety of fabrics, including velour, silk, stage linen, scrims, and stage netting. They also have dance floors, theatrical risers, and platforms. You may want to investigate their *Scenographer's Source Book*, a seven-pound collection of fabric and material samples, brochures, and sample hinges.

I. WEISS—Stage Curtains, Rigging, and Supplies

www.i-weiss.com

Tradition is a major part of I. Weiss. Founded in 1900 in the heart of what was becoming the Broadway theatre district, it has been managed by several generations. It offers a wide variety of theatrical products such as custom draperies, projection screens, fiber-optic curtains, counterweight rigging, suspension hardware, rentals, hardware, and much more.

NORCOSTCO

www.norcostco.com

This Atlanta-based company offers so many different types of theatrical supplies that its information is applicable to all theatrical designers. *Norcostco* says it is the largest supplier of theatrical goods in the Southeast, and you'll find pages for costume, lighting, drapes, drops, scrims, hardware, stage equipment, scenic materials, props, makeup, special effects, sound, and more. Its link to FAQ and Fun led to only a few entries—how to make a mask, how to make a

Individual Scene Design Web Pages

Design Image Online—Scenic Design (*<www.performance-design.com/dol/desscene.html>*) lists almost 70 sites put together by individuals and groups, allowing you to see what other designers are doing and to note techniques you may wish to consider for your personal page. More sites are at *Netscape* (*<http://directorysearch.netscape.com/Arts/Performing_Arts/Theatre/Stagecraft/Set_Designers>*).

phone ring, and lighting fixture tuneup—and although it promised more to come, the last update was almost two years old.

ENCYCLOPAEDIA BRITANNICA

www.britannica.com

At the *e-Brit* site you can find a scholarly examination of the historical development of scene design along with an essay on contemporary practices. There are cross-references to relevant materials such as stock settings. See also *e-Brit* discussions of lighting and scenery. The search engine will find details.

LIGHTING DESIGN

You'll find more resources for lighting than for scenic design. Some are excellent. For example, *Axiom* (*<www.axiomlight.com>*) has stunning pictures of lighting design for various professional productions. There also are numerous vendor sites.

Organizations for Lighting Designers

The professional union for lighting designers is listed at the beginning of this chapter. Because a talented lighting designer isn't necessarily restricted to theatre work, here I include organizations not focused on theatrical design whose work contains ideas and expertise adaptable to the stage.

ASSOCIATION OF LIGHTING DESIGNERS

www.ald.org.uk

A U. K. organization, ALD represents lighting designers in the United Kingdom and the rest of the world. About ALD describes its five major goals, including furthering the art of lighting design and offering advice about equipment while also calling manufacturer's attention to problems. Its Directory takes you to an alphabetical list of members with links to their personal pages. Corporates is for industry members, but there are no links to the companies.

PROFESSIONAL LIGHTING AND SOUND ASSOCIATION

www.plasa.org

PLASA, also a U. K. organization, intends to be the premier online information resource for those working within the entertainment and presentation technology industry. It has links and informational material to a number of countries. The site is crisply laid out and quickly accessed. Place your cursor on the left menu to open each category's contents.

Each month members receive *Standards News*, an e-mail newsletter, and PLASA's magazine, *Lighting & Sound International*. Members also have directory listings, can enroll in an insurance program, and receive free (up to 15 minutes) legal advice.

INTERNATIONAL ASSOCIATION OF LIGHTING DESIGNERS
www.iald.org

Although they are interior and exterior lighting professionals and not *theatrical* lighting designers, IALD nonetheless may interest those who bring light to theatre. Certainly their designs show the impact of lighting, as you'll see in the picture on their first page. Stay there and watch the changing display of striking images, which show a way of painting with light.

For the same reasons, you may want to visit *The Lighting Resource* (<*www.lightresource.com/index.html*>).

Resources for Lighting Designers

Talented lighting designers can fashion careers that include not only theatre but also commercial design for stores and companies, as you'll note from some of the sites here.

THE LIGHTING SHOOTOUT
http://home.earthlink.net/~arnflux/shootout.html

Shootout is a well-chosen name because here a number of automated lighting choices are evaluated. Controversial? Sure. After all, stage lighting designers naturally enough have their favorite equipment, and this site undoubtedly challenges some deeply held assumptions. Arnold Serame, a freelance lighting programmer and designer, lists the results of his study and describes its background:

> The foundation for all of these opinions was the original lighting shootout held over at The Obie Company in January 1996. At that point, we had every DMX mirrored light on the market hung in the demo room and evaluated. Subsequently, I've seen all the yoke lights in that demo room. BUT, unless otherwise noted, *all of these reviews are based on seeing these lights in an actual show situation.*

You can use the table of contents to access areas that most interest you. Serame discusses both generic and brand-name equipment, the latter including various companies such as Martin, Vari-Lite, Coemar, and others.

AXIOM LIGHTING PORTFOLIO
www.axiomlight.com

Axiom is led by Chris Parry, a multi-award-winning designer who also teaches lighting at the University of California, San Diego. (Among his winning designs is a 1993 Tony for *The Who's Tommy*.) Sharing the honors is Trevor Norton, also an active professional lighting designer.

Their site shows that theatrical lighting designers can use their talents in other ways, such as commercial lighting for stores. The first page has a clever and appropriate lighting effect. Place your cursor over any of the links on the left menu and—zap!—a spotlight comes on.

Clicking on Portfolio takes you to pictures of various theatrical lighting designs for plays such as *Blue Angel* at the Royal Shakespeare Company; *Twelfth Night* at the Old Globe Theatre; *The Who's Tommy*, presented in several countries; *The Gambler* at Milwaukee Rep; and more. All are compelling, but instead of showing one photograph per production, I wish they had included a number of pictures of the individual shows.

WESTERN AUSTRALIA ACADEMY LIGHTING LINKS
http://waapa.cowan.edu.au/lx

A distinctly international flavor seasons these links to organizations, companies, forums and discussion groups, health and safety information, utility programs, special effects and pyrotechnics, and reference information. The list of sites is impressively long, and careful surfing is likely to uncover sites you'll find interesting.

THEATRE AND CONCERT LIGHTING DESIGNERS' WEBRING
www.geocities.com/Broadway/Stage/5429/ldringhm.htm

(Some places list this site under a somewhat different title: *Stage and Concert Lighting Designers' Webring*.) Although relatively small in comparison to other theatrical rings—when I visited there were not quite 30 participants and ringmaster Richard Grevers says it is still in its infancy—the ring deserves attention because many of the sites belong to lighting designers who share their work for theatre, dance, film, concerts, or television. It is a safe bet the ring will grow, and you may wish to join.

CRESCIT SOFTWARE
www.crescit.com/

Crescit has Professional Lighting Design Software and Educational Lighting Software for PC/Windows or Mac operating systems. You'll need to register to access the Demo section. They also offer software for sound designers.

LIGHTING AND ELECTRONICS, INC.
www.le-us.com/

This commercial site offers informational materials beyond the company's catalog materials. Designers will want to look at Lighting Math Formulas, Safety Guides, and links to other sites.

WWW.LIGHTING DESIGNERS.COM
www.lightingdesigners.com/

Representing independent lighting designers, the site offers them a place to put their home pages and résumés. When I last visited, there were six designers.

STAGE LIGHTING MATH
www.le-us.com/lgtmath.htm

This clear and straightforward site contains math formulas for lighting designers and electricians.

ETEC—Lighting Dimensions Magazine
www.etecnyc.net/ld.html

For lighting professionals, the monthly *Lighting Dimensions* contains articles about the creative use of light in theatre, dance, and opera as well as in other entertainment areas such as film, television, concerts, museums, and theme parks. The site shows current articles about productions and other designs, and you also can visit archives. If these tempt you, you can subscribe online to the magazine for $39.95 annually.

ENCYCLOPAEDIA BRITANNICA
www.britannica.com/

The online *Britannica* has references for various aspects of theatre. Of the various design arts, Stage Lighting has the largest number of entries. Using the search engine, you'll find scholarly articles on Historical Development, Electrification, Light Sources, Illumination Sources, Projections and Special Effects, Lighting Controls, and Lighting Design. Many have cross-references to relevant individuals and movements. The historical overview and development of technology are neatly organized, although curiously there are no links to such innovators as Inigo Jones, Adolphe Appia, or Gordon Craig.

THE SCIENCE OF LIGHT—The Dark Sucker Theory
www.reed.edu/~markelc/science.html

Maybe you believe that electric light bulbs emit light? Nope. Here you'll see that they suck dark. Therefore we'll call bulbs dark suckers. Oh, you want proof? Here's the logic:

> A candle is a primitive dark sucker. A new candle has a white wick. You will notice, that after first use, the wick begins to turn black. This represents all the dark which has been sucked into it. . . . Dark has mass. When dark goes into a dark sucker, friction from this mass generates heat. Thus, it is not wise to touch an operating dark sucker.

And to think there are people who say the Internet can't be educational! We owe a debt—of something or other—to Reed College (Portland) for this, um, enlightenment.

Lighting Suppliers and Vendors

Some vendors listed here, despite their titles describing lighting, also offer supplies for props, scenery, and sound.

HIGH OUTPUT, INC.

www.highoutput.com/

Offering rentals and sales of "everything from inkies to 18kw HMIs, dollies to generators, and expendables from A to Z," *High Output* has offices throughout New England. Their healthy list of credits includes theatre, feature films, schools and universities, sporting events, and television. Jobseekers will be encouraged to know they had advertisements posted for jobs in their company when I last visited.

ELECTRICS LAND

www.geocities.com/Broadway/2736/index3.html

A collection of theatrical lighting and sound links on the Web that used to be called *Stagecraft Central*, this is a good source for lists of commercial suppliers and organizations. The site also offers a list of some theatrical training institutions. When I last visited, the most recent update was about a year old.

From the main page you can click on Other Resources and find links to theatrical and lighting pages, including Cue Sheets by Fred Hopke (for both sound and lights). Retailers leads you to companies, organized by geographic areas, and Manufacturers is a lengthy alphabetized listing of companies, all with links. Fun Stuff allows you to open The Cyber Theatre, which has various links from an interesting graphic of a stage.

CITY THEATRICAL

www.citytheatrical.com/

Although there are many pages, *City Theatrical's* site has a clean and efficient organization. Click on a category on the left menu—such as Lighting Accessories, Moving Light Accessories, or General Accessories—and you'll instantly see the relevant subdivisions.

Some of the products, like AutoYoke, are innovative and offer new solutions to old problems. Among other helpful entries that you'll find is Lightwright, called the professional's paperwork tool, which tracks all aspects of selecting and arranging, numbering and comparing, assigning and footnoting lighting paperwork. Blacktac Light Mask Foil creates patterns or controls spill light.

ETEC—Entertainment Technology

www.etecnyc.net/default.html

Clicking on Industry Resources on the left menu takes you to "complete. Industry Resources and Buyers Guides" to find companies and latest product information. Before accessing that, you might want to explore the site to see special workshops like the Broadway Lighting Master Classes.

BRENDAN'S PAGE OF LIGHTING RESOURCES
http://members.home.net/2828056091/home.html
The site lists a number of computer programs for lighting designers, although reviews would be helpful. There also is an extensive list of major companies and organizations, almost all dealing with lighting.

STRAND LIGHTING
www.strandlight.com/
Strand manufactures lighting, dimming, and control systems. The first page shows you a world map of *Strand's* international coverage. Click on your country and you'll find links to Products, Industries, and Service. For opportunities to attend one of their programs to learn about equipment maintenance, programming moving lights, and so forth, open Training. Tech Info leads to links for CAD Symbols, Operating Manuals, and their Product Specifications.

ROSCO
www.rosco.com/
Rosco is a major supplier of scenic paints, lighting color filters, stage hardware, special effects machines, and other items. Their site gives you links to all their products. Technotes has advice and problem-solving discussions for designers to help them achieve particular effects.

TECH THEATRE LINKS
www.iwaynet.net/~phantom/theatrelinks/
This is sort of a mini-mega-site of vendors. Clicking on Lighting from the left menu will take you to long list of lighting suppliers (or go there directly with this address: <*www.iwaynet.net/~phantom/theatrelinks/lights.htm*>).

LIGHTSEARCH.COM
www.light-link.com/
With guides to Lighting Specifiers and Buyers, *LightSearch* helps you find lists of suppliers of lighting equipment, although not all are directly related to theatre.

Sites to Buy or Sell Used Lighting Equipment
Granted, everyone wants the very latest equipment, but not all budgets can meet those demands. Those who are used to shopping for used cars may want to kick the fresnel lenses of used lights.

LIGHTBROKER.COM
www.lightbroker.com/
Lightbroker offers a place to buy and sell used lighting gear. Not all of the listings are used; some are closeouts. It also offers a guarantee.

More Information About Suppliers and Design

For more information about design, look in (<*www.stetson.edu/departments/csata/thr_guid.html*>) and USITT (<*www.culturenet.ca/usitt/home.htm*>), which have lists you may wish to explore. *Artslynx* has lists of theatre design and technology sites (<*www.artslynx.org/theatre/design.htm*>). For lists of companies that offer theatrical supplies, see *Scott's Theatre-Link.com* (<*www.theatre-link.com/*>), and you can also find materials at *Entertainment Technology Communications Group* (<*www.etenyc.net*>). For a list of manufacturers, Netscape has more than 40 sites (<*http://directory.netscape.com/Business/Industries/Arts_and_ Entertainment/Equipment/Manufacturers/Lighting/Theatrical*>).

Individual's Websites

Design Image Online—Lighting Design lists more than 100 personal and group Web pages (<*www.performance-design.com/dol/deslx.html*>), valuable for finding what others in the field are doing and for looking for models to use for your personal page.

SOUND DESIGN

We read that back in the days of radio drama—yep, that's right, drama with no pictures—there was one of those goofs that becomes legend. On one live show the hero, in grave risk, told the villain: "All right. You leave me no choice! I have to shoot you! Take that!" *Silence. No sound effect.* "I said, I'm going to shoot you! Take that!" *More silence. The hapless sound engineer couldn't get the sound effect to work.* Desperate, the actor ad-libbed: "No, the gun is too noisy. Instead, I'm going to use this knife and stab you to death! Take that!" *The actor grunted with the exertion of each thrust of the knife.* "And that!" Then the sound engineer got the sound to work. *Bang!*

That sort of mistake can't happen today with our modern computerized equipment, right? Right.

Organizations for Sound Designers

The groups here are focused on helping you learn the science of sound, protecting your interests, and providing you a chance to associate with others who share your interests.

THE ACOUSTICAL SOCIETY OF AMERICA

http://asa.aip.org

We speak in general terms of a theatre building's acoustics, using phrases such as "this theatre has excellent acoustics" or "the acoustics are poor under the balcony," but most often we're making highly subjective observations. In fact, acoustics is an objective study of sound, a field so broad it encompasses, as the *Society* says, "physics, electrical, mechanical, and aeronautical engineering, oceanography, biology, physiology, psychology, architecture, speech, noise and noise control, and music." Whew. Sound designers must, somehow, apply relevant portions of that study to their work. This site may help.

There are some 7,000 members of the *Acoustical Society of America*, representing America and other countries, all involved in one or more aspects of "sound," both theoretical and applied, and more recently some members have been involved in a study of "noise." They receive the monthly *The Journal of the Acoustical Society of America* (JASA).

UNION OF STAGE EMPLOYEES—Local One, IATSE
www.iatse-local1.org

In 1999, the Theatrical Sound Designers Association, Local 922, merged with Local One. The International Alliance of Theatrical Stage Employees are the ones who control sound, lights, scenery, and props for the legitimate theatre, as well as for television studies, hotels, and arenas. If you're planning a professional career in any of those areas, you'll want to explore this site.

PROFESSIONAL LIGHTING AND SOUND ASSOCIATION
www.plasa.org

As we noted earlier in Lighting Design, PLASA membership consist both of sound and lighting designers who work in the entertainment and presentation technology industries. This U. K. organization has links to and informational material for a number of countries. The site is crisply laid out and quickly accessed—when you place your cursor on the left menu, each category's contents open. Members receive the monthly *Standards News*, an e-mail newsletter, and PLASA's magazine, *Lighting & Sound International*. Members also have directory listings, can enroll in an insurance program, and receive free (up to 15 minutes) legal advice.

Resources for Sound Designers

The Net grants more treasures to sound designers than it gives lighting and scenery designers. For you, the Net has a number of excellent sites that offer valuable information and resources, as you'll discover by exploring the pages listed here.

KEN'S LINKS
www.prosoundweb.com/kenslinks/

AUTHOR'S CHOICE Ken Berger, cofounder and CEO of Eastern Acoustic Works, which designs and manufactures loudspeaker systems, offers a list of links to websites for music and audio materials. The site has more than 750 links, which may well make it the largest and most comprehensive available. You start by selecting from one of some 20 different categories. Each leads to a list of sites, some directly related to theatrical sound and others more broadly based.

THEATRE SOUND DESIGN DIRECTORY

www.theatre-sound.com/tsindex.html

AUTHOR'S CHOICE   Charlie Richmond of *Richmond Sound Design* has put together this mega-site with careful organization. International in scope with some two dozen different countries represented, the site's contents are impressive in size and depth. It obviously is the result of diligent research, and you're bound to find information you seek in its estimated 500 sites.

Valuable folders include Computer Audio (slightly under 100 pages that offer guides), General References (almost 100 sites, including half a dozen about copyright plus many on problem solving, even a Whistling Man who can whistle anything you want!), Manufacturers (such a large list it is difficult to believe any are missing), Organizations (almost 20 entries), Sound Designers (over 100 individual pages), and Sounds on the Web (over 70 entries, including some with royalty-free sound).

THEATRICAL MUSIC AND SOUND EFFECTS

www.teleport.com/~mjgallag/

AUTHOR'S CHOICE   M. J. Gallagher's personal website has two valuable informational pages. If you're interested in sound design, both pages deserve your attention because they show a professional designer's process.

The first is Theatrical Music and Sound Design, which explains what a sound designer does and the goals of sound design. It more than explains; it illustrates. In what Gallagher calls "an 'aural window' into the creative process of the sound designer," there are .WAV files that you download to hear examples.

The second page is The Business of Sound Design, which is "devoted to the real task of staying alive while trying to create art." Here you find a number of techniques and approaches for sound designers, primarily centered around using the Internet for both the creative process of designing sound and—important for jobseekers—marketing your talents. There also is a good bibliography.

The site also illustrates one possible structure of a designer's résumé, which can help you design your own. Surely any producer seeking a sound designer would be impressed with Gallagher's knowledge and clear devotion to the art, as illustrated in this home page.

KAI'S SOUND HANDBOOK

www.harada-sound.com/sound/handbook/

A Glossary of Sound Terminology is one of the features of this site. Among other topics are Basics of Sound, Input Devices, Crash-Course Guide to Wireless Microphones, and more. Although the opening page sounds flip, the interior is, well, er, sound.

THEATRE SOUND DESIGNER AND COMPOSER RING

www.ashland.net/madrone/tsound_ring.html

This ring is a good start for those looking for resources or suppliers. It consists of sound designers and companies that provide sound effect libraries, equipment, and playback equipment. To access members' sites on the ring, you can simply click on Next on the ring box. Because you don't know where that will take you, you may prefer the more efficient system of clicking on List Sites. There were almost 40 ring members when I last visited.

More Information on Sound
Netscape, like other mega-directories, has a category of Sound you may want to explore (<*http://directorysearch
.netscape.com/Arts/Performing
_Arts/Theatre/Stagecraft/Sound*>).

If you have a website concerning sound, you'll see an invitation to join the ring. The webmaster examines submissions to be certain they are appropriate.

THEATRE-SOUND MAILING LIST

www.brooklyn.com/theatre-sound/

An impressively large number of people—almost 600 from a dozen countries—participate in this cooperative communication system to ask questions and offer answers or opinions about theatrical sound.

THE AURAL IMAGINATION

http://homepages.enterprise.net/micpool

This U. K. site is "a resource for students of sound design" and is run by Mic Pool, Director of Creative Technology at the West Yorkshire Playhouse in Leeds. You'll find articles that deal in general terms with fundamentals, such as a Step by Step Guide to Sound Design For Drama and Art and Craft in Theatre Sound Design, plus technical essays like A Cue Based MIDI Theatre Sequencer for the Apple Macintosh, and GIF Files of Drawings and Plans and Plots from Recent Shows.

Sound Suppliers and Vendors

Some pages in the Resources Category, which appeared earlier, can help you find vendors. Other websites are listed here.

TECH THEATRE LINKS

www.iwaynet.net/~phantom/theatrelinks

This is, the site says, "the world's largest technical theatre link." It certainly has a large number of sites. Click on Sound from the left menu and you'll find a long list of suppliers (or go there directly with this address: <*www.iwaynet
.net/~phantom/theatrelinks/sound.htm*>).

SOUND IDEAS

www.sound-ideas.com/

Sound Ideas says it is "the world's largest publisher of professional sound effects." Its libraries are used around the world. Their site offers music as well as sound effects, and an audio demo file lets you audition their materials.

TVMUSIC.COM
www.tvmusic.com/index.html

Not only does Valentino Production Music and Sound Effects Libraries have music and sound effects, they also let you preview their materials, for which you'll need MP3 (<*www.mp3.org/*>). Valentino says it has arranged with major play publishing companies to make available "all of the necessary music and sound effects cue used in virtually all major plays produced for Broadway, regional dinner theatre, College and high school productions, 'straw hat' amateur productions, and all other applications."

With more than 500 titles, ranging from *Anastasia* to *You Can't Take It with You*, likely they may have the sound you need—and if they don't, they say they'll make sound for you. They have online catalog services.

More Vendors for Sound
The Theatre Sound Mailing List has a list of vendors (<*www.brooklyn.com/theatre-sound/index.html#net*>).

CRESCIT SOFTWARE
www.crescit.com/

Crescit has "Pro Audio and Sound Effects Software" for either Mac or PC/Windows operating systems. A demo is available, but you have to register to use it. They also supply software for lighting designers.

TELEPHONE RING GENERATOR
www.users.dialstart.net/~gbg

To make phones ring authentically on stage, here's an electronic device that simulates the cadences of both British and American telephones. They say it even actually rings Bell-type phones.

JOHN MILLS-COCKELL—Scoring and Sound Design
www.musicplanet.com/jmc/profile/

If you're looking for a job, here's a neat model. This page doesn't give you instructions on finding employment, but it does show how one enterprising Canadian designer parlayed his talents into a full career in film, dance, radio, television, and film.

PROPERTY DESIGNERS

Property designers and running crews need to be creative, inventive, resourceful, and well organized. They also need to be patient and good team workers because they must work with a group of others—the show's director, actors, scene designer, technical director, and production stage manager. A missing prop can throw the whole production askew, but when well planned, props contribute to the show's success more than the audience ever can recognize. I still marvel at the property designer for one of my shows, which required *two* sit-down dinners for eight characters, surely an intensely challenging task. The designer handled it all with such smoothness, grace, and positive good nature that we all felt totally secure. And blessed.

Although some of the sites below were still a-building when I last visited them, I expect they will grow by the time you read this.

S*P*A*M—Society of Prop Artisan Managers
www.geocities.com/Broadway/2938/home.html

Here's a site with a wry sense of humor—how often do you see SPAM as a positive organization? Unfortunately, when I last visited there was only a home page with the ubiquitous "under construction notice," and none of the links worked. It looks promising, however, with sites called Educational Opportunities for a Career in Professional Theatre and so forth, so I list it here hoping it'll be active when you go look.

PROPPEOPLE.COM—The Online Home for the Props Professional
www.PropPeople.com/index.shtml

AUTHOR'S CHOICE Proclaiming that "this site is one of the only places on the Web aimed exclusively at prop people," it is full of pages you'll want to investigate. You can sign up for a Newsletter you'll receive via e-mail, join in the Discussion board, and see what's happening on the Props Listserv. The list of Vendors was still being formed when I last visited.

Although still building, PropPeople is an effective site. Webmaster Sean McArdle sees a significant need for an authoritative online page, saying that one goal

> is to give students interested in props a source of information. It is well
> nigh impossible to get a formal education in the area of props, and what
> instruction exists is sometimes difficult to find. My hope is that this site will
> help point future prop people in the directions they need·to start a career
> in this field.

Properties Suppliers and Vendors

Searching for e-suppliers of properties uncovers many companies that provide props for catalog photography, movies, television, or magic. That focus doesn't necessarily negate their potential usefulness for theatrical productions.

THE PROX WERX
www.propwerx.on.ca

Located in Toronto, this relatively new site deals with the creation of all kinds of props for theatre, film, special events, or advertising. They offer a wide range of services, from custom props to sets to makeup work.

Additional Information for Property Designers

Sets, Props, Costumes, Stunts, Special EFX has a lengthy list of vendors (<*www.creativedir .com/html/18.html*>), as does *The Professional Lighting and Sound Association* (<*www.plasa .org*>), described in this chapter under Lighting. Also look at Netscape's entries (<*http://directory.netscape.com /Arts/Performing_Arts/Theatre /Stagecraft*>).

NON-STOP PROP SHOP

www.nonstoppropshop.com

The *Prop Shop* says, "If we don't have it, we'll find it. If we don't find it, we'll build it!" They offer props, furniture, settings, even clothing. Although their main focus is on catalog and advertising, the quality of their work may attract theatrical prop managers.

THE PROPPER SOURCE

www.proppersource.com

An Atlanta company that has props for movies, television, photography, and stage, the interestingly named *Propper Source* both rents and sells its equipment. The site has a search engine to speed your process. Although a search for *rifle* pulled up, of all things, *Ronsonol Lighter Fuel* (to use to remove tape residue), other searches were more effective.

PROPTOLOGY—The Journal of Props Professionals

www.arvotek.net/~props

This Canadian publication—$15 annually—is designed for property folks. The site lists some past articles, although not recent ones.

10

Theatre and Dance Arts Management

Managing theatre and dance organizations is a complex and difficult task. Perhaps this remarkable statistic can contribute to morale:

> Spending on performing arts events was roughly 1.6 times greater than spending on either admissions to motion pictures or spectator sports events between 1992 and 1997.

You'll find that and other encouraging facts on *The Business Committee for the Arts*, one of the strong management sites discussed in this chapter (<*www.bcainc.org*>).

Arts managers tend to be unobtrusive, unseen, unheard, unnoticed (except when things go wrong), and underappreciated. But without the supportive umbrella of effective management, creative folks would find themselves working without a plan, budget, audience, maybe even without a roof.

One endless management goal is searching for funds. In this chapter you'll find information about finding local, state, governmental, and public sources for grants and support. Another goal is publicizing your organization. For that task, you'll want to look at sites we examine in this chapter, such as *Open Studio—The Arts Online* (<*www.openstudio.org*>) and other marketing homes like *Arts Marketing Online* (<*www.artsmarketing.org*>). If you're seeking an education in arts management, the *Association of Arts Administration Educators* (<*www.artsnet.org/aaea*>) lists undergrad and grad colleges and universities for you to consider. For future seminars to improve your skills and allow you to network with other managers, check *Theatre Communications Group* (<*www.tcg.org/*>).

ORGANIZATIONS FOR ARTS ADMINISTRATION

There seem to be fewer support organizations for arts administration than for, say, acting or design. The reason is probably best explained by the *Association of Arts Administration Educators* when it points out that "recognition of arts administration as a profession is a recent development," and therefore it still is "in its adolescence." More sites will arrive as people in arts administration begin to exploit the Net.

THE INTERNATIONAL ALLIANCE OF THEATRICAL STAGE EMPLOYEES
www.iatse.lm.com

The labor union "representing technicians, artisans and craftspersons in the entertainment industry, including live theatre, film and television production," IATSE has more than 100,000 members in the United States and Canada. I mention it here because members include those who work in such areas as Treasurers and Ticket Sellers; Publicists, Press Agents and Managers; Stage Technicians; Costume Design/Set Design; Wardrobe; or Hair and Makeup. To discover membership benefits, click on An Introduction to The IATSE, and on the next page open Membership Services.

ASSOCIATION OF ARTS ADMINISTRATION EDUCATORS
www.artsnet.org/aaae

AAAE represents graduate and undergraduate programs in arts administration. An international organization, the *Association of Arts Administration Educators* believes that college/university programs will grow to satisfy the increasing need for arts administration personnel.

If you are looking for graduate or undergraduate training in arts administration, scroll down the left menu and you'll find a list of almost 40 graduate degree institutions, and five with undergraduate work in the field. They're located in America, Canada, Australia, and other countries.

AAAE publishes a *Guide to Arts Administration Training and Research*, which contains information about job posting services, arts service agencies, graduate research theses, and more. You can order it ($12.95) here.

THEATRE COMMUNICATIONS GROUP
www.tcg.org/

I've mentioned *Theatre Communications Group* (TCG) several times elsewhere in this book, indicative of its importance as a national theatre service organization. One of its services offers professional development to theatre leaders. From its opening page, click on Programs and Services. You'll find Management Programs. This leads to a broad range of services, which TCG says

> improves the managerial expertise of the field by providing research and resource information to theatre managers and trustees, giving national visibility to the condition, needs and achievements of the theatre community, and by disseminating TCG-conducted research on finances and practices of the American not-for-profit theatre.

On the Programs and Services page you can also click on Artistic Programs, then scroll down to Observerships. That section describes programs for artistic and management personnel—monetary support for travel and expenses—to aid in their personal growth and improve their contributions to their theatrical institution. TCG also offers theatre managers its research and resource information about finances and practices of the American not-for-profit theatre.

TCG sponsors workshops for artistic and management leaders, such as the recent human resource training seminar titled "Expanding the Theatre Manager's Repertoire." Illustrating the broad range of a manager's responsibilities, the seminar topics included "Coaching and Developing," "Managing Conflict," "Your Role as Influencer," and "Your Role as Change Agent." If interested in future seminars, you can watch TCG's site for announcements, and perhaps you may wish to encourage them to continue that program.

For theatrical employers and job searchers, TCG publishes *Art*SEARCH, the first-choice employment publication for theatre.

CENTER FOR ARTS MANAGEMENT AND TECHNOLOGY
www.artsnet.org/camt

The Carnegie-Mellon CAMT "exists to link the artist of today with the technology of tomorrow." Click on Services and then Initiatives to find Arts Over America, which includes an online cultural calendar. It offers a nicely organized Automated Grants Management System for filling out forms online. Its *ArtsNet* (below) has valuable resources.

ARTSNET
www.artsnet.org/index.html

From the Master of Arts Management Program at Carnegie Mellon University, this page gives you access to *ArtSites*, a directory of arts and culture sites on the Web that operates with a search engine. The search engine works best from the pull-down menu, where you'll see categories that include Dance and Theatre.

ArtsNet offers access to a wide range of sites, some directly related to management and others more broadly based. One interesting menu leads you to arts such as theatre, dance, and opera organized by states. Another section contains Arts Management Resources. Once there, a pull-down menu takes you to a database of information about management.

THEATRE MANAGEMENT JOURNAL
www.artsnet.org/ATHEEJ

This 'zine offers you articles dealing with aspects of management. Given the breadth of coverage, you'll likely find articles that apply to your organization. For example, one recent publication discussed time management, audience development, arts advocacy, handling required theatre attendance for students in introductory classes, and working with volunteers.

NATIONAL ARTS STABILIZATION

www.artstabilization.org

Stabilization? Although the title may sound less like the arts and more like a device to keep ships from tossing and turning in stormy seas, that's not a bad analogy. For the arts to weather storms, NAS believes there must be a base foundation consisting of strong management. To that end, this nonprofit organization offers arts organizations training, planning, and technical assistance programs tailored to meet their individual requirements. Clicking on Stabilization Projects gives you insight into their goals as you look into various pages.

RESOURCES FOR ARTS MANAGEMENT

Funding and marketing publicity necessarily preoccupy arts managers. Several sites offer help.

Recommended Book for Theatre Management

A major resource for managers is *Theatre Management and Production in America: Commercial, Stock, Resident, Community, and Presenting Organizations*, by Stephen Langley (Drama Book Publishers, 1990). Although it is out of print, you may be able to find it at book sites like *Big Words* (*<http://bigwords .com>*) or *Ecampus.com* (*<www .ecampus.com>*), both of which sell used textbooks at discounts, or at one of the other book sites discussed in Chapter 12.

Funding

One problem you may face is finding "grantmakers"—foundations or organizations that offer grants—appropriate for your goals. In the past, researching possibilities was a daunting task because there are some 50,000 grantmakers. The Net decreases the difficulties and speeds the process.

Sites such as *The Foundation Center On-Line*, *Artslynx*, and others (discussed below) give you detailed information about a large number of such groups. You still need to research each organization to see if you fit their criteria, but thanks to the Net you can click on their home sites for details. Often you can find information about grants they've awarded in the past, which gives you a basis for comparison about your proposal's acceptance. You even can find keys to filling out those pesky application forms.

THE FOUNDATION CENTER ON-LINE

http://fdncenter.org

AUTHOR'S CHOICE *The Foundation Center* is so extensive it is almost a Library of Congress for funding. It appears to list everything grantseekers could possibly want (except, of course, a blank check).

Quite valuable, perhaps unique, is its offer to give reference assistance: "Our professional staff will consult our library resources to help answer your questions." It invites you to phone its Grantmaker Services or e-mail questions to an online librarian.

The site is a bit complex because it focuses on both those who make grants and those who seek them, and unfortunately the home page doesn't show all that is here. I suggest the best approach is first to click on About Us. You'll then see Starting Points for Grantseekers, divided into Orientation to Grantseeking and Guide to Funding Research. Both deserve your careful attention. Orientation is a nicely detailed and quite thorough online tutorial divided into two paths, one if you're an individual grantseeker, and a second if you represent a nonprofit organization seeking funding. The user-friendly Guide also is constructed with the reader in mind and has well-organized and richly explicit information.

One particular strength of the site is Foundation Finder, frequently updated, with information on some 50,000 private and public foundations and links to their websites. Additionally, there is an Online Library with Resources that includes a Bookshelf, Reading Lists, and perhaps most helpful, Prospect Worksheet and Common Grant Application Forms.

For books and articles on arts funding, look in Literature of the Nonprofit Sector Online, a bibliographic database. Once there, use the search engine or alphabetical index. This site is quite serious about thorough detail, evidenced by more than 18,000 full bibliographic citations.

ART AND CULTURE—Philanthropy Search
www.philanthropysearch.com/art.html

Calling itself "the first search engine serving the nonprofit and philanthropic sector," this is a mega-site of the editors' recommended links, a mixture of arts companies, arts sites, and a few sources for grantmakers. If you scroll down to the bottom of the page, you'll find a search engine that accesses their entire database.

ARTSLYNX
www.artslynx.org/

I've mentioned *Artslynx* before in connection with its extensive lists for actors, dancers, designers, and technicians. Here it is appropriate for management.

From its home page you can click on Arts Admin (or go there with this address: *<www.artslynx.org/admin>*) for Arts Administration Resources, where you will find a number of varied categories. Of them, you may wish to start with *Artslynx Library of Arts Funding Resources Online* or *Guidestar*, which has a list of nonprofit organizations.

General arts funding (*<www.artslynx.org/funding.htm>*) has links to mega-directories or individual sources.

Dance funding (*<www.artslynx.org/dance/funding.htm>*) lists websites that specialize in helping fund the arts and arts-related projects.

THEATRE SOURCES DOT COM

Using the *Artslynx* search engine to find *theatre management* led to an outside site with a complicated address (<*http://intra.whatUseek.com/cgi-bin/intrasearch ?crid=7898450c0e19b11a&slice_title=&query=Management&session=96338061*>) with 10 sites that have some relevance to managers.

BOLZ CENTER FOR ARTS ADMINISTRATION
www.bolzcenter.org/
One of America's graduate programs for arts administration, the *Bolz Center* is in the School of Business at the University of Wisconsin–Madison. From its home page you can look at its program and examine its research projects. Valuable is General Resources for arts professionals.

PHILANTHROPY NEWS DIGEST
http://fdncenter.org/pnd/current/index.html
PND is a weekly news digest of new articles related to philanthropy as taken from various media. Each publication follows a reporting pattern, with the front page listing current headlines and giving you access to book and web-site reviews, a job corner, and links of interest. You also can examine the PND archives. If you want to receive a free e-mail version each week, submit your e-mail address.

PRESIDENT'S COMMITTEE ON THE ARTS AND HUMANITIES
www.pcah.gov/
Created in 1982, *The President's Committee* seeks to solicit private sector support of the arts and to increase the public's awareness of the value of arts and humanities. For those reasons, a strong advocate for the arts might want to explore the site to learn how to support the projects.

The opening page gives you access to Publications, Children and the Arts and Humanities, and Creative America. To access many reports you'll need the *Adobe Acrobat Reader* (free at <*www.adobe.com/products/acrobat/readstep.html*>). From this site you can access the *Arts Education Partnership* (<*http://aep-arts.org*>), where you can look at Task Forces and Advocacy, Gaining the Arts Advantage, and the Arts Report Card (which requires patience due to an inordinate amount of clicking to get anywhere).

ARTS MARKETING ONLINE
www.artsmarketing.org/home.shtml
Deceptively simple at first glance, the site has several valuable departments. It says it intends to be the preeminent resource for arts marketing resources online, and undoubtedly it will continue growing. At the home page you are given four options. Essays contain thoughtful pieces about the arts. Forum is particularly interesting because it has contributions from people who are actually involved in arts management. They identify themselves and their organizations—far preferable to some chat rooms where people are anony-

mous—and discuss such matters as season tickets and drawing audiences. Books is a nice bibliography, and Links has a wide variety of sites, although some appear at best marginally relevant to actual arts.

Business and the Arts

Business executives, by the nature of their responsibilities, have considerable expertise with budgets, funding, and marketing. They also have extensive personal contacts with other executives and therefore are able to make a good pitch for corporate donations to the arts. Wouldn't it be nice if they volunteered their skills and talents to help arts organizations? As a matter of fact, they do, and we in the arts are grateful beneficiaries.

THE BUSINESS COMMITTEE FOR THE ARTS, INC.

www.bcainc.org

BCA brings business and the arts together, offering its considerable resources to assist businesses in supporting the arts. BCA is for businesses, not the arts, and membership is restricted to business.

That said, you'll find that it is well worth visiting, and you'll pick up some good material to quote when you're soliciting funds from businesses. For example, the section titled Why Business Invests in the Arts has fascinating statistics, such as:

□ The arts account for 6% of the U. S. Gross National Product. The construction industry accounts for 4.8%.

□ The arts employ 2.7% of the American workforce, or 3.2 million individuals. Agriculture employs 2.6%.

And a most significant point when you approach businesses for support:

□ Employees involved in the community activities of their employers, like volunteering for arts organizations the company supports, are 30% more likely to want to continue working for that company, and to help it succeed.

Consider, too, this intriguing statistic:

□ A telephone survey of the first 400 companies on the 1997 Forbes 500 list revealed that 84% of the respondents support the arts.

These and other interesting concepts await you on this BCA site. Imagine how you might use them when making your pitch to business executives.

ARTS AND BUSINESS COUNCIL, INC.

www.artsandbusiness.org/home.htm

ABC says it seeks to "keep the arts in business" with partnerships between corporations and nonprofit arts groups. Its major program—Business Volunteers for the Arts—"places corporate executives as *pro bono* management consultants with nonprofit arts groups." Centered in New York, it is a national program. It has a network of 21 affiliates that have generated nearly $100 million in donated services and resources for the arts.

While much of this site is focused on New York, you can look into its links for national programs by scrolling down the right-hand menu. Links can be especially valuable. It includes entries for funding (governmental and private) and sites for Arts Management Resources and Service Organizations.

It also has a National Arts Marketing Project to train arts professionals. This includes such programs as Basic Marketing Workshops to develop audiences, and an Advanced Audience Development Training and Granting Program, which also makes participating organizations eligible for a grant up to $25,000 to implement their marketing plans. It started *ArtsMarketing Online* (listed in the next section) in January 1999.

An E-Presence: *Publicizing Your Organization on the* Net

What's the sense of mounting a magnificent production if no one knows? Promotion, advertising, and publicity are crucial. In this era of the Internet, I suggest that a well-managed arts organization absolutely must have a strong Net presence. The key is a carefully designed informational site that has an artistic flair appropriate for the organization and that features interesting pages—yet opens quickly.

The arts management needs to take steps to ensure that the audience knows the address to access the site. It also must be faithfully kept up to date—in my surfing I was dejected to see site after site that discussed last year's season or, worse, a season that happened four years past. Wake up and move on, guys!

The following site offers you guidance in creating a presence on the Internet.

OPEN STUDIO—The Arts Online

www.openstudio.org

Evidence of the Net's importance is the *Open Studio* focus on providing Internet access and training to nonprofit arts organizations. Collaborating with the National Endowment for the Arts, *Open Studio* offers you a Toolkit with a Trainer's Lounge that has tools and tutorials to help you create a Web page for your organization. Field Trip shows you how other arts use the Net and includes a focus on funding resources. Marketing and Publicity and Arts Services Online are aids to thinking of your website, and the Trainer's Lounge has valuable materials that deal with getting online and planning, creating, and publicizing your site.

Advocacy

We know, of course, that many organizations, businesses, and special interest groups fill the halls of Congress as they lobby for legislation supporting their goals. Who lobbies for the arts in Congress? Fortunately, we have some dedicated souls who undertake that responsibility, such as those listed next. In the interest of art, you may want to consider joining their efforts.

AMERICAN ARTS ALLIANCE

www.artswire.org/~aaa

The *American Arts Alliance* intends to be an advocate for nonprofit arts organizations. To view an example of their arguments in favor of the arts, click on Myths and Facts about National Support of the Arts and Culture. There you'll find potent statements such as "Cultural funding is less than one one-hundredths of one percent (.001%) of the federal government's multibillion dollar budget, and a mere 36 cents per capita," and "A recent Lou Harris poll indicated that 79 percent of Americans believe that 'the federal government should provide financial assistance to arts organizations, such as arts museums, dance, opera, theater groups, and symphony orchestras.'"

You also will want to look at Fact Sheets, which present arguments for support of NEA, NEH, and other cultural programs. By opening Read Legislative Alerts and Become a Cyber Advocate, you can learn how you can support the lobby effort.

AMERICANS FOR THE ARTS

www.artsusa.org/

Americans for the Arts has three main goals, which it states simply: "More money for the arts; Arts education for every child; and Community development through the arts." It says that it "works with cultural organizations, arts and business leaders and individuals to provide leadership, education and information that will encourage support for the arts and culture in our nation's communities."

To better understand some of the organization's actions, on the home page you can click on Press Releases to see its stance on controversial issues involving the arts and government. Also along the left-hand menu are Publications and Arts Advocacy. Clicking on Research and Information leads you to studies about the impact of the arts. Arts and Education also has interesting materials and recommendations.

FINANCIAL GRANTS FOR THEATRE AND DANCE

All of our problems would be solved if only we had adequate funds, right? Well, no, they wouldn't. But the arts are haunted by constant concerns about funding. As an arts manager, one of your goals is seeking—and finding—financial support for your organization's operations. Naturally enough, you think of grants from federal programs, foundations, and your city and state governmental agencies. Yet the process is daunting. Who do you ask? How?

The directories listed here can help you with user-friendly guides to find funds for dance and theatre organizations as well as for individual artists.

Mega-Directories of Charitable Foundations and Organizations

Several sites attempt to coordinate all possible philanthropies into a master mega-databank. The advantage to using such sites is that you can discover organizations you didn't know existed. The disadvantage is that you'll need to weed through discouragingly long lists to find grants for which you are eligible and that fit your particular needs and goals.

FOUNDATIONS ON-LINE

www.foundations.org

The focus of this Directory of Charitable Grantmakers is its detailed list. Click on Directories on the first page and you'll see sites you can explore. Corporate and Private Foundations, and Grantmakers Directory has an alphabetical list of foundations of well-known national companies such as The Ben & Jerry's Foundation, the Carnegie Corporation of New York, and William H. Gates Foundation.

The Community Foundations Directory lists foundations by geographic areas, allowing you to find those in your neighborhood. Government Grants has only three listings, but you might want to explore them. There even is a listing for *Moneyupthewazoo.com*, a name that's hard to resist clicking. It is primarily for venture capital sites, although you'll also find Scholarship and Charitable Foundations.

ARTS WIRE ARTQUARRY

http://camt.nyfa.org/artquarry

ArtQuarry maintains a database of the online arts community, and it encourages submissions from arts organizations. For arts managers, the search engine can be helpful. From the first page, click on Search. You then have options of searching for a keyword or phrase appearing in a site's title or in its description. When I used the engine to look for grants, I found two sites with *grant* in the title and almost 60 with the word in the site's description.

You also can click on Index from the front page and you'll see broad categories. Arts Funding, Marketing and Management Topics took me to more than 400 sites, but many seemed irrelevant and some were dead. More valuable to an arts manager would be locations organized by states or metropolitan areas.

FUNDSNET SERVICES—List of Arts and Culture Funders

www.fundsnetservices.com/arts01.htm

This no-nonsense site plunges directly into its focus: an alphabetical list of funding opportunities for the arts. Both corporations and private foundations are included. When I visited there were more than 80 listings that included regional and national programs. The site apparently is regularly updated.

Federal Government Programs

The federal government's primary source for us in theatre and dance is the *National Endowment for the Arts*. In certain instances, the *National Endowment for the Humanities* may be worth considering if you have a specialized research proposal, perhaps dealing with history of arts, but it does not support productions.

NATIONAL ENDOWMENT FOR THE ARTS
http://arts.endow.gov

The NEA has taken a lot of flack over recent years. Quite undeserved flack, if you'll accept my opinion. It's tough to be a political football. Its statement of its goals is impressive:

> The arts reflect the past, enrich the present, and imagine the future. The National Endowment for the Arts, an investment in America's living cultural heritage, serves the public good by nurturing the expression of human creativity, supporting the cultivation of community spirit, and fostering the recognition and appreciation of the excellence and diversity of our nation's artistic accomplishments.

So what's wrong with that?

Its site is well organized with the reader in mind. You'll want to explore many of the pages. Most are available to view as is, but one or two will require the *Adobe Acrobat Reader* (free here: <www.adobe.com/products/acrobat/readstep.html>).

If you're considering applying to NEA for a grant, a helpful page is Basic Facts. It takes you to brief information about annual grants that NEA awarded, helping you guesstimate your particular proposal's chances. Click on Creation & Presentation to see awards to theatre and dance. Also look at its special theatre page (<www.arts.gov/artforms/Theater/Theater1.html>), which for some reason doesn't show up on its master site.

To understand the grants process, you will want to examine NEA's *Lessons Learned: A Planning Toolsite* (<www.arts.gov/pub/Lessons/index.html>). It takes you to informative materials about the planning process plus case studies of the way arts organizations have changed and improved their operations.

NATIONAL ENDOWMENT FOR THE HUMANITIES
www.neh.fed.us/

NEH makes a number of major grants. For example, recently it awarded almost 295 grants totaling $30.5 million for projects involving cultural preservation, educational technology, curriculum development, and scholarly research.

Unfortunately for us, the possibility of NEH support is limited—it does not fund creative or performing arts. Eligible, however, are critical, historical, and theoretical studies of the arts, and conscientious arts managers may want to encourage members of their organization to consider working on a proposal for one of these highly prestigious awards. A good place to start is Who We Are on the home page. That leads you to a Fact Sheet with examples of NEH programs and a page for Frequently Asked Questions.

State, Regional, and Metropolitan Arts Commissions and Agencies

Likely you know of your state's and city's arts commissions, but check to see if you are in an area also covered by a regional group. There are too many individual agencies to list here, but these excellent sources will help you locate those in your geographic area.

NATIONAL ENDOWMENT OF THE ARTS

http://arts.endow.gov

An excellent source to locate regional arts commissions is the NEA. From the home page, click on State and Regional Arts Agencies (or go there directly with <*http://arts.endow.gov/artforms/RAO_SAAs.html*>).

FOUNDATIONS ON-LINE

www.foundations.org/

You'll find lists of arts commissions at the Community Foundations Directory.

NATIONAL ASSEMBLY OF STATE ARTS AGENCIES

The NASAA home page (<*www.nasaa-arts.org*>) spotlights special activities in various states. A search engine (<*www.nasaa-arts.org/new/nasaa/aoa/saadir.shtml*>) will lead to agencies in individual states.

Examples of Public Foundations That Support the Arts

Organizations focused on supporting cultural activities reflect sensitivity to the arts' contributions to society. Indeed, some foundations, convinced that arts are essential for excellent quality of life, want to focus donations to arts in geographic areas where they have offices or plants so their employees can benefit.

To illustrate the possibilities, I list selected foundations below. This is *not* a list of all grantmakers, because that would fill a book itself. It does suggest the policies of larger foundations, all with websites you can explore.

To judge if you should consider applying for support, check the foundations' statements and guidelines. To get an idea of their preferences, look at their records of organizations and projects they've supported in the past.

DORIS DUKE CHARITABLE FOUNDATION ARTS PROGRAM

http://fdncenter.org/grantmaker/dorisduke/ns/index.html

During her lifetime, Doris Duke was deeply interested in modern dance. Her foundation supports dance with program development, planning, commissioning new works, endowments, and capital improvements. In 1997 and 1998, the Arts Program awarded nearly $23 million in twelve grants to performing arts organizations in modern dance and jazz. The Duke Foundation also provides support for theatre and talented students in the arts.

PRINCESS GRACE AWARDS
www.pgfusa.com
The *Princess Grace Foundation* USA assists emerging young artists in dance, film, and theatre with grants, scholarships, apprenticeships, and fellowships. As the site says, "The Foundation's trustees share Princess Grace's dedication to supporting the arts and they believe, as She did, that cultivation and training of emerging young talent in America is a priority to ensure sustained excellence in the arts." You can find application guidelines and information at this site.

THE FAN FOX & LESLIE R. SAMUELS FOUNDATION
www.samuels.org/perform.htm
The *Foundation* is a major supporter of Lincoln Center for the Performing Arts in New York. It also supports programs that provide arts education in New York City public schools, programs for students working toward careers in performing arts, and young professionals. In addition, this foundation makes a limited number of special project grants that will help the performing arts community address important issues such as audience development, access for the disabled, preservation, and the effects of the AIDS epidemic.

At the bottom of its home page you can click on such topics as Dance, Theater and Performance, Professional Education and Development, Special Projects, or Arts In Education. Each is a financial report that shows you organizations the foundation has supported.

AMERICAN EXPRESS
http://home3.americanexpress.com/corp//philanthropy/
We know not to leave home without American Express, of course, but perhaps we aren't aware that the New York City–based financial services firm supports visual and performing arts institutions, the development of new audiences for the arts, and the preservation of major historic arts sites. At its site you can click on What We Fund to see its policies. An examination of the list of Grant Recipients gives you insight into priorities—and, yes, there are theatres and dance organizations listed, and the list is impressively long. Finally, How to Apply gives you brief guidelines.

AT&T FOUNDATION—Arts and Culture
www.att.com/foundation/programs/arts.html
The Grapes of Wrath, by Frank Galati, produced by Chicago's Steppenwolf

THEATRE SOURCES DOT COM

Theatre Company . . . *Seven Guitars*, by August Wilson, produced by the Goodman Theatre in Chicago . . . *Once on This Island*, by Lynn Ahrens and Stephen Flaherty, produced by Playwrights Horizons in New York City . . . *Love! Valour! Compassion!*, by Terrence McNally, produced by the Manhattan Theater Club (and winner of the 1996 Tony Award for Best Play) . . . these share one thing in common. All are AT&T: OnStage productions, characteristic of its support of living artists and contemporary art.

You can find its Funding Guidelines on its opening page. Grant Search takes you to a search engine to find specific recipients. You also can look in its programs for Education, Arts and Culture, and Civic and Community.

PHILLIP MORRIS
www.philipmorris.com/philanthropy/culture/culture.asp

Phillip Morris has an interesting home page. You first see statements that so strongly support the arts you might think for a moment it is a page for an arts advocacy group instead of one created by the food and tobacco giant. The page describes arts that the company has supported, with a focus on innovative programs and dance, but I suggest you go to the site map to find information about grants (or go here directly: <*www.philipmorris.com/philanthropy/grants/grant_guidelines.asp*>), where you'll discover you are to write the New York office directly for more information.

THEATRE DEVELOPMENT FUND
www.tdf.org/

We who work in theatre and dance can wish that this New York organization would inspire comparable programs in other cities, especially our own. Theatre buffs are familiar with the TKTS booths—you can buy discount tickets for plays and musicals—in Times Square and in the World Trade Center; knowledgeable theatre fans know that the office at the World Trade Center has markedly shorter lines. Those discount booths are one function of the *Theatre Development Fund*.

Each year, TDF says, through TKTS it sells approximately 2.5 million theatre seats at discounted prices to an audience that might not otherwise be able to afford the unique experience of live performance. Additionally, TDF provides programs to build audiences and support performing arts in New York City. The site points out its accomplishments:

> Since its inception in 1968, TDF's remarkable record encompasses more than 48 million theatre seats filled; subsidy support given to more than 600 plays including 17 Tony Award winners and 23 Pulitzer Prize honorees; and more than 600 million dollars in revenue returned to theatre, dance, and music organizations.

ALLEN FOUNDATION FOR THE ARTS

www.paulallen.com/foundations

Microsoft cofounder Paul Allen established six different foundations, and his *Allen Foundation for the Arts* serves the Pacific Northwest performing arts community. Its goal is to support organizational and artistic excellence, innovation, diversity, and access. You can access that foundation from the home page, where you find guidelines and a list of past recipients. (You'll also find a reflection of Allen's interest: From the home page you also can open Free Fonts, which takes you to Microsoft Typography.)

THE FORD FOUNDATION

www.fordfound.org/

Clicking on Media, Arts, and Culture leads you to a page where you click on the same title again and find that the *Ford Foundation's* goal is to "strengthen opportunities for artistic creativity and cultural expression that will generate the hope, understanding, courage and confidence needed for societies to help citizens fulfill their potential."

At the top of the page you'll see Guidelines for Grantseekers, which encourages you to write to the New York office to see if your proposal fits their current plans and available funds. Only rarely are grants awarded for ordinary operating costs or bricks-and-mortar proposals.

WALLACE—READER'S DIGEST FUNDS

www.wallacefunds.org/

The opening page has an intriguing design, and you'll want to examine such areas as Overview and Programs, then look at the FAQs. Included in the various projects that the fund supports are programs for the arts. It prefers to give grants for both proven and innovative artistic practices that "enable arts and cultural institutions to diversify, broaden and deepen relationships with their audiences." Although unsolicited proposals are rarely funded, it encourages inquiries to its New York office.

JOB LISTINGS FOR ARTS MANAGERS

I conclude this examination of management sites with a brief list of places you might look to find a job.

BACKSTAGEJOBS.COM

www.backstagejobs.com/

Despite the title, this site has categories for job openings in management. Scroll down a bit on the second page (click Backstage Jobs) and you'll find a box for Management and Administration with listings for Box Office Managers, House Managers, and Theatre Managers. It had about 25 job listings when I last looked. You'll see Public Relations, Marketing, Building Managers, Webmasters, Secretarial, and Sales.

As you'd expect, there was a wide variety of jobs—several Shakespeare festivals looking for managers, a ballet company, some lighting companies, and the like.

ARTSWORK

www.artsandbusiness.org/programs/artsworkny.html

Sponsored by the Arts and Business Council, this site lists arts management jobs in New York City.

ARTJOBS

www.artjob.org/

This is a subscription site. Jobseekers need to register and pay a fee according to the length of their subscription—three months ($25), six ($40), or one year ($75). For employers, posting a job description costs $75, with a discount of 40 percent for nonprofit organizations. The site has such categories as Academic, Artist Opportunities, Arts Organizations, Internships, Grants, Commissions, and Fellowships. Specific disciplines, such as theatre or dance, are not indicated. Without actually joining, I saw no way to find out how many job descriptions are available overall or by categories.

THEATRE COMMUNICATIONS GROUP

www.tcg.org/

ArtSEARCH, the TCG bimonthly bulletin, is the most important and consulted publication in the field. Arts management jobseekers will want to check it frequently. If you're still in college, quite likely your department subscribes to it.

11

Netting a Job

More Than 40 Sites to Help Theatre
and Dance People Find a Job

No one can promise that there is an easy way to find a job—and I'm talking about working in theatre *and* as a temp while you wait for your big break—but this chapter contains helpful techniques and resources you can use. Plan a three-pronged attack. First, to net a job, explore Web pages that list theatrical jobs. Second, look at ways you can start your personal website, thinking of it as an e-advertisement. Finally—if you're still in college—use your campus Career Planning Office.

USING THE NET TO FIND JOBS ON- AND OFF-STAGE

You can find an encouragingly large number of sites—over 40 are listed in this chapter—that lead you to listings of job opportunities in theatre and dance. I discussed some of them in earlier chapters (e.g., in our discussion of acting and dance I listed sites for those areas), but many sites contain jobs in more than just a single category and instead have listings for both on- and off-stage. Therefore, for your convenience, I gather them all together here along with some new ones.

As you explore what each offers, you'll discover that often *audition* does *not* refer to actors only but instead can include dancers, singers, designers, and technical personnel. Equally, some sites that label their jobs page for technical theatre will, in fact, also include listings for performers. Browsing each site will help you decide which are most useful for your needs. Because most are updated frequently, it is a good strategy to return often to find new information.

It's difficult to identify one "best" site. Instead, plan to investigate all, and bookmark those that are most applicable to you. Note that some offer an opportunity to file your personal website with them. If you're hunting for a theatre job, consider using those offers to get your résumé in front of prospective employers.

ACTORS' EQUITY ASSOCIATION

www.actorsequity.org/home.html

At this site for professional actors you'll see Casting Call, which leads to Audition Hotlines of contacts in theatrical cities. See also the long list of Audition Notices, which are organized in pull-down menus by state, type of contract, and type of job.

ACTOR SITE

www.actorsite.com/

Scrolling down the left menu leads you to Equity Casting Call. A click and you find Audition Hotlines of phone numbers in selected cities. Note that this site offers you free website help so you can post your personal e-self.

ACTORSOURCE

www.actorsource.com/

This is a rich site, and you can mine quantities of information about agents, casting directors, headshots, and much more. Resources leads you to agents, casting directors by states, show-biz places where you might get a temp job or an internship, theme parks and their wages, screen-writing talent agents, talent unions, voiceover studios, and more. Getting Started and Service have valuable first-person advice.

ACTORS WORLD LINK

http://members.aol.com/AWorldLink

"We give actors a great looking Web page where you can display your headshot and résumé along with your own Web address, all for around 20 cents a day," announces the first page. Before deciding, you can browse around the site to get a feel for the place and see how other actors have used this service.

AMERICAN ASSOCIATION OF COMMUNITY THEATRE

www.aact.org/

AACT offers many programs for the community theatres we find in virtually every town. There's also a program for jobseekers. On the left menu click on Job Listings. When I visited there were jobs for managing director, technical director, lighting designer, and others. Most were recently posted.

Avoid the common mistake of thinking community theatres are small operations that never pay their people. One ad on this site described a theatre that presents nine productions yearly and has an annual operating budget of $325,000. Some jobs paid in the high $30s.

AMERICAN THEATRE RESOURCES

www.theatre-resources.net/

ATR is a good source for regional theatre information. You'll find Job Openings, which includes auditions, production, and management. When I've visited there weren't many listings. The top of the page lists theatres alphabetically, with links for every state, where you can find details about individual theatres. Although not all companies are included, this can be an excellent way for you to start research into places you'd like to work—and, of course, those that have given you a job offer.

AMERICAN THEATRE WEB
www.americantheaterweb.com/
Visit the Callboard for announcements about auditions. It also has lively exchanges about finding audition materials, locating a place to live in theatre cities, and opinions about various productions.

Playwrights will find callboards, too. There's Call for Scripts, which also contains contest announcements. A second invites you to post your script.

AMERICAN THEATRE WORKS
www.theatredirectories.com/
Not everything is on the Internet. A number of books guide you to career development. At *American Theatre Works'* home page, click on Theatre Directories and you'll find eight books of pragmatic advice and valuable information about regional theatres, a summer theatre directory, information on constructing a résumé, and even a tax record-keeping system (for those fortunate enough to have income!). Prices are less than $20 each. See also Special Reports for other publications. A secure server allows you to order online.

Playwrights needing a quiet retreat may want to look at The Dorset Colony for Writers, a historic three-story home in a friendly small village in southern Vermont, some four hours from New York. It has eight private writers' rooms, plus communal spaces. You can access information from the home page.

The Dorset Theatre Festival operates June through September and holds auditions for Equity actors and non-Equity apprentices. Information is on the site.

ARTSLYNX—INTERNATIONAL ARTS RESOURCES—ARTS LINKS TO THEATRE, DANCE, MUSIC, AND MORE FROM ARTSLYNX
www.artslynx.org
—or take a short cut directly to the theatre location—

ARTSLYNX INTERNATIONAL THEATRE RESOURCES
www.artslynx.org/theatre/index.htm
Artslynx is a primary source for theatre and dance materials. Follow the links to Employment and Jobs. From the home page click on Theatre, then examine the large number of links. Theatre Employment Resources is a good place to look.

ARTJOBS

www.artjob.org/

This site lists jobs in various arts. They are arranged in categories such as Academic; Artist Opportunities; Arts Organizations; Internships; Grants, Commissions, Fellowships; and others. This is a subscription site with fees ranging from $25 for three months to $75 for a year.

ARTSWORK

www.artsandbusiness.org/programs/artsworkny.html

For management jobs in New York City, *Artswork* is an excellent resource. A clever jobseeker may use information here to try to wangle a temp job with a theatre group, which would bring the added benefit of making contacts with important people.

ARTS WIRE

www.artswire.org/current/jobs.html

This site has announcements for job positions in all arts, not just theatre. That said, it does contain listings for theatre management, technical directors, and so forth. It is updated weekly, and every time I visited I was struck by the large number of jobs of all types.

BACKSTAGE.COM

www.backstage.com/

This is a membership site costing $9.95 monthly or $119.40 annually, but access to basic audition information is free. You can skip the opening page—although it is full of interesting links—and go directly to audition information, which opens quickly (<*www.backstage.com/casting*>). You'll find casting information from Chicago, Florida, and both coasts. Click on Casting to find listings that include not only dancers, singers, and actors, but also staff and tech. Playwrights will want to explore Post Your Play.

BACKSTAGE WORLD

www.backstageworld.com/

If you're looking for a backstage job as a designer or crew member, *Backstage* publishes a list of jobs available and also gives you an opportunity to post your résumé. Unfortunately, few job listings have dates, so it is difficult to tell the age of any given ad. However, they have websites so you can find out more information. From its opening page click on Job List.

CALLBOARD

http://vl-theatre.com/

You need to dig a bit here. Use the search engine to find *auditions* and you're led to An Industry Callboard Posting Area and Casting.Com. Alternatively, search for *callboard*.

CANADIAN ACTORS' EQUITY ASSOCIATION
www.caea.com/index.htm

Auditions lists job openings and allows members to sign up for regular e-mail announcements of forthcoming auditions, and Opportunities leads to a broadly diverse number of workshops, competitions, and announcements. While there, you might want to explore Infoculture on Dance and Theatre.

CASTING NETWORK.COM
www.thecastingnetwork.com/

Developed by actors for actors, *Casting Network.com* is a membership site that provides online databank resources for casting directors and talent agents. It claims to have more auditions in its databank than any other site, and it offers you a chance to try out the site by paying the first month's dues ($9.95) and looking around for 48 hours. Note that they extend your membership unless you specifically cancel.

THE CASTING NETWORK
www.castingnetwork.net/

Although the name is similar to the site above, this is a different organization. Based in Studio City, California, TCN says it is dedicated to providing "top quality cold reading and prepared scene showcases for professional performers who meet our standards and are committed to career advancement." It requires actors to audition for entry and thereafter encourages them to attend various workshops with casting directors.

CULTURE NET
www.ffa.ucalgary.ca

This excellent site deals with the arts throughout Canada. From the opening page, select your language—English or Français—then scroll down to Notice Boards. As you'd expect with a site that deals with all of the arts, the Job Board (*<www.fc.culturenet.ca/Job-Announcements>*) has listings for more than theatre. On my last visit there were almost 20 jobs, six that were dance-theatre related. All were recent.

DIRECTORY OF SUMMER THEATER IN THE UNITED STATES
www.summertheater.com/

Actors and dancers have numerous war stories about experiences in summer theatres—the typical barn theatre, the lack of air conditioning, the housing—but they also have fond memories of opportunities, growth, positive audience response. This site allows you to search by geographic region or by alphabetized listings.

DRAMA AND THEATER CONNECTIONS

http://libweb.uncc.edu/ref-arts/theater/

Once you've opened the page, see Jobs on the left menu. Although it had few links when I last visited, the high quality of the site suggests that the jobs page quite likely will grow.

ELAC THEATRE LIBRARY—Theatre Links

www.perspicacity.com/elactheatre/library/links.htm#Employment

This address takes you directly to Employment links. You'll be led to such categories as Agencies, Internships, Job Listings, and Training Programs. Frequently updated, they are worth investigating regularly.

EPERFORMER.COM

www.eperformer.com/

From the front page click on Auditions and you'll be taken to information about auditions divided into Theatre, Music, Dance, Film and TV, Other, and Tech.

ENTERTAINMENT TECHNOLOGY ONLINE

www.etecnyc.net/default.html

Designers, technicians, shop foremen, electricians, and other backstage workers will want to open Classified on the left menu. There also are listings for internships for designers.

THE INSTITUTE OF OUTDOOR DRAMA

www.unc.edu/depts/outdoor

Some 125 outdoor theatres, located around the country, offer summer jobs for actors, dancers, singers, designers, management workers, and technicians. This site describes them and gives you audio and video pieces of those productions. From the home page click on Auditions, where you'll see that a number of those companies annually join in one place to seek their summer staff.

MR. SHOWBIZ.COM

http://mrshowbiz.go.com/

Some will think of this Disney-affiliated site's design as mod. The word *busy* comes to my mind. Worse, speaking as one who hates cookies and disables the cookie-reception, Mr. *Showbiz* is sternly dedicated to sending cookies—and sending and sending. The site is all about flicks, but if you scroll down to the very bottom of the page, you'll see small type announcing Job Openings.

NEW ENGLAND THEATRE CONFERENCE

www.netconline.org/

Actors, singers, dancers, designers, technicians, and production staff personnel may be interested in the annual NETC auditions, which bring together directors, talent agents, and training institutions from the New England area to seek theatre people for positions in summer and year-round professional theatres. From the opening page click on Auditions.

ONStage—The Actor's Resource
www.onstage.org/

Designed for professional stage and screen actors, this site has helpful guides, although you have to register—free—to access everything. An Auditions section covers numerous cities, and there are valuable links you'll want to explore (although some services charge for what should be free information). Classified has about everything for big cities like New York, San Francisco, Los Angeles, and Chicago: rentals and sublets, employment, and items for sale. See Public Service Announcements for auditions. You can view home pages of theatre folks and post your own site.

OPEN CASTING
www.opencasting.com/

This bulletin board—free to both those seeking information and those announcing auditions—contains casting notices, auditions, and crew calls. Select a page to visit from the menu at the top of the home page. Callboard has hundreds of jobs listed for actors, dancers, tech, engineers, and production, and there is also information for internships. Rogues leads you to Rogues Gallery, a very long list of actors on the Net. You can visit their sites to get an idea for your own page, and you can post your link there. Classified leads to many ads.

SCOTT'S THEATRE-LINK.COM
www.theatre-link.com/

On the home page scroll down to Casting and Contract Services Link (or go there directly with <*www.theatre-link.com/casting.html*>) and you're led to Casting and Contact Services, which offers a wide variety of links. Look for Theatre and Technical Jobs. You can post your information here, too.

PROP PEOPLE.COM
www.proppeople.com/index.shtml

The site says this is the only place you'll find jobs for property specialists. From the home page enter Job Board. When I last visited there were more than a dozen jobs offered for Prop Masters, Artisans, and Interns at LORT and rep theatres. It is regularly updated.

SETC—The Southeastern Theatre Conference
www.setc.org/

SETC holds annual conventions, which include auditions as well as seminars, workshops, and displays from a large number of theatres, training schools, publishers, and others. Some 100 theatre companies gather to audition actors, often as many as 900 or so. It is a potent early-career opportunity, popular with students. At the conventions, too, there is a Job Contact Service for staff and technical positions, and—if you are an SETC member—you can sign up to interview with companies. From its opening page, click on Auditions.

SPECIAL EFFECT SUPPLY
www.fxsupply.com/

This commercial supplier offers job listings, too. On the opening page scroll down (and down) to open Employment Opportunities, where you'll find listings for the entertainment industry. There are divisions for Cable, Feature Film, Special Effects, and the like.

PLAYBILL ON-LINE/THEATRE CENTRAL
www1.playbill.com/

For professional theatre notices, *Playbill on-Line/Theatre Central* has rich materials. On the opening page, scroll down and click on Casting and Jobs on the left menu. To access Job Openings you need to sign up for a membership—it is free—in The Playbill Club. Once you're a member, on the opening page scroll down to Job Search on the left menu. Clicking on that, you find categories such as Performer, Technical, Design, Administrative, Academic, and Other. Note that you can add your theatre link or enter yourself in the Connections Database.

THEATRE COMMUNICATIONS GROUP
www.tcg.org/

TCG publishes ArtSEARCH, perhaps the single most significant national publication of job listings, which posts more than 6,000 openings annually in a number of varied theatre companies, colleges and universities, summer theatres, and more. If you're a college student, check the theatre office to see if your department subscribes to ArtSEARCH. Most do.

DRAMA AND THEATRE CONNECTIONS
http://libweb.uncc.edu/ref-arts/theater/

Actors and Acting (Biographies, Jobs) on the left menu takes you not to listings of specific jobs but instead to resources to help you find them through the Internet.

THE THEATRE DESIGN AND TECHNICAL JOBS PAGE
BACKSTAGEJOBS.COM
www.backstagejobs.com/

This is one of the better job-listing pages. Formerly *The Theatre Design and Technical Jobs Page*, "this site is designed to help the 'behind-the-scenes' people in the live entertainment industry find work, and to help entertainment groups fill their job openings." It is updated frequently. Despite the title, it posts listings for more than design and tech, and you also find jobs for Choreographers, Directors, Management, Box Office, Internships, and links for Actors.

THEATREJOBS.COM

www.theatrejobs.com/

Click on Guests for a listing of this site's offerings of online job placement for theatre and related areas. It includes special sections for summer stock, festival listings, internships, assistantships, apprenticeships, and fellowships. Note that you can post your résumé here. Annual membership costs $35 for students and $75 for others.

THE THEATRE RESOURCE

www.theatre-resource.com/

Theatre Resource is a valuable site with numerous categories such as training institutions, theatre consultants, suppliers and vendors, and more. People and Webrings offer links you can explore. Jobseekers will want to visit Theatre Jobs, and For Actors, Directors, and Playwrights to find links to other sites.

THEATRE SERVICES GUIDE

www.theaterservicesguide.com/

On the bottom of the left menu click on Call Board and you'll find notices for actors, stage managers, technicians, and others.

More Sites for Jobseekers

CastingNotices.com (<*www .castingnotices.com/*>) offers a wide variety of services, directories, and information, and you can click on More Casting Sites to investigate other possibilities. *Showbizjobs.com* (<*www.showbizjobs .com/*>) has information for film, television, and attractions job markets. Not for jobs but to keep up with news of professional theatre around the country, see *Talkin Broadway* (<*www .TalkinBroadway.com/*>).

In addition, Chapter 3 contains a list of Web rings. Use the ring that applies to your specialization and examine all the sites. You may find jobs discussed.

UNIVERSITY/RESIDENT THEATRE ASSOCIATION

www.urta.com/

Using unified auditions—actors and directors congregate in one location—U/RTA offers jobs in universities, summer theatres, and resident professional theatres. Auditions leads to another page, where you're to click on a box marked NUAI (National Unified Auditions/Interviews), which describes the process.

UNITED STATES INSTITUTE FOR THEATRE TECHNOLOGY

www.culturenet.ca/usitt/

Designers, technicians, costume and wardrobe, makeup, and backstage folks find that USITT is a major organization. See Classified Ads for job openings.

You also will want to consider attending its conferences to meet potential employers.

AN IMPORTANT JOB TOOL:
CONSTRUCTING YOUR PERSONAL WEBSITE

A well-designed personal home page can be a valuable tool for those seeking a job on- or off-stage. I'm not talking about those "me, my family, and my calico cat" sort of chitty-chatty places, but a professional e-presence that lists your résumé, credentials, experience, photographs of you on stage or renderings of your design, and contact information. It should reflect your personality—which means there is no single perfect design—and you'll want to keep it up to date. Examining other Web pages can give you a good idea of what you might want to do with your own.

While your first venture may be frustrating, making a personal Web page gets easier as you learn the techniques. One such technique is HTML—HyperText Markup Language—which can be daunting for beginners. At its simplest, it is merely a method of embedding special tags that make things happen on your site (like blinking words, color changes, italics, internal anchors on places that let the visitor jump to letters of the alphabet or items in a table of contents, and more complicated commands that get into multimedia). HTML can be a tricky bugger, however, and you'll see the chaos theory firsthand if you goof up. The good news is that you don't need to use HTML. Instead, there are places—on the Net, of course—that offer you help. Some are free. Better equipment will cost you somewhere between $50 to $350, but the higher-priced materials are less for individuals and more for full-fledged webmasters.

THEATRICAL MUSIC AND SOUND EFFECTS
www.teleport.com/~mjgallag/

Yes, this site is for sound designers, but any theatre jobseeker can find valuable tools here. Clicking The Business of Sound Design takes you to a well-thought-out and detailed discussion that webmaster Martin John Gallagher says "will mostly deal with finance, marketing, communications, and contacts." You first see an outline that allows you to pick and choose sections of particular interest. For our discussion here of personal websites, notice Building Web Pages: Meet the World and its four subdivisions. Design Concepts Used in Creating Your Web Page will give you valuable concepts, and Search Utilities—How People Find You lists specific steps to get your Web page on the Net.

The No-Cost Approach

Free Space and Templates

Your Internet service provider may offer you free space and easy-to-use templates that give you a basic design that doesn't require computer knowledge. AOL, for example, gives you 12 megabytes at no charge (<*http://hometown.aol .com/*>), and you have the option of selecting from some 50 different fill-in-the-blank templates that don't require HTML, although some are in the awfully cute category or, worse, they are give-me-a-break! patterns. (My Wrestling Page?!)

AOL is far from being the only free service. Asking you "What kind of Website do you want to build?" *Homestead* (<*www.homestead.com/*>) gives you 16 MB of free space that you can fill without knowing a thing about HTML or programming, and its templates allow variety. (*Homestead*, however, is one of those sites that continually sends cookies, an irritant for those who gear their computers to refuse the cookie monsters.) Another example is the similar *Geocities* (<*http://geocities.yahoo.com/home*>), which has a Page Wizard to guide you. It also shows you other websites to give you suggestions, and it gives you the option of using more advanced techniques with a built-in HTML editor. *Tripod* (<*www.tripod.lycos.com*>) is another free service that gives you 50 MB of space, a site builder that doesn't require HTML as well as an advanced system with HTML, and domain registration (annual cost is $25 and up).

These are but representative examples, and you'll find other freebies. It is a good idea to check sample pages on those places to see how fast they load, if the ads are intrusive, and if you like the way the sites look.

Free Ways to List Your Site

Listing your personal page on a Web ring is a good idea. And they are free. Open the ring that pertains directly to your special interests (see Chapter 3), and look for the instructions about adding sites.

There are also techniques to get your website on search engines. For example, *Yahoo!* offers you a way to suggest your site to them so they'll include it in their listings about theatre. First go to their theatre folder (<*http://dir.yahoo.com/Arts/Performing_Arts/Theater*>). Then select your field—acting, playwriting, whatever—and open that file. Scroll down to the very bottom and you'll see Suggest a Site. Of course, the site you'll suggest is your own. Click on that and follow their instructions to fill in the blanks. Other places have similar openings.

Is there a catch to these freebies? Yup. Often your site will have the company's advertisements. Not everybody objects to those, and they even seem to be ingrained in our social structure. For illustration, think of the many times you see people wearing clothing with the maker's ad plastered over the front. You'd think we'd charge *them* for being walking signboards.

A Bit More Pricey

Free systems are effective but not sophisticated. For advanced work, you'll need to use HTML codes for animated effects, editing programs, and highly personalized custom work. And you may have to pay for the service.

One of the better tutors is CoffeeCup HTML Editor (<*www.coffeecup.com/*>), which will, for $49, teach you HTML online with a split-screen device that lets you see how codes change appearances. Also available online is Allaire HomeSite 4.5 (<*www.allaire.com/products/homesite/index.cfm*>), highly recommended by professional webmasters, which has an intuitive WYSIWYN (What You See Is What You Need) interface for $89.

If you prefer software programs, consider Microsoft Front Page (which a careful e-shopper can find for slightly over $100) or the more complicated Dreamweaver 3/Fireworks 3 Studio, a Macromedia product (around $350). If you're new to Net design, these high-powered tools may overwhelm you unless you've got a good Web-page-design buddy to guide you through the process.

The point here is that the free sites and uncomplicated systems mean there really is no reason for you not to have a personal page to enhance your career. The advantages are many. You can keep your site up to date, in contrast to those materials you sent out last year. As you move about the country, you can post your current contact information. Including your page's address on all communications with agents, casting directors, or producers encourages them to see what you've been doing recently. The standard headshot and one-page résumé tend to be pretty static, but your Web page can reflect your personality, as you'll see with some actors' personal sites that include professional links. All in all, your site can be a helpful tool to use in the Great Job Hunt.

COLLEGE STUDENTS: THE CAREER PLANNING OFFICE

College students should contact their campus Career Planning Office. *Early.* Professionals in such offices say that the beginning of your sophomore year is not too early. The last semester of your senior year is woefully late.

Career Services offers numerous valuable aids—aptitude tests that help you identify your interests, statistics about professions, lists of jobs. They often host companies visiting to find employees. Conveniently, at your request they'll send to prospective employers your personal file of transcript and letters of recommendation (which means you need to ask faculty only once for a recommendation).

But you say you don't need those services because you're going to get a theatre job? Okay, but that office is ideal if you're looking for a nontheatre job to fill in while you're auditioning and making the rounds. Think temp services, which are one of the theatre person's best jobs because they allow you to arrange for free time for that big audition or interview. They're much better than saying, "Do you want fries with that?"

Ask the career personnel how to best prepare yourself for a temp job. (This is one of the many reasons you go there early in your college career.) You may discover that you should take advantage of work-study jobs that colleges offer students—perhaps doing word processing or computer design—so you'll learn skills that will prepare you for a cushy temp job.

If you're seeking a theatre job, your campus career office likely will not have access to all possibilities—your theatre faculty will know more about techniques to find a theatre job—but the folks who specialize in career guidance and counseling can give you valuable advice about transcripts, interviewing tactics, preparation, and much more. Like so many aspects of campus life, the career office has a great advantage: It is free.

WHAT THEATRE MAJORS LEARN
http://faculty.wm.edu/lecatr/majorslearn.html

Forgive the lapse of modesty as I suggest a page on my website that intends to help you get a nontheatre job, whether temp or full-time. *What Theatre Majors Learn, or, What Can You Do With a Theatre Major?* suggests that if you're searching for a nontheatre job you have more than two dozen advantages over those who majored in other disciplines. My experience indicates that theatre majors aren't aware of their edge. Unfortunately, employers may not know either, so you need to teach them. This site intends to raise your consciousness of your value as an employee.

12

An E-Shopping Spree

Bookstores, Play Publishers, Publications,
Shakespeare, and Gifts

Playwrights, directors, dramaturgs, actors, designers, technicians, managers—*all* of us in theatre—improve our art and craft by reading plays, reading plays, reading plays, as well as by reading other materials about theatre.
A number of online services have plays and books available for you. E-publications of books offer interesting choices, and e-zines have stimulating articles. Play publishers are eager to help you select and get permission to present a play. There even are theatre gift shops where you can buy "break a leg wishes" for your colleagues on opening night.

Caveat Emptor
If you're like me, you are unwilling to give anyone your credit card information unless you are quite comfortable that the order form is secure and safe. Before making a purchase, see the site's announcement about security, and also look at your Web browser's toolbar to see if the padlock is closed.

BOOKSTORES

Although I hate to see mega-bookstores pushing specialty dealers out of business and I prefer browsing in a real bookstore where you can actually leaf through the books and talk with book-loving salespeople, virtual bookstores are luring customers with huge stocks, convenience, and substantial discounts. Just remember to consider shipping costs.

THE DRAMA BOOK SHOP, INC.
www5.playbill.com/playbill/html/drama.html
AUTHOR'S CHOICE *The Drama Book Shop* is my favorite bookstore to visit when I'm in New York. Close to Times Square at the corner of 7th Avenue and West 48th Street, it has been in business for three-quarters of a century, making it the oldest theatrical bookstore. That experience makes it an ideal place

to ask questions. The staff is extremely helpful, and you feel they've read every book in the place. The store has some 40,000 titles—playscripts, dance, film, musical theatre, design, costume, makeup, and puppets, plus dialect tapes, vocal scores, and videos.

AMAZON
www.amazon.com/
See description for *Borders.com*, below.

BARNES AND NOBLE
www.barnesandnoble.com/
See description for *Borders.com*, below.

More About Theatre Books
See also a list of theatre books at *Books at T2K* (*<www .theater2k.com/books1.html>*).

BORDERS.COM
www.borders.com/
Frankly, these three mega-e-bookstores blur in my mind, and I have difficulty telling one from the other. The only difference I've seen is that searches on *Borders* often gives me Error 503, which I suspect is computerese for "our disk drive is on coffee break." All three have hype on the opening pages that may make you think they focus only on national bestsellers, but each has a well-organized menu and a search engine to help you find other books by title, author, or category.

THEATRE BOOKS
www.theatrebooks.com/
This Toronto bookstore offers books and software dealing with theatre as well as with opera, film, and dance. Its stock comes from large and small publishers, North American and British. Established in 1975, the bookstore is in an attractive building on Thomas Street. When I last visited its site there was the ubiquitous "under construction sign," but it shows promise of becoming a significant Net source.

BUYPATH.COM
http://buypath.com/
Want an easy way to compare prices of various items, books in this instance? *Buypath.com* gives you a quick way to find the least expensive e-site. Enter either the book title, author name, or the ISBN number—full details make the process quicker—in the search engine on the opening page and you're quickly taken to a list of online e-book sellers. The list provides purchase prices, shipping method and cost, and the total price. You can click on a vendor to go directly to its site. *BuyPath* has similar services for other items, and it includes a list of book e-vendors (*<http://buypath.com/books>*) with thumbnail descriptions and links that allow you to visit them.

Textbooks

Textbooks often are astronomically expensive. One reason is that lavish illustrations are expensive, and some books contain copyrighted plays and other materials that increase production costs. There are e-alternatives you may wish to explore in place of a trip to the college bookstore. The advantage is that often books are much less expensive; the disadvantage is that you need to plan ahead because the books won't arrive immediately. You don't have to be a student to use these sites, by the way. Many so-called textbooks are ideal for anyone interested in theatre.

VARSITYBOOKS.COM
www.varsitybooks.com/

College texts are featured here at discounts "up to" 40 percent. A pull-down menu lets you choose your campus (although there are a limited number of listings of colleges and universities), click on your major, select your classes, and order required books. Another search engine lets you find books by author or title.

BIG WORDS
http://bigwords.com/

Used college textbooks—not only on sale but even for rent—are found on this site, which has a fun, breezy style. The books, you are assured, are in the industry's Grade-A condition (and what does *that* tell you about the study habits of the original owner?). If you can wait five to eight business days, shipping is free; faster delivery is moderately priced. There is no charge for tax, except in California. The search engine seeks author, title, or the identifying ISBN number.

ECAMPUS.COM
www.ecampus.com/

Their motto is "We know you're broke. We try to make you less broke." The site claims it is "The Globe's largest college bookstore." It offers discounts—in a few cases up to 50 percent—for new and used textbooks, fiction and nonfiction general trade books, clothing with college emblems, supplies, and more. Shipping was once free; now UPS standard shipping is $2.99 plus $.99 for each item, with higher charges for speedier delivery. A search machine lets you look for author or title, and another is engineered by course name (although it sends you to colleges and seems inefficient). Best-seller fiction and nonfiction, it says, "always is 50 percent off list price." There's also an auction site that sells general stuff (and *eBay* it isn't). After you're finished with the books, *ecampus.com* says it will repurchase them (for significantly less).

A1 BOOKS
www.a1books.com/cgi-bin/a1books/a1Front?a1code=YFTTGHGJ

A general e-bookstore, it also has special prices on textbooks. From the opening page click on Attention Students. You're taken to an alphabetical list of states, and you can look to see if your college is there. Select it and you'll find book titles. Perhaps you'll find some that fit your needs (although my experience wasn't all that hot, and the list of books was short even for major universities).

Out-of-Print Books

An "out-of-print" (OP) book is a forlorn ghost no longer loved by its publisher, which has stopped publishing it (usually when sales drop). Therefore, typical booksellers won't have a copy for you. Just because a publisher no longer wants to support the book doesn't mean it is invalid, however, and many of us search out favorite books in the "after market"—the used book sites.

BOOKFINDER.COM
www.bookfinder.com/

AUTHOR'S CHOICE Not a bookstore itself, *BookFinder* searches major used-book dealers. It says it connects with the databases of "over 15,000 booksellers from around the world" so there are "over 20 million new, used, rare, and out of print books at your fingertips." For a service like this to work, it must have an efficient search engine. *BookFinder* does. A search will quite quickly locate one or more bookshops that stock the book you seek, and it tells you the book's price and condition. For purchases, you deal directly with the bookseller, not *BookFinder*.

REDDING BOOK STORE
www.redding-bookstore.com/searchdb.htm

California-based *Redding Book Store* has almost 200,000 titles, and if the book you seek isn't among them, it invites you to use its free locator service. You can start with the search engine or by browsing their catalog.

RECOLLECTION USED BOOKS
www.eskimo.com/~recall

The primary strength of this site is its listing of used theatre and dance books. However, that portion of the site is difficult to locate, so you may wish to go there directly with this link: *<www.eskimo.com/~recall/cats/drama.htm>*. *Recollection* has a distinct political point of view, and if you have time, wandering through its links can be interesting.

HARVEST BOOK COMPANY
www.harvestbooks.com/

"Any author, any title, no matter how old or how recent," says this site about locating out-of-print books. It will find a copy of the book, then tell you its condition and price. At that time you can decide whether to buy it.

E-PUBLICATIONS

You may not be a fan of e-books in general, but some sites have such a quantity and mixtures of books that they lure you in to read. Directors may wish to consider downloading a play to print it for a production.

THE INTERNET CLASSICS ARCHIVE
http://classics.mit.edu/

AUTHOR'S CHOICE   In a single word: *Wow.* You find here more than 400 works of classical literature by some 60 different authors. Most are Greco-Roman, with a few Chinese and Persian. All are in English translations. Granted, not all the materials are plays, and few deal with theatre. But some do, and you'll find such playwrights as Aeschylus (7 plays), Aristophanes (10), Euripides (19), and Sophocles (7), among others. Aristotle is also present—not only his *Poetics*, a foundation for all theatre, but almost 30 other works.

Each work has an accompanying discussion area where visitors express theories and opinions. *Medea*, for example, has almost 200 comments. Not surprisingly, many focus on the question of whether killing is justifiable, and others look at Medea's motivations. The discussions are rather like being in a seminar class—but without a moderator—and occasional points are interesting.

PROJECT GUTENBERG
http://promo.net/pg/

AUTHOR'S CHOICE   A second *Wow.* For pure fun, enlightenment, and education, *Project Gutenberg* is hard to beat. It has a large collection of books, plays, essays, reference books, and more. It is dedicated to adding materials regularly. You won't find the latest books here due to copyright rules, but you'll see a large library of classics.

It classifies entries into three categories. Light Literature includes *Peter Pan*, *Aesop's Fables*, and those Tom Swift novels that prompted the Tom Swifties ("I won the daily double," Tom cried hoarsely, or "I'll try and dig it up for you," Tom said gravely). Heavy Literature refers to the Bible, *Moby Dick*, and *Paradise Lost*. Reference includes almanacs, dictionaries, and the like. Theatre buffs will find Aristotle's *Poetics* (the Butcher translation), 167 postings of Shakespeare's plays (there are multiple copies of individual plays), and more.

If you're new to this site, good places to start are What Is PG? and Help and FAQ. The search engine works best when you enter the title or author's name. Generic searches are less effective. When I entered *plays* I got *Pinocchio* (how did that nosey kid get into that category?); *theatre* got no responses; and *drama* pulled up 160 entries. You also can browse through alphabetical lists.

THE ON-LINE BOOKS PAGE
http://digital.library.upenn.edu/books/

The advent of e-publishing is challenging concepts of books as tangible material. This site certainly pushes the envelope. It has a number of e-books—more than 11,000 and growing. The Features section is impressive, too. Articles on banned books—always a sobering topic—and women writers are well researched and carefully written.

For theatre interests, this site offers plays. You can find folio editions of Shakespeare along with other playwrights whose work is not copyrighted. The search through so many titles is eased by a convenient engine that will look for authors or titles, but unfortunately there is no way to search for categories such as dramas or comedies. The alphabetical listing can be fun to browse.

THE INTERNET THEATRE BOOKSHOP—Plays and Musicals
www.stageplays.com/

The first thing you notice is that this is a well-designed site. No hoopla, no drop-down ads, no specials de jour. Instead, the bookshop allows you quick access to its search engines and categories. It offers an international catalogue of plays, including those that are out of print and difficult to find, plus a wide variety of books that deal with various aspects of theatre. You can make purchases online on a secure server. What the home page fails to tell you is that this is a British site, and you'll have to deal with the monetary rate of exchange.

There is a briskly efficient search engine so you can look by title or author. At the bottom of its home page you can click on Plays by Nation, Dance, Music, Stagecraft, or Biography. Plays by Genre gives you special search capabilities, and Study and Theory lists books according to subject.

Playwrights can list their plays and websites here at no charge and can participate in The Playwrights' Forum and The Playwrights' Noticeboard. To see websites of playwrights from around the world, scroll down to the bottom of the home page to the small type and click on Playwrights on the Web.

SHAKESPEARE ON THE NET

Given the popularity of our friend Will of Stratford, you won't be surprised to discover that there are a number of websites about him and his plays. Here I list several, including some that focus on denials that Shakespeare wrote Shakespeare.

MR. WILLIAM SHAKESPEARE AND THE INTERNET
http://shakespeare.palomar.edu/

AUTHOR'S CHOICE Whether you are just starting your exploration of Shakespeare or are familiar with his works, this well-designed site is an excellent first stop for e-Shakespeare. It intends to be the complete annotated guide to

More Information on Shakespearean Festivals
Yahoo! lists almost 70 festivals that present Shakespeare (<http://dir.yahoo.com /Arts/Humanities/Literature /Authors/Playwrights /Shakespeare__William__1564 _1616_/Shakespeare_Festivals>). I'd guess there are at least that many not listed.

scholarly Shakespeare resources on the Internet. The Shakespeare Time Line alone is fascinating, and there are well-organized guides to other areas.

The webmaster doesn't merely grab a bunch of sites on the premise that more is better. Instead, valuable Five Diamond labels call your attention to the "best" Shakespeare sites. The webmaster's choices are sound and effective, and you'll want to examine these if you are searching for more about Shakespeare.

Go to Other Sites (which the webmaster calls "sites your mother should have warned you about"), and you'll find what happens to his plays when they are made into movies or when Will is warped into Star Trek. You'll also find Book a Minute, which sums up Hamlet in 11 words: "Whine whine whine . . . To be or not to be . . . I'm dead."

The Criticism section is still growing. Although it has a good start, more is needed. As the webmaster says, "There is still a desperate need for more, higher quality criticism to be published on the web."

The site also has access to Shakespeare's Festivals, and although it is incomplete, it does have an international flavor and can link you to some 100 various producing organizations in Australia, Canada, England, and the United States.

PROPER ELIZABETHAN ACCENTS
www.renfaire.com/Language/index.html

Thou goatish weather-bitten harpy, thou mammering folly-fallen maggot-pie, thou dissembling beetle-headed whey-face. . . . Nay, nay, gentle friend, I speaketh not at thee. I merely quote some of the insults from this site.

One major question actors and directors face is handling Shakespeare's language. The premise of this website is simple: "Learning to speak passable faire Elizabethan is easy. It simply requires some practice of the pronunciation, and some memorization of common vocabulary." The approach is also direct: "Start by learning where the sounds of Elizabethan differ from modern English. This has the side effect of teaching you many short words. Then work on some other words and learn the terms of address for the different people you might meet."

To achieve the goals, your webmaster divides his site into Pronunciation, Pronunciation Drills, Vocabulary, Grammar, Forms of Address, Insults and Cursing, and Songs of the Times.

Cyber-Shakespeare: The Bard's Plays Online

Several sites offer you the Bard's plays. Although as far as I'm concerned, an actual book is much more convenient than an e-version on the monitor, these sites are popular and convenient. Directors may want to download pages for productions.

THE COMPLETE WORKS OF WILLIAM SHAKESPEARE

http://tech-two.mit.edu/Shakespeare/works.html

This site divides Shakespeare's works into Comedy, History, Tragedy, and Poetry. Once you select a play, you have the option of accessing it by scenes or to have the entire play show up. You will also find an explanation for why you will find differences in various versions of his plays:

> There are many varying "original" editions of Shakespeare's plays, and it is only in a few cases that one can claim that a particular edition is more "authentic" than another. It is also important to realize that in most Elizabethan texts the punctuation was decided by the printer more often than by the author; punctuation varies significantly from copy to copy and it is likely that manuscripts and prompt books had little or no punctuation.

There also is a lively Discussion area, with a separate forum for each individual play. Many of the posts are from students, usually asking for help (you can hear "term paper" hanging over their heads!).

Shakespeare Greetings by E-Mail
If you want to send someone a Shakespeare e-card, try *Sealingwax Greeting Cards* (<*www.sealingwax.com/*>).

THE PLAYS OF WILLIAM SHAKESPEARE

www.theplays.org/

The *Electronic Literature Foundation* offers you the plays of William Shakespeare. You select a play, then click on scenes. Each play also has a search engine, concordance, quotes, and other information. In addition to Shakespeare's plays, the site also has his Sonnets. The split screen unfortunately makes navigation difficult.

The Globe Theatre

If we want to understand Shakespeare, we need to understand the physical theatre for which he wrote. After all, he thought of that theatre while writing, and surely it greatly influenced many of the scenes he wrote and the effects his plays require. Now, after centuries of questions about that theatre, we have it for all to see—the Globe.

SHAKESPEARE'S GLOBE THEATRE

http://shakespeares-globe.org/home.htm

The famous Globe was built on Bankside in 1599 and suffered a disastrous fire. It was rebuilt in 1614, but disappeared again. As hundreds of years passed, the Globe faded into vague memory, and no one could say authoritatively what it was like. This new Globe is the product of historians who gathered evidence for an authentic re-creation of Shakespeare's theatre, only yards from where the original Globe stood. Leading the reconstruction of England's most famous theatre was, of all nationalities, a Yank—the American actor and director Sam Wanamaker. As the site says about him:

> He founded the Shakespeare Globe Trust, and International Shakespeare Globe Centre—the final attempt to build a faithful recreation of Shakespeare's Globe close to its original Bankside, Southwark location. He also established the Shakespeare Globe Museum. While many have said that the Globe reconstruction was impossible to achieve, he had persevered for over twenty years, overcoming a series of monumental obstacles. At the Royal Unveiling of two sections of the Globe in June 1992, Sam Wanamaker saw clearly that his life had come full circle. The Globe was opened by HM the Queen in June 1997.

The site gives details, provides admission information, and sells a guidebook.

Who Wrote Those Plays Attributed to Shakespeare?

Shakespeare didn't write those plays by Shakespeare. At least, that's the position of a number of societies. Queen Elizabeth wrote them. No, Ben Jonson did. Wrong, the author was Edward de Vere. Hey, you're all mistaken, it was Chris Marlowe.

One fears that skeptics doubt that the Stratford native wrote such glorious plays because he did not attend a university, and (they would have us believe) only university-trained scholars could have known so much about Greek drama, English history, folklore, falconry, naval warfare, and so forth. Furthermore, he was a mere commoner. Talk about a snobbish attitude!

More on Who Wrote Shakespeare

To see an argument that Bacon wrote Shakespeare, check out <http://fly.hiwaay.net/~paul/contents.html>. And a novel argument: Shakespeare wrote Shakespeare (<www.clark.net/pub/tross/ws/will.html>).

SHAKESPEARE OXFORD SOCIETY

www.shakespeare-oxford.com/

These folks hold that the true author of "Shakespeare's" plays was Edward de Vere, the 17th Earl of Oxford (1550–1604). The premise is interesting: "For those who believe that Edward de Vere wrote Shakespeare, you must believe in conspiracies. For those who believe that the Stratford actor was the author, you must believe in miracles." I'm not convinced, but the arguments are well presented.

SCRIPTS: MUSICAL AND PLAY PUBLISHERS–LEASING AGENTS

To produce a play, you turn to a play publisher–leasing agent to obtain legal copyright permission (most often by paying royalties) and to buy copies of the script for the director, actors, designers, and technicians who will be involved in the production. A number of companies publish acting editions of plays and musicals. They also serve as leasing agents, based on contractual arrangements with playwrights and composers that authorize them to charge royalties and enforce copyright laws. You purchase scripts for plays. For musicals, more often you rent scripts and scores.

For plays, two of the major companies are Samuel French (*<www.samuel french.com/>*) and Dramatists Play Service (*<http://dramatists.com>*). For musicals, two of the large agents are Music Theatre International (*<www.mtishows.com>*) and Tams-Whitmark (*<www.tams-witmark.com/>*). Some other companies specialize in works for children. We discuss play publishers below.

Preliminary Steps to Presenting a Play or Musical Production

Before a theatre decides to produce a play, it must first be sure the play actually is available. Even if the play is listed in a publisher's catalog, that does *not* necessarily mean you can present it, because there may be restrictions. Check before announcing you'll put it on next year's season.

> **More Information About Legal Issues**
> Dramatists Play Service explains Rights and Restrictions, including Copy Cats, Permissions, and Copyrights (*<http://dramatists.com/text/home.html>*).

The theatre must also arrange to purchase scripts and pay royalties. The site listed next tells you how to arrange to present a specific play.

OBTAINING RIGHTS TO PRODUCE A PLAY OR MUSICAL
www.utsystem.edu/ogc/intellectualproperty/perform.htm

The process of presenting plays or musicals requires following a number of specific steps. Rachel Durkin of the University of Texas at Austin outlines the procedure nicely and accurately here. Of importance to sound designers, she also lists the process of using recorded music in theatrical or dance productions.

Musical and Play Publishers–Leasing Agents

A surprising number of play publishers do not have websites. I've added their snail-mail addresses to the sidebar appearing in this section.

BAKER'S PLAYS
www.bakersplays.com/

Baker's offers classic full-length plays by such authors as Brecht, Ibsen, Shaw, Chekhov, and García-Lorca, mixed with lighter-fare revues, short plays, and works for young audiences. *Baker's* also sells books on various theatrical subjects and has links to other aspects of theatre. The site's search engine has seemed fluky when I've visited.

BROADWAY PLAY PUBLISHING, INC.

www.broadwayplaypubl.com/

Service here is excellent, and e-mails are answered promptly, often by an executive. BPPI is an excellent source for contemporary American plays, primarily full-length but also one-acts and musicals. Representative titles include Tony Kushner's *Angels in America*, George C. Wolfe's *The Colored Museum*, and Naomi Wallace's *In the Heart of America*. It also has interesting lists, such as The Ten Most Significant Plays of the Century as compiled by two major organizations. You might want to check those lists to see if you agree with the choices.

CENTERSTAGE PRESS

www.cstage.com/press/index.html

CenterStage specializes in family musicals, with such classics as *Hansel and Gretel*, *Tom and Huck*, and *The Wizard of Oz*, as well as originals. They appear to offer something under 20 full-length and one-act scripts. Many have flexible casting and simple staging. They also have recorded music tapes so the cast works with a full orchestra from the first rehearsal.

CHILDRENS THEATRE PLAYS

www.childrenstheatreplays.com/

This is an attractive and well-laid-out site featuring children's plays by Kathryn Schultz Miller and Barry Miller. Their list of awards is impressive. Particularly valuable are the links to reference materials that follow each play's descriptions, bound to be extremely helpful to producers, directors, and teachers.

DRAMA SOURCE PLAYS AND MUSICALS

www.dramasource.com

Specializing in plays and music with G-rated content, *Drama Source* has plays, melodramas, and musicals for young people. In addition, it encourages playwrights and composers to submit works for consideration. The site has a number of links to bulletin boards, theatre sites, and a list of What's Playing.

DRAMATIC PUBLISHING COMPANY

www.dramaticpublishing.com/

The company's search engine is more flexible than many you find, allowing you to look for title, author, cast size, or category—such as Young Audiences, Comedy, Drama, Holiday, Fantasy, Full-length, One-Act, or Musical. A file of Best Sellers offers plays by subdivision such as Stock Theatre, Community Theatre, Young Audiences, Middle School, and High School.

DRAMATISTS PLAY SERVICE
http://dramatists.com/text/home.html

Dramatists tends to handle plays that have had successful professional Broadway productions, such as *Dinner with Friends*, by Donald Margulies; *How I Learned to Drive*, by Paula Vogel; *Three Tall Women*, by Edward Albee; and *The Kentucky Cycle*, by Robert Schenkkan. Those plays also indicate another characterization of works you find at *Dramatists*: It has a large number of plays that have won major awards such as the Tony or Pulitzer (the four plays mentioned are all Pulitzer winners). There's a well-organized index to its more than 2,000 titles, and PlayFinder searches for plays by title, author, or cast size.

MUSIC THEATRE INTERNATIONAL
www.mtishows.com/

MTI is a major force in musical theatre, and I've always found its staff dedicated and helpful. It has scripts and musical materials such as *Guys and Dolls*, *West Side Story*, *Fiddler on the Roof*, *Les Misérables*, *Annie*, *Little Shop of Horrors*, *Follies*, and many more, including works by Sondheim, Lloyd Webber, Bernstein, Schmidt and Jones, and Bock and Harnick. MTI also offers a wide range of resources—study guides, cast recordings, promo logos, production slides, recordings, and of course full musical scores. Its RehearScores allow rehearsal accompaniment on an interactive computer program. Video Conversation Pieces, 30- to 60-minute videos, take you to Broadway directors, lyricists, composers, and writers. Its latest development is The Broadway Junior Collection, which promises Musicals Made Easy.

PIONEER DRAMA SERVICE
www.pioneerdrama.com/

Pioneer publishes musicals like *The Secret Garden*, *Tom Sawyer*, and *The Wind in the Willows*, as well as Gilbert and Sullivan musicals such as H.M.S. *Pinafore* and *The Mikado*. Its full-length plays include *Big Boys Don't Cry*, *The Boy with No Name*, *Bride of Frankenstein Goes Malibu*, and *A Connecticut Yankee in King Arthur's Court*. It also publishes short plays and plays for Christmas or other special occasions. Its opening page directs you to its search engine. Neat Theatre Links has good entries. Playwright's Corner invites you to send scripts.

RODGERS AND HAMMERSTEIN ORGANIZATION
www.rnh.com/theatre/index.html

Look here for musicals such as *The Threepenny Opera* (Bertolt Brecht and Kurt Weill), *Song and Dance* (Andrew Lloyd Webber), and of course the famous Rodgers and Hammerstein musicals—such as *Carousel*, *Flower Drum Song*, *The King and I*, *Oklahoma!*, and *South Pacific*. The site recently improved its search capabilities, a great improvement. An added bonus is that you can listen to excerpts of musical numbers of the shows.

More Information on Publishers Without Websites

Other play publishers without websites, as far as my searches indicated, are:

- Anchorage Press, Inc., PO Box 8067, New Orleans, LA 70812; phone (504) 283-8868.
- Contemporary Drama Service—Meriwether Publishing LTD, 885 Elkton Drive, Colorado Springs, CO 80907; phone (719) 594-4422.
- The Dramatic Publishing Co., 311 Washington Street, Woodstock, IL 60098; phone (815) 338-7170.
- Encore Performance Publishing, PO Box 692, Orem, UT 84059; phone (801) 225-0605.
- I. E. Clark, Publisher, Saint John's Road, PO Box 246, Schulenburg, TX 78956-0246; phone (409) 743-3232.
- J. W. Pepper & Son, Inc., PO Box 850, Valley Forge, PA 19482-9985; phone (800) 345-6296.
- KMR Scripts, 116 N. 5th Street, Medford, OK 73759-1002; phone (405) 395-2990.
- New Plays, Inc., PO Box 371, Bethel, CT 06801-0371; phone (203) 792-4342.
- Players Press, PO Box 2231, Studio City, CA 91604; phone (818) 789-4980.

SAMUEL FRENCH, INC.

www.samuelfrench.com/

French is the world's largest play publisher–leasing agent. It handles plays that have had amateur productions as well as those that have enjoyed professional exposure. Under Special Plays you'll see a list of 25 Pulitzer Prize–winners that French handles, such as Charles Fuller's A *Soldier's Play*, Edward Albee's A *Delicate Balance*, August Wilson's *Fences*, and D. L. Coburn's *The Gin Game*. French also has musicals. From its home page you can order posters for selected plays, see the application form to receive a quote for a musical, or order original cast recordings of musicals. French also has a Bookshop that stocks publications other than its own.

TAMS-WITMARK MUSIC LIBRARY, INC.

www.tams-witmark.com/

Tams-Witmark, like *Music Theatre International*, is one of the major companies you'll contact to produce a musical. *Tams* represents well over a hundred musicals ranging from *Anything Goes* to *Your Own Thing* and including recent shows as well as many from the past.

From the home page, clicking Musical Shows takes you to a list of the musicals it has available. When you click a title, you find a Quick Review of the story line that is more a publicity blurb, a list of awards it earned, a Brief History of its professional life, a Synopsis outline, Orchestration, and Optional Additional Material, such as a stage manager's guide.

Also on the home page, Special Features has reports from creators or producers of a few musicals, such as *Titanic* and *Bye, Bye, Birdie*.

For royalties and rental charges, however, you'll need to contact them directly and fill out a form that deals with ticket prices, auditorium size, and the like.

GIFTS, CARDS, AND SOUVENIRS

Need a gift for a friend's opening night? Interested in souvenirs from your favorite play or musical? Many of us think it is great fun to collect or give theatrical memorabilia such as posters, T-shirts, cups, and buttons. Commercial sites await your orders.

BROADWAYNEWYORK.COM
http://BroadwayNewYork.com/

You feel like you're in a Times Square shop wandering through aisles of gifts, New York souvenirs, books, vocal scores, programs, CDs, and more. The Gift Shop has a large collection of Broadway materials, posters, videos, recordings, programs, show T-shirts, magnets, mirror stars saying *Dancer* or *Superstar*, and other items, and a search engine organized by shows.

FOOTLIGHTS THEATRE GALLERY AND GIFTS
www.footlightsgallery.com/

Think of owning a signed, numbered Al Hirschfeld drawing or lithograph! *Footlights* also sells posters of your favorite Broadway shows, recent or past.

SHOWBITS
www.showbits.com/

Gifts with a theatre, music, or dance motif can be ordered from this "Theatre Shop on the Internet."

TRITON GALLERY—Broadway Posters.com
http://BroadwayPosters.com/

Here's a source for theatrical posters if you want to give your home or greenroom a Broadway flair. *Triton Gallery* says they have "the largest collection of theatrical posters in the world, including current Broadway shows, national tours and foreign productions as well as obscure collectibles which you thought were unattainable." The posters come in various sizes, from 14-by-22-foot window cards to larger paper posters to seven-foot advertising posters. Prices seem to be around $15, although a photo reproduction of the original poster for *Cabaret* was $90. To use this site you'll have to have a

Additional Gifts Sources

You also can find theatre materials for sale on *eBay* (*<www.ebay.com/>*) by clicking on Books, Movies, and Music, then scrolling down the Memorabilia list. *Broadway New York* (*<www.broadwaynewyork.com /about.asp>*) describes theatre gift stores such as the famous One Shubert Alley, Theatre Circle, and more.

good knowledge of who was in the original production or the revival, because there is a decided lack of descriptions and information.

TALKIN' BROADWAY

www.TalkinBroadway.com/

An interesting way to find theatrical gifts and memorabilia is Shoppin' at *Talkin' Broadway.* Individuals use a forum to sell, look for, or buy materials from favorite shows. (Go there directly with *<www.TalkinBroadway.com /shoppin>*). Autographs, posters, CDs, playbills, and other items are available.

ONLINE MAGAZINES

With the advent of the Internet, electronic magazines are becoming increasingly popular. Most have a specific focus, such as health or politics. There also are interesting cyber-publications for theatre, as you'll discover when you dig into the sites listed here. They fall into two broad categories: the e-version of a print magazine, and a magazine that's only available online.

VARIETY

www.variety.com/

Variety became famous for its snappy headlines such as "Stix Nix Hic Pics," which described how small towns were rejecting movies about rural life. This is the e-version of that printed show-biz newspaper.

The magazine tracks the entertainment industry, covering film, television, theater, and music, making it a must-read for working professionals. It includes articles, news, columns, announcements of awards, box office income reports, a calendar of future entertainment events, and reviews from the daily print edition. There also are selected features from the weekly edition. Little icons by headlines identify stories as Music, Film, and so forth. The icon for Theatre is a sketch of an actor with arms outstretched for a bow (at least I think that's what it represents).

For those bemused by its slang, there is a Slanguage Dictionary of *Variety* language, some of it reminiscent of the famous Damon Runyon fiction (the source for *Guys and Dolls*). *Bird* is *satellite, boffo* is *outstanding, chantoosie* is a female singer who *chirps* (sings), and *ankle* is a verb, as in "The star *ankled* off the set." It claims to be the originator of *corny, deejay,* and *sitcom.*

Although you can read headlines, a recent change in policy means that you'll need to be a subscriber to open the stories. Subscribers to the print version have free access. For others, there is a free thirty-day trial. For a twenty-four-hour "day pass," the charge is $2.95; a yearly subscription is $59.

BACKSTAGE
www.backstage.com/index.asp

A weekly trade paper, *BackStage* has a large site, filled with professional information for actors. The site is updated daily, and news headlines deal with contemporary events. *BackStage* calls itself "the complete online performing arts resource," and complete it is, indeed. Regular weekly columns offer commentary on actors, theatrical events in New York and Los Angles, plus a question-answer site. The site is updated daily, and news headlines deal with contemporary events.

It offers news about casting calls, divided geographically into West Coast and East Coast, with subdivisions for Chicago and Florida. Members ($9.95 monthly) can post headshots and résumés and have their own websites listed.

The Performing Arts Directory is full of valuable resources for the professional, ranging from acting schools and coaches, voice and diction, tax preparation, talent portfolios, photographic services, models, voiceovers, and—in an ironic commentary on the business of acting—temp services. The Broadway Cash Register indicates weekly box office revenues.

STAGE DIRECTIONS MAGAZINE
www.stage-directions.com/

Designed for "small theatres," for a dozen years *Stage Directions* has discussed practical and technical aspects of theatrical operations. Articles typically examine lighting, fundraising, noise control, and technical innovations. Especially valuable is its Stage Directory, which is a mega-site of directories for children's theatre, musical theatre, organizations, and technical aspects for costumes, makeup, lighting, scenery, and so forth.

PROJECT MUSE
http://muse.jhu.edu/journals/

An impressively large and thorough site, *Project Muse* is a directory of journals. Scholars will enjoy studying the various publications. Theatre journals included are *The Drama Review, Theater, Theatre Journal,* and *Theatre Topics.*

TDR—The Drama Review
http://muse.jhu.edu/journals/the_drama_review/

Edited by Richard Schechner, TDR emphasizes experimental and avant-garde works in dance theatre, performance art, and more. There is a strong focus on the social, political, and economic contexts of performances. A search engine allows subscribers to look through the archives.

THEATER

http://muse.jhu.edu/journals/theater/

Theater has been the first publisher of plays by writers such as Adrienne Kennedy, August Wilson, and Athal Fugard. Its special issues have dealt with theatre and revolution, and Soviet revolution.

THEATRE JOURNAL

http://muse.jhu.edu/journals/theatre_journal/

The *Theatre Journal* publishes analyses of productions and articles on social and historical studies. If you're a subscriber, its search engine allows you to select a particular section or browse through its files.

THEATRE TOPICS

http://muse.jhu.edu/journals/theatre_topics/

Focusing on topics such as dramaturgy, performance studies, and pedagogy, *Theatre Topics* seeks to keep readers in touch with recent events on stage and in the classroom. Subscribers have access to a search engine to search the files.

PAJ—Performing Arts Journal

http://muse.jhu.edu/journals/performing_arts_journal/

PAJ has coverage of the visual arts, such as video, photography, and multimedia performances, as well as new works in theatre, dance, film, and opera. You can browse through archives.

ARTS JOURNAL

www.artsjournal.com/

This site is especially interesting because it both contains daily art news and has a distinctly international vision, drawing reports from more than 100 newspapers, magazines, and e-publications from a number of countries. The front page has brief stories, with connective links to the source. The left menu has topics such as theatre, dance, music, publishing, and issues involving arts.

AISLESAY

http://aislesay.com/

The *Internet of Stage Review and Opinion* is an e-zine that offers reviews of professional productions in Toronto, Canada, and major American cities. This is one of the older theatrical sites, and instead of showing age, it displays the advantages of experience. The critics are knowledgeable and insightful, and they do not pull punches. Materials are updated weekly.

You may tend to think the reviews are relevant only if the productions are in your own city, but they can offer broader insights that may make you rethink your opinions. For example, a sensitive review of a Minneapolis production of four Tennessee Williams early one-act plays sent me back to reread those scripts and consider them for production. Additionally, the review of a bewildering gender reversal version of *The Taming of the Shrew* (Kate played by a man, Petruchio by a woman) spoke about the confusion that results when a director (Sarah Stanley, in this case) seems to have an agenda but not a creative vision.

OOBR—The Off-Off-Broadway Review

www.oobr.com/

Off-off-Broadway can be excitingly innovative or tired tail-end avant-garde. OOBR helps you distinguish between the extremes and guides you to productions you'd like to experience. There are regular reviews, archives from the past, and lists of current productions.

DRAMATICS

www.etassoc.org/dramcov.htm

Dramatics magazine is oriented toward high school productions, although theatre professionals and professors often write its articles. This site lists contents of the lively monthly magazine.

THE ELIZABETHAN REVIEW

www.elizreview.com/

A nice surprise awaits you when you open *The Elizabethan Review*: period music. Excellent writing highlights the site. For example, when you click on About *The Elizabethan Review* at the bottom of the home page, you'll find statements such as these: "Our editorial embrace includes related Elizabethan topics as they evolved on the European Continent during the 16th and early 17th centuries." Visually, too, the site carries out the period approach: The pages look like old parchment paper.

The scholarly journal looks at the English Renaissance, including what it calls "the century-old contention of the Shakespeare authorship to the wars of the Counter-Reformation." There are interesting links, including Research Newsletters of the Shakespeare Oxford Society (1939–1992), or the Shakespeare Fellowship in England (1943–1985), both of which investigate the authorship case for the Earl of Oxford.

AMERICAN DRAMA

http://blues.fd1.uc.edu/www/amdrama/

It is difficult to tell if this site is alive. It says, "American Drama is published twice yearly by the American Drama Institute. It is funded by the Helen Weinberger Center for the Study of Drama and Playwriting and by the College of Arts and Sciences, both at the University of Cincinnati." Published twice yearly? When I visited the site it said it finally is making available a Fall 1996 issue, four years old. Too bad. The focus was an in-depth look at Arthur Miller, and if that's an indication of the site's potential, I'd like to see the promise fulfilled.

More Magazines and Publications Online

Artslynx lists hundreds of journals and magazines for theatre (<*www.artslynx.org /theatre/journals.htm*>) and dance (<*www.artslynx.org/dance /mags. htm*>). See also the list at Theatre Central (<*www1 .playbill.com/cgi-bin/plb/central _res ?cmd= show&code=2043*>). Also see McCoy's lists of primary research sources and e-publications (<*www.stetson.edu /departments/csata/thr_guid.html #Primary*>).

LIGHTING DIMENSIONS—ETEC

www.etecnyc.net/ld.html

Website for "The Magazine for the Lighting Professional," it offers you a chance to sample news from its pages.

STAGE DIRECTIONS

www.stage-directions.com/lvsd/articleSplash

A journal containing practical information for regional, academic, and community theatres, it offers a regular "tip of the day" about production techniques. You also may want to look in its various categories, such as Lighting Effects, Theater Space, and Fundraising for All. Spotlight highlights theatrical organizations, Onstage Buzz offers news and tips, and The Play's the Thing suggests books. Stage Directory leads to sites for suppliers of books, sets and scenery, props, plastics, paints, lights, fabrics, and many other items.

13

Copyright Law for Theatre

Our consciousness of copyright law was raised when the heavy metal band Metallica brought suit against Napster, an online music source, for copyright infringement. As part of its suit, Metallica said it planned to release more than 300,000 names of Internet users it claims broke copyright laws by swapping songs online, and the band sued three universities that allowed students to use Napster, charging that they were assisting in copyright piracy. All three institutions quickly blocked or sharply restricted use of the software on their campuses. Metallica and Dr. Dre also included slots in their suits for unnamed students and universities, saying they would be added later as the musicians obtained more information.

A similar case involved MP3.Com, which allows consumers to create virtual music libraries online. Accused of copyright infringement by Warner Music Group and BMG, two recording industry giants, MP3.Com had to settle by paying more than $20 million to each company.

Copyright law, like that invoked by Metallica and Warner-BMG, is the subject of our discussion here. *That same law applies directly to theatre.*

Prior to the development of the Internet, searching out details of copyright laws required long hours digging through heavy books in dusty libraries. Not any longer. Details are online, including the single most authoritative source—the United States Copyright Office—which is charged with the responsibility of enabling and enforcing laws passed by Congress. Not only is that office now easily available for Netters, it has handy quick clicks to basic information, FAQs, and forms. You'll find it and other relevant copyright sites in this chapter.

THE IMPORTANCE OF COPYRIGHT LAW TO THEATRE PARTICIPANTS

My goal here is to clarify, at least to some extent, complex copyright laws that relate to theatre folk. Those laws are important to us for a number of reasons, directly affecting our process of writing, selecting, preparing, and performing plays. In addition, there are stiff penalties for infringement, which I'll discuss later. Although copyright laws can seem as complicated and hard to master as theatre, websites can give us at least some direction.

A wide variety of theatre workers need to understand copyright:

- For *playwrights*, copyright offers significant legal protection against misuse, misappropriation, or outright theft of their plays.

- For *theatre managers, producers, artistic directors*, and *directors*, knowledge of copyright laws can prevent violations that may bring major legal problems, including tiresome hassles and even hefty fines.

- *College and university theatre department chairs and instructors of theatre courses, especially those focused on play direction, management, and sound design*, need to understand—and apply—copyright laws that pertain to their responsibilities and courses. They will want to ensure that they properly instruct their students and set appropriate legal and ethical examples through actions and attitudes.

- Because of penalties for infringement, *high school drama teachers, principals*, and even *school boards* should carefully understand the legal ramifications of presenting plays, especially who may be sued when copyright laws are violated.

- For *directors*, copyright laws have double significance. First, as mentioned above, to avoid legal hassles a director must know the laws that pertain to producing a play. Second, there is an interesting question about whether directors may enjoy copyright protection for their work.

- For *scene designers* and *costume designers*, copyright laws apparently have mixed applications. As I discuss later, scene designers can copyright their work, as has been proved through court decisions, but apparently costume designers cannot; the law considers clothing to be of a utilitarian nature and not copyrightable.

- For *sound designers*, copyright laws can present tricky obstacles.

For all of us in theatre, copyright law is important because it both protects the playwrights and outlines our legal responsibilities to plays protected by copyright. The latter point is a matter of great importance to theatre managers, artistic directors, theatre departmental chairs, and directors. I discuss those responsibilities later.

I start the discussion with definitions of copyright laws that are related to our job of producing plays. I then look at how *playwrights* enjoy copyright protection from the moment their plays are finished, and I show how dramatists register scripts with the U. S. Copyright Office. Information about copyright protection for directors and scene designers, plus problems for sound designers, follows. The chapter focuses on copyright laws affecting what we in theatre legally can—and cannot—do to the plays we present.

WHAT IS COPYRIGHT?

Copyright is protection provided by the laws of the United States (title 17, U. S. Code), granting authors and other artists the *exclusive* privilege to control reproduction, distribution, performance, or displays of their creative works. Part of a larger legal family known as *intellectual property*, which also includes siblings trademark and patent law, copyright safeguards creators of *original works of authorship*—such as dramatic, musical, artistic, and certain other intellectual work. Copyright law also is the legal foundation that protects companies that publish books, develop computer software, and produce movies and music recordings.

Copyright can be thought of as comparable to laws that protect ownership of homes and personal property (such as cars) because it is exclusive possession, full ownership with no reservations. A significant goal of copyright law is to give financial and moral encouragement to authors to invest time and effort in creating new works. For us in theatre, encouraging playwrights to continue creating new plays should be a primary concern, and even if copyright laws did not exist, wise theatre leaders would follow the principles anyway to ensure a flow of new plays and to extend to playwrights the same respect urged to all colleagues in the production process.

While our copyright is provided by the laws of the United States, it is international in scope. Through agreements such as the Berne Convention, many other countries share the premise that those who create such intellectual works are entitled to the same basic legal protections given inventors, manufacturers, or entrepreneurs. As a result, America has cooperative mutual agreements with more than 100 countries to honor citizens' copyrights.

Copyright Established in the U. S. Constitution

The basic authority for American copyright laws is expressed in Article I, Section 8, of the Constitution:

> To promote the progress of science and useful arts, by securing for limited times to authors and inventors the exclusive right to their respective writings and discoveries.

Impressive. Not only is that in our Constitution, it is in the *first* article, which includes major concepts about Congress, taxation, declaring war, providing military forces, and more. Our nation's founders believed so deeply in the rights of creators of "useful arts"—*authors* now means *artists*—they crafted this language in the Constitution.

Authoritative Websites for Copyright Information

The primary and official source for information about copyright is the *United States Copyright Office*, which has an efficient and informational website. You'll want to start your research into copyright here.

UNITED STATES COPYRIGHT OFFICE
http://lcweb.loc.gov/copyright

This thorough site offers you insights into copyright laws and processes. A good place to begin is to click on Copyright Basics, appropriately the first link you'll see, and scroll down the lengthy table of contents to find areas that interest you. You'll also want to explore the valuable FAQs, which are carefully constructed to address most concerns you may have.

MSN ENCARTA—Copyright
http://encarta.msn.com/find/Concise.asp?ti=04A06000

Authoritative—but couched in less formal legalistic terms—is this *Encarta* research resource. You'll find definitions and examples. Worth opening is the History of Copyright, which traces the concept back to the development of the printing press. More important is Copyright in the United States, most especially the subdivisions of Subject Matter, Rights of Copyright Owners, and Infringement.

COPYRIGHT RESOURCES ON THE INTERNET
http://groton.k12.ct.us/mts/pt2a.htm

A well-designed and thorough meta-index of valuable copyright sites, this is part of the Groton Public Schools Copyright Implementation Manual. The first part has links to specific parts of the Copyright Office documents, in particular those dealing with fair use, which are relevant to educators. Section 5 is Obtaining Permission, which contains Licensing Organizations and includes music, theatre, and musicals along with some clues to finding copyright holders. There also are numerous links that focus on new copyright law, significant with the growth of the Internet.

THE COPYRIGHT SOCIETY
www.law.duke.edu/copyright/index.htm

Duke University School of Law hosts this society for the study of copyright law and rights in theatre, literature, art, music, motion pictures, and other forms of intellectual property. Clicking on Research leads to valuable sites, such as Case Law and Courts, General Copyright and Licensing Information, and more. Searching Sites leads to mega-search engines. Licensing Organizations helps you find groups such as ASCAP and BMI, which you may want to contact to use copyrighted music.

FREE ADVICE.COM
www.freeadvice.com/

Legal information of all sorts is this site's specialization. Insurance law. Immigration law. Criminal law. Estate planning. Along with those categories, there is a folder for Intellectual Property, which contains informational material for Copyright Law and other significant regulations. It is worth investigating. Set up with questions and answers, it addresses many facets of copyright. For example:

If I Buy a Copyrighted Work, Why Can't I Do Anything with It I Want?

Ownership of a copyright is not the same as owning the copyrighted object. For instance, you can go to a bookstore and buy a book. You now own the book and can read it, write in it, or even rip it up. However, you cannot copy the material in the book, or prepare a derivative work from it or engage in any conduct that violates any of the rights of the copyright owner that are set out above.

There are multiple questions and answers, and leafing through the various pages can clarify questions and de-murk some gray areas.

INFORMATION ON COPYRIGHTS
www.bpmlegal.com/copyrt.html

The law firm of Brown, Pinnisi & Michaels, PC, discusses copyright and answers your questions. The Links page directs you to a number of other sources, including an interesting international list of copyright information. Valuable are the Copyright Qs and As.

NOLO.COM LEGAL ENCYCLOPEDIA—PATENT, COPYRIGHT, AND TRADEMARK LAW
www.nolo.com/encyclopedia/pct_ency.html#Subtopic115

If you're interested in knowing the differences between patents, copyrights, and trademarks, this well-known legal encyclopedia makes them clear. Under Copyright you'll find seven areas to click for valuable information such as this: "Copyright is a legal device that gives the creator of a work of art or literature, or a work that conveys information or ideas, *the right to control how that work is used*" (emphasis mine to stress playwrights' legal right to object to misuse or misappropriation of their creations).

THE INTELLECTUAL PROPERTY LAW SERVER
www.intelproplaw.com/

Intellectual property law encompasses patent, trademark, and copyright. This site is popular with writers, and a popular writers' magazine lists it as one of the top 100 places for writers. It also is recommended as one of the top 50 sites for legal professionals. The site offers recent news stories about copyright, a forum where you can ask questions, and a Copyright Page.

The following sites also are worth visiting for more information about copyright and intellectual property. I describe them only briefly here.

COPYRIGHT AND INTELLECTUAL PROPERTY

http://arl.cni.org/info/frn/copy/copytoc.html

The Table of Contents leads you to an impressive list of information about copyright.

LAWGIRL'S COPYRIGHT BASICS

www.lawgirl.com/copyright.shtml

An informational guide provided by a California attorney answers questions, lists procedures, and defines terms regarding copyright law.

AMERICAN LIBRARY ASSOCIATION—Copyright and Intellectual Property

www.ala.org/work/copyright.html

The ALA site provides links to major resources in the area of copyright and intellectual property.

LEGAL INFORMATION INSTITUTE—Berne Convention

www.law.cornell.edu/treaties/berne/overview.html

To help us understand the international copyright laws, the *Legal Information Institute* at Cornell offers the full text of the 1971 Berne Convention for the Protection of Literary and Artistic Works. It is the most important international treaty concerning copyright law.

WEBSITES FOR LAWYERS, ATTORNEYS, AND LAW FIRMS

http://attorneysforcopyrights.com/

If you're searching for a lawyer who is a specialist in copyright laws, this site will direct you. The search requires you to use a pull-down menu for your state and fill in the blank for city. Because copyright law is not a common specialization, expect to search a number of cities.

THE UT SYSTEM CRASH COURSE IN COPYRIGHT

www.utsystem.edu/OGC/IntellectualProperty/cprtindx.htm

It is our loss that this site doesn't address copyright for theatrical issues, because it thoroughly discusses the topics it *does* address. This *Crash Course*, like many sites we find on the Net, focuses more on the thorny Web questions. Still, it is worth investigating to enrich your understanding.

TIMELINE: A HISTORY OF COPYRIGHT

http://arl.cni.org/info/frn/copy/timeline.html

Prepared by the Association of Research Libraries, this is an excellent history of copyright from England's 1710 "Statute of Anne" to the present, with references to significant cases such as Fair Use and links to important laws like the Berne Convention.

INTELLECTUAL PROPERTY ISSUES
www.negativland.com/intprop.html

Enter this site understanding that the sponsors have a distinct bias against aspects of the copyright laws. That said, the site has interesting views and links.

WHAT CAN BE COPYRIGHTED?

A number of creative works are eligible for copyright. Certain prerequisites influence eligibility. The work must be *tangible, fixed* in some form. Inherent are concepts of *creative work*. The copyright office divides such works into eight basic categories. Four of the eight are especially relevant to us in theatre and dance:

1. literary works;
2. *musical works, including any accompanying words* (emphasis mine);
3. *dramatic works, including any accompanying music* (emphasis mine);
4. *pantomimes and choreographic works* (emphasis mine);
5. pictorial, graphic, and sculptural works;
6. motion pictures and other audiovisual works;
7. *sound recordings* (emphasis mine; important to sound designers); and
8. architectural works.

A BRIEF INTRODUCTION TO COPYRIGHT
www.netfunny.com/brad/copyright.html

Brad Templeton, a copyright lawyer, informally explains aspects of copyright. Two of the major questions he tackles are "creative work" and "tangible form":

> The first big issue involves defining what it is to make a creative work. The law requires that it exist in some tangible form—it can't just be in your head or sailing through the ether, it has to be on disk, paper, carved in stone (sculpture) or the like. It has to be creative (that's a tough one for lawyers to define) and that means it can't just be factual data.

What Cannot Be Copyrighted

Copyright laws specify what can, and cannot, be protected by copyright. We can better understand copyright by knowing what isn't eligible for protection.

- ☐ A *title* cannot be copyrighted because it is not, in itself, a "work." This explains why you often see duplicated titles of novels, poems, and plays. No law prevents you from calling your play *Death of a Salesman*—just don't copy Miller's story or plot.

- *Facts*, such as news or histories, are not creative but are public information, and therefore cannot be copyrighted. A magazine's specific arrangement and interpretation of those facts, however, can be copyrighted. For example, if you use a source like the *National Geographic* to research facts for a play about life in the Congo, you violate no copyright law if you shape the facts into a play. You can't duplicate the *Geographic*'s story, though.

- *Governmental informational materials*, such as official publications, are also noncreative (let's not comment about the stories some of our officials tell us). Instead, they are public information.

- *Ideas* are not eligible for copyright because one requirement is that the material specifically exist.

- *Names* do not receive copyright protection. While various brand names—like Kleenex and McDonalds—are legally protected from misuse, that's a *trademark* law, not copyright.

- *Characters* are not protected by copyright. However, if they have been popularized in comics and movies—Batman, say—there very likely will be a *trademark* protection. Moviemakers such as Disney spawn dozens of action figures and toys, and woe to anyone who tries to jump on that business bandwagon.

Copyright Protection of Plays and Musicals

Copyright protection begins at the time the work is finished in a fixed form—**immediately,** emphasizes the Copyright Office in rare boldface type—and it is the property of the author who created it. In the case of authors of a joint work, all are co-owners unless there is an agreement to the contrary. Copyright protection extends not only to published works but also to unpublished creations.

Assignment of the Playwright's Rights

Quite often artists assign rights to a designated agent. Musicians, for example, rely on BMI or ASCAP (both discussed later under Sound Design). Playwrights can assign rights to a play publisher–leasing agent, such as Samuel French or Dramatists Play Service, which will represent the playwright and is empowered to publish and sell copies of the script, handle requests for performances, collect royalties, and actively protect the dramatist's rights, if necessary, through vigorous legal recourse. For playwrights, the company's service represents freedom from paperwork and requests, a way to circulate their creations to a wide audience, and a system to produce income from royalties, perhaps even enough to support continued playwriting. For those of us who are involved in presenting plays, the publisher–leasing agent is a convenient method to obtain scripts and permission to produce them, while following relevant laws.

Regardless of whether the playwright is professional or amateur, experienced or beginner, represented by a publisher-agent or not, the law is absolute in its protection. Says the U. S. Copyright Office (<*www.loc.gov /copyright/circs/circ1.html*>): "It is illegal for anyone to violate any of the rights provided by the copyright law to the owner of copyright."

Work for Hire

I've said that authors own copyright of their work. There's an exception, however: *work for hire*. If the author is writing for an employer, that author will not be able to copyright his or her work unless special contractual arrangements are made in advance. The employer will hold the copyright. Typically, for example, television writers will not own copyright of their scripts because they work for hire. Most likely the network owns all copyrights. (Most TV writers get residuals—payment each subsequent time the show is aired—but that's a contractual agreement that has nothing to do with copyright.)

As I shall discuss later under the category of Copyright for the Director, the work-for-hire concept often prohibits stage directors from seeking copyright protection. But not always. Again I quote the U. S. Copyright Office Basics (<*www.loc.gov/copyright/circs/circ1.html*>):

> In the case of works made for hire, the employer and not the employee is considered to be the author.
>
> Section 101 of the copyright law defines a "work made for hire" as:
> (1) a work prepared by an employee within the scope of his or her employment; or
> (2) a work specially ordered or commissioned for use as a contribution to a collective work, as a part of a motion picture or other audiovisual work, as a translation, as a supplementary work, as a compilation, as an instructional text, as a test, as answer material for a test, or as an atlas, if the parties expressly agree in a written instrument signed by them that the work shall be considered a work made for hire. . . .

How Long Does a Copyright Last?

Copyright has a fixed life. How long? That's complicated because the copyright laws have evolved through a number of changes. Here's an explanation from FAQ Number 46 of the United States Copyright Office (<*www.loc.gov /copyright/faq.html#q46*>):

> The Sonny Bono Copyright Term Extension Act, signed into law on October 27, 1998, amends the provisions concerning duration of copyright protection. Effective immediately, the terms of copyright are generally extended for an additional 20 years. Specific provisions are as follows:
>
> □ For works created after January 1, 1978, copyright protection will endure for the life of the author plus an additional 70 years. In the case of a joint

work, the term lasts for 70 years after the last surviving author's death. For anonymous and pseudonymous works and works made for hire, the term will be 95 years from the year of first publication or 120 years from the year of creation, whichever expires first;

- For works created but not published or registered before January 1, 1978, the term endures for life of the author plus 70 years, but in no case will expire earlier than December 31, 2002. If the work is published before December 31, 2002, the term will not expire before December 31, 2047;
- For pre-1978 works still in their original or renewal term of copyright, the total term is extended to 95 years from the date that copyright was originally secured.

That's complicated. For a neat diagram that illustrates the duration of copyright, see the following website:

WHEN WORKS PASS INTO THE PUBLIC DOMAIN
www.unc.edu/~unclng/public-d.htm

This chart, prepared by Lolly Gasaway, gives the most clear statement of copyright time periods that I've seen. Laid out in chronological outline form, it sums up the various revisions of the American copyright laws.

Copyright and Public Domain

Not all plays are protected by copyright. Some are "in the public domain," which means copyright laws do not pertain to them; they are owned by the public. Early plays, such as those by Sophocles, Shakespeare, or Moliére, for instance, are clearly in the public domain because they were created before copyright laws existed. However, *a translation* of a play by Sophocles or Moliére may be copyrighted. That quite likely will be the case for any translation you'd care to use for production. For example, Edmund Rostand's glorious *Cyrano de Bergerac* was written in 1897 and therefore now is in public domain. There are some two dozen translations from French to English, and the majority is in public domain, but only two or three of them are strong enough to interest you—and they are recent and copyrighted.

Equally, a play like Tom Stoppard's *Rosencrantz and Guildenstern Are Dead*, even though based (very loosely!) on Shakespeare's noncopyrighted *Hamlet*, is protected by copyright because that is Stoppard's creation. While you can present *Hamlet* without permission, you will need to contact Samuel French to arrange permission—and pay royalties—before you can produce Stoppard's play.

Also in the public domain are plays for which the copyright has expired due to time limitation. For example, certain early George Bernard Shaw plays fall into that category. However, before assuming that any given play is now in the public domain, check the catalogue of the publishing-leasing agent that handles plays by that author. In the case of George Bernard Shaw scripts, look in the Samuel French catalogue. You'll discover that although some of his plays were written long enough ago that they would fall into the public domain, his later revisions put them back under copyright protection.

Searching for Plays in the Public Domain

As a broad generalization, any play written more than 75 years ago may now be in the public domain. In close calls, we should check. I know of no single, authoritative list of plays for which copyright has expired. Most of us search carefully through catalogues of the various play publishers–leasing agents. The Library of Congress, which is responsible for this country's copyright records, has no such list but will search their records for a fee of $65 an hour. Should you wish to search the records yourself, there is no fee, if you go to its Washington, D.C., location.

COPYRIGHT FOR PLAYWRIGHTS

Technically, playwrights do not need to register their plays to be protected. Under current copyright law, your work belongs to you regardless of whether you formally copyright it. Some playwrights believe they can prove ownership by mailing their scripts to themselves, never opening the envelope and preserving the postmark until such time they may need to certify a date of creation. Others wait until their play is published by a play publisher–leasing agent such as Samuel French or Dramatists Play Service, which will arrange copyright. Still others register their works with one of the literary organizations, such as the Writer's Guild of America, but it provides only proof of authorship and requires you to renew within five years.

Better is a formal copyright. Think of it as insurance. In a worst case scenario, when the author needs to take legal action, registration with the Copyright Office is *prima facie* evidence of ownership. As the Copyright Office says in its FAQs:

> In general, registration is voluntary. Copyright exists from the moment the work is created. You will have to register, however, if you wish to bring a lawsuit for infringement of a U. S. work.

Given that obtaining a copyright is relatively inexpensive—the fee now is $30—the insurance policy makes sense if you intend to submit your play to a number of potential producers or directors. (Some of us enjoy framing our first copyright document and mounting it above our work space. Now we have legal proof we are playwrights!)

THE DRAMATISTS GUILD—Dramatists' Copyright and Intellectual Property Rights
www.dramaguild.com/doc/rights.htm

Playwrights sometimes are concerned about perceived invasion of their rights by directors and dramaturges. *The Dramatists Guild*, which says it is the only profession association for playwrights, composers, and lyricists, states clearly its position about the sanctity of the author's rights:

> It is the artistic heritage of the playwright and a long-standing principle of The Dramatists Guild of America that the dramatist owns and controls the intellectual property, including the copyright, of the author's script and of all changes of any kind whatsoever in the manuscript, title, stage business or performance of the play.

The *Guild* takes a stand against others asserting rights to the playwright's work:

> The Council of the Guild has become aware that directors, dramaturgs and other theatrical collaborators have from time to time claimed copyright and other ownership interests in any such changes or contributions for which they claim to be responsible.

One device such people use, the *Guild* says, is making videotapes of performances and filing them with the Copyright Office to attempt to establish their claim. The *Guild* strongly opposes such records:

> in furtherance of the artistic and legal rights supported by the Guild for its members, the Council of the Guild for and on behalf of its membership restates that no Dramatists Guild member should allow his or her script, or any taped performance of his or her script, to be used to establish or promote ownership or control by any theatrical collaborator over any claimed changes or contributions.

The Guild promises to support any actions members must take to protect their legal rights.

How to Copyright Your Play

To have your work legally protected, you need to register it with the United States Copyright Office. Go to its site (<*http://lcweb.loc.gov/copyright*>) and click on Application Forms (or go directly to that page at <*www.loc.gov/copyright/forms*>).

You'll see a number of forms. As a dramatist, you want Form PA for Performing Arts, which is used to register works intended for performance before an audience, such as plays, screen plays, and radio scripts. (It also is used for works that require a mechanical device or process, such as lyrics, musical compositions, or multimedia.) A form is needed for each individual work.

You can view and print copyright forms from this site. For that, you'll need the Adobe Acrobat Portable Document Format, which lets you fill in and submit PDF forms online. If you don't have it on your computer, you can download it free from Adobe Systems (<*www.adobe.com/products/acrobat/readstep.html*>).

Should you prefer to order Form PA by snail-mail, the website gives the office address. It also lists the phone number for Public Information Specialists, who can answer questions about complex copyright issues.

Displaying the Copyright Symbol

At one time a copyright notice was required for copyright protection, and undoubtedly you've seen plays that have a copyright announcement, often including the symbol ©. Technically, this is no longer required. For all works published after March 1, 1989, the copyright notice is optional to receive copyright protection, because now your work is immediately copyrighted when it is completed in fixed form.

However, as I've noted, making sure that you've filed the correct papers with the Copyright Office is invaluable. Remember, if you don't register your play, you can't bring suit in a Federal court for infringement. Furthermore, it makes sense to announce clearly that your play is copyrighted. That way, no one can claim, "Oh, I didn't know it was copyrighted." After you've registered your work, place a statement of copyright in a prominent place on your script, such as the cover page. You can use the letter *c* inside a circle © or include the word *copyright*— or do both. Also list the year and your name as copyright holder. It would look like this:

© Copyright 2003, I. M. Dramatist.

The Copyright Office offers a number of free helpful publications on this and other matters. You can view them at Copyright Information Circulars and Form Letters (<*http://lcweb.loc.gov/copyright/circs*>). Again, you'll need the Adobe Acrobat Reader to view and print PDF versions of the circulars.

FRIENDS OF ACTIVE COPYRIGHT EDUCATION
www.csusa.org/face/index.htm
FACE offers information for those who need copyrights. Playwrights will want to click on Words and then go to Copyright Basics and Words FAQs.

COPYRIGHT FOR STAGE DIRECTORS AND CHOREOGRAPHERS

Copyright protection is available to more than playwrights and other authors. It also includes pantomimes and choreographic works; pictorial, graphic, and sculptural works; and motion pictures and other audiovisual works. Do those categories include theatrical directorial creations? Yes. No. Well, probably— the answers get tricky.

THE COPYRIGHT WEBSITE
www.benedict.com/

San Francisco copyright lawyer Benedict O'Mahoney's authoritative site focuses on complex questions of copyright in the e-age. As he says, "This site seeks to encourage discourse and invite solutions to the myriad of copyright tangles that currently permeate the Web." A major portion of his site shows "notorious pillagers of copyright" in Visual, Audio, and Digital Arts. You can see and hear the thefts.

His headlines section (<*www.benedict.com/news/headlines/headlines.htm*>) refers to an article in the American Bar Association Journal (October 1995). He summarizes the article:

> Stage Directors claim that their individual interpretation of a play is embodied in their stage directions, which concern such things as placement of actors, positioning and intensity of spotlights, and other nuances of stagecraft. However, copyright protection for stage direction generally has not been an issue because traditionally Stage Directors have worked under "work for hire" agreements, which meant that they received credit for their work, but no copyright protection.
>
> Recently, collective bargaining agreements have resulted in the stage directors retaining copyright ownership of their work. As a result, several stage directors have registered their works with the Copyright Office. An|d| earlier this year, director Gerald Gutierrez settled a lawsuit against the producer and director of the 1994 Chicago production of "The Most Happy Fella." Gutierrez alleged that artistic innovations had been appropriated from his 1992 Broadway revival without consent.

THEATER, STAGE DIRECTIONS, AND COPYRIGHT LAW
www.kentlaw.edu/student_orgs/lawrev/text71_3/freemal.htm

A different point of view is expressed in this article by Beth Freemal, which appeared in the *Chicago-Kent Law Review*. This thorough and well-documented discussion of copyright law for the director has careful and detailed organization, as you'd expect considering where it was published. Part I examines copyright law, Parts II, III, and IV conclude that stage directions can't be copyrighted, and Part IV states that directors should instead use *contract law* to protect their work.

COPYRIGHT FOR SCENE AND COSTUME DESIGNERS

As we know, law is based on precedents. A given legal action in one court reverberates in other jurisdictions. Scene designers can study a certain case, described below, to help them come to decisions about their work.

UNITED SCENIC ARTISTS LOCAL 829—Designers and Artists for the Entertainment Industry
http://frontpage.shadow.net/usa829fl

Designers will want to go to the Copyrights page, which you access from the left-hand menu. Once there you'll find a discussion of one scene design controversy that ended in court—The Case of the Stolen Stage Designs.

> In the spring of 1996 Caldwell Playhouse, in Boca Raton Florida, completed the run of the first regional production of *Love! Valour! Compassion!* A storm of controversy erupted over this production concerning the stage designs and stage directions. The physical production and staging at the Caldwell so closely resembled the original Broadway production that a legal battle developed over this issue.

As you'll note when reading the summary, the original designer won in court.

Not discussed here are the director's rights. If that production used the stage directions, one wonders if the director also had a case.

Costume designers will want to look at this site, too. It expresses an opinion that their designs are not eligible for copyright. My guess—a very nonlegal opinion—is that this isn't true and at some point that opinion will be tested in a court case.

COPYRIGHT FOR SOUND DESIGNERS

For sound designers, copyright has a different application than for playwrights or designers. The sound designer is concerned with *others'* copyrights. You're designing sound for a dance or theatrical production and want to use recorded music. Can you simply download recordings from the Net or borrow CDs from a library? Nope. Not legally. As SESAC (a performing rights organization) points out:

> In order to comply with the U. S. copyright law, any establishment that plays copyrighted music is legally required to secure permission to use copyrighted music, whether in a live performance or by mechanical means. A music user can do this by securing licenses from the three performing rights organizations recognized by the U. S. Copyright Act of 1976.

Any establishment? BMI lists some 75 different "businesses" that certainly indicate a wide scope of copyright areas. Telephone music on hold. Theme parks. Casinos. Restaurants. RV parks. Sports. Beauty pageants. Dance studios. Yes, *any establishment* seems to be the correct description!

If you want to play a copyrighted song for a public theatrical performance, you need to contact the composer's and lyricist's representative and the publisher for permission. The Internet is an excellent way to find out who the representatives are. ASCAP (<*www.ascap.com*>), BMI (<*www.bmi.com*>), and SESAC (<*www.sesac.com/open/html*>), commonly called *performing rights societies*, are the three major performing rights organizations that represent songwriters, composers, and music publishers, and they license the public performing rights for musical compositions.

Steps to Obtain Rights

Getting rights to use copyrighted music isn't easy. Understand that ASCAP, BMI, and SESAC are primarily focused on *major* organizations that produce high revenue. We're pretty small potatoes in their eyes, and getting them to answer our questions will be time-consuming. Instead, start with some of the sites listed next.

OBTAINING RIGHTS TO PRODUCE A PLAY OR MUSICAL OR USE MUSIC IN LIVE PERFORMANCES

www.utsystem.edu/ogc/intellectualproperty/perform.htm

This is a fine location for basic information about getting rights. The first half of the site deals with script permissions. The second part is valuable for the sound designer. Rachel Durkin, manager of the performing arts center at the University of Texas, describes legalities and procedures to obtaining rights to use music in live performances. She stresses the difficulties:

> The process of obtaining rights to use music in live performance is never an easy one. Unlike obtaining the rights to produce a play, there is no central clearinghouse for music clearance. Two major pieces of advice I can offer are, one, give yourself plenty of time to go through this process and two, always have a back-up plan if you are not successful in obtaining the rights.

She also discusses college-university processes to get rights:

> One of the biggest misconceptions about music rights is that if you are working at, or are a student at a college or university, the rights are already taken care of by the educational institution. This is true, but only in a limited sense. While most colleges and universities do pay a licensing fee to ASCAP and BMI, the licenses are very narrow in terms of what's covered by that fee. What is never covered by these standard university licenses is "grand rights" which is defined as the use of music in a dramatic setting. This means that if you are presenting a play or dance performance, you cannot legally use any copyright protected music without first obtaining permission.

However, you should also check the BMI information for colleges (<*www.bmi.com/iama/business/entertainment/artsqa.asp*>), which seems to make a different statement about the rights colleges and universities have: "If the college or university holds a BMI license and is also the presenter of the event, a separate license is not necessary." If you're a sound designer at such an institution, a visit to your campus business office makes sense. Given that there will be a large number of campus organizations using copyrighted music, try to convince the administration to pay these licensing fees and negotiate the terms in your theatre's behalf.

Sites to Help You Determine Copyright for Selected Music

You've selected the perfect musical pieces for a theatrical production or dance performance. Now you want to get copyright permission. How do you find the appropriate company? Slowly. Expect to have to search. The sites listed here can help you. Quite likely the pieces will be in ASCAP, BMI, or SESAC. Look in their sites or try one of the general search centers.

COPYRIGHT SEARCH CENTER

www.mpa.org/crc.html

If you need to find the copyright holder of music, perhaps this guide can help you. There also are links to a few informational sites dealing with copyright laws.

SONGFILE

http://songfile.snap.com/

SongFile says it has a database of more than two million songs and the most complete CDs and tapes search on the Internet. It offers opportunity to view lyrics of some 62,000 songs and has a comprehensive guide to sheet music resources and artists. It has a search engine, but I found it flaky. (After inserting the title, I was taken to a link that is supposed to provide buttons to click for Lyrics, Listen, CDs, Sheet Music, and License. I couldn't get it to work.) Underneath the search engine is a button for Browser Requirements for SongFile. That took me to a "no such page announcement." I include the site here in case it kicks the bugs out of its system.

THE AMERICAN SOCIETY OF COMPOSERS, AUTHORS AND PUBLISHERS

www.ascap.com/

ASCAP has more than 80,000 composers, songwriters, lyricists, and music publishers. It seeks to "protect the rights of its members by licensing and paying royalties for the public performances of their copyrighted works." Sound designers will want to search this site to find composers or recording artists they wish to use.

BROADCAST MUSIC, INC.

www.bmi.com/

BMI says it represents more than 4.5 million songs. It has a strong search engine—HyperRepertoire Internet Database—to help you see if BMI represents the artists you need for your sound design. Also check the small menu at the top of the page. Clicking on Businesses Using Music will lead you to a long list and perhaps one will apply to you. The home page lists a number of activities needing licenses, but nothing for theatre. However, a bit of clicking through the FAQs leads you to Q and A for Performing Arts Presenters (<*www.bmi.com/iama/business/entertainment/artsanswers.asp#3*>), which contains valuable information for us.

More Information for Sound Designers

Sound designers may wish to explore a forum that addresses their interests (<*www.brooklyn.com/theatre-sound*>). It has some 600 participants from 17 countries who frequently discuss copyright issues and other areas of sound. There are searchable archives.

SESAC

www.sesac.com/open.html

A menu on the left takes you to various internal information. If you need to find one or more musical artists, clicking on Repertory Online leads you to a search of the SESAC database for titles, composers, and authors. Heavy in graphics, it opens slowly but dramatically.

Music in the Public Domain

You may have some luck finding music you like that now is in the *public domain*, a legal term that refers to creative and intellectual works that no longer are copyrighted. For such music you don't need permission, nor do you pay a royalty.

MUSIC IN THE PUBLIC DOMAIN

www.pdinfo.com/

This site lists music for which copyrights have expired, available for your use without seeking rights (or paying royalties). You may want to check the link to the *Dover Book Catalogue*, where you can find republications of interesting old music now in the public domain. You can also find sites for music publishers.

COPYRIGHT INFRINGEMENT

Because there is such emphasis on the rights of the copyright holder, you won't be surprised that violating those rights can result in legal punishments that range from injunctions to fines, even to imprisonment. The following sites explain the legal process.

Playwrights have legal recourse if their plays are presented without permission or if the plays are produced in a way the authors believe violate the work. The Copyright Office (<*www.loc.gov/copyright/faq.html#q55*>) spells out some steps:

A party may seek to protect his or her copyrights against unauthorized use by filing a civil lawsuit in Federal district court. If you believe that your copyright has been infringed, consult an attorney. In cases of willful infringement for profit, the U. S. Attorney may initiate a criminal investigation.

Encarta, which I mentioned earlier (<*http://encarta.msn.com/find/Concise.asp?ti =04A06000&MSID=b963307e395511d498880008c7d9e3db*>), defines infringement and explains possible legal consequences:

> An infringement of a copyright is the reproduction, distribution, performance, or display of any copyrighted work without permission of the copyright owner or without a compulsory license. For example, . . . performing a play without permission would be [an infringement].

Encarta discusses the legal process:

> Copyright infringements are usually dealt with in civil lawsuits in federal court. The law provides several remedies to copyright owners who prove infringement against their work. In such a case, the court may order an injunction against future infringement, which requires the infringing party to refrain from committing further violations of the copyright. The court may also order the destruction of infringing copies; reimbursement for any financial loss suffered by the copyright owner; transfer of profits made from the sale of infringing copies; and payment of specific damages, plus court costs and attorneys' fees. If the infringement was intentional, *the infringing party can be subject to criminal penalties as well, which include fines and possible imprisonment.* (emphasis mine)

The Legal Repercussions of Copyright Violations

The dangers of breaking the law are real. Federal copyright law establishes statutory fines for each act of copyright infringement, ranging from a minimum of $500 for "innocent" infringement to a maximum of $100,000 for "willful" infringement. Most licensing agreements define *any* unauthorized changes as willful infringements.

Who Can Be Fined?

An impressively large number of people could be charged for a single violation of copyright. The Federal Copyright Act extends "joint and several" liability for each infringement. *Each individual involved* could be held responsible for the *whole* amount of the fine—the director, the theatre's artistic director and chair, individual members of the production staff, each member of the student cast and crew (or their legal guardians), the school (acting as producer), the owner of the building in which the performances take place, and in the case of public schools, the school board or district. Serious? You bet.

Myths About Copyright

Urban myths are alive and well in theatre, perhaps nowhere as much as pertaining to permissions and royalty:

> *If we don't charge admission, we don't have to get permission or pay royalty.* Wrong. Audience = performance. Performance = permission required. Most often, permission = royalty payment. I confess I don't know why directors and producers try to rationalize what actually is stealing from the playwright. After all, in the large scheme of theatrical budgets, royalty expenses for a comedy or drama are relatively inexpensive. Some theatres spend more for cast parties.

> *No one will know if we do the play without permission.* Wrong. "No one will ever know" is, first, a defensive posture based on admitted deliberate violation. Second, it is incorrect. Publishers and agents take active steps to protect their property, including subscribing to clipping services that focus on finding every mention of plays in newspapers (both campus and general) and magazines. Think of this, too: Publishers have experienced copyright lawyers on retainer, but because copyright law is an unusual specialty, an infringer may have difficulty finding a local expert to defend a case.

10 BIG COPYRIGHT MYTHS EXPLAINED

www.templetons.com/brad/copymyths.html

Attorney Brad Templeton selects ten "myths" and debunks them. For example, his second myth is often heard by those presenting plays in, say, a Lab Theatre or religious environment: *"If I don't charge for it, it's not a violation."* Templeton makes the record clear:

> False. Whether you charge can affect the damages awarded in court, but that's essentially the only difference. It's still a violation if you give it away—and there can still be heavy damages if you hurt the commercial value of the property.

For playwrights considering adapting another's work, his sixth myth is applicable: *"If I make up my own stories, but base them on another work, my new work belongs to me."* His reply is clear:

> False. Copyright law is quite explicit that the making of what are called "derivative works"—works based or derived from another copyrighted work—is the exclusive province of the owner of the original work. This is true even though the making of these new works is a highly creative process. If you write a story using settings or characters from somebody else's work, you need that author's permission.

For directors, the statement also is pertinent. Who can change a playwright's work? Only the playwright. As the owner of that original work, the playwright alone has exclusive rights to make "derivative works."

Two Examples of Playwrights Evoking Copyright Laws

Several illustrations show the copyright law in action and illustrate the playwright's absolute ownership. I cite two authors to represent all.

Playwright Edward Albee evoked copyright law to control productions of his plays such as *Who's Afraid of Virginia Woolf?*; *The American Dream*; *The Death of Bessie Smith*; and *Zoo Story*. They each include this notice: "[This play] may be leased only for amateur productions at which the audience is unsegregated." Of course we today quickly agree with that concept, even wonder why it needs to be said. Remember, however, that he wrote during a turbulent civil rights period when it was not unheard of for audiences to be segregated. The point here is an illustration of playwrights' rights. Does Albee have a legal right to make such a demand? Absolutely. It is his play and his rights are absolute. What would happen to a producer or director who violated this stipulation? Legal actions are possible, and the copyright infringer should expect to lose the case. That premise applies to *any* infringement of copyright.

Directors who claim they have a "right" to change plays ignore the law. For one example, Samuel Beckett took legal actions to prohibit a theatre from producing his *Waiting for Godot* with an all-female cast. "Had I wished those characters to be female, I would have said so," he said icily. The theatre was close to opening its production, but it was forced to cancel.

Equally, Edward Albee took legal action to stop a production of *Who's Afraid of Virginia Woolf?* in drag, stating, "That is not the way I wrote it." Again, although rehearsals were well along, the production never took place.

Copyright and Stage Directions

Some directors preach that the director should cross out all stage directions before beginning to prepare the play for production. That's a violation of copyright. Samuel Beckett was appalled when a production of his *Endgame* ignored his specific stage directions and instead sought to place it in a railway station. He was going to prevent the production but finally let it continue. Later, however, his estate forced the cancellation of a production of *Footfalls* for not following the author's stage directions.

Publishers' and Leasing Agents' Stipulations

Producing a play without obtaining permission—which in the case of copyrighted works almost always involves paying royalties—is theft. No matter what alibi one presents, the cold fact is clear. Refusing to pay the royalties is stealing, stealing from the playwright, stealing from the agent, stealing from the play publisher or leasing agent.

Before we select a copyrighted play to produce, we necessarily must be aware of the conditions that govern receiving permission. When we select that play, we enter into a contract. Note the following examples of stipulations in contracts of major play publishing companies that supply us scripts and arrange for legal permission to produce the play.

DRAMATISTS PLAY SERVICE
www.dramatists.com/

The statement from Dramatists Play Service is typical of all play publishers–leasing agents. From its home page, click on Enter, then scroll down to Information and click on How to Apply for Performance Rights (or go there directly at <*www.dramatists.com/text/anp.html*>). You'll find these warnings:

> *Any unauthorized performance of these plays constitutes an infringement of the copyright and a violation of the Law, with possible serious consequences for the infringer* [emphasis mine]. No play listed may be produced unless written application is made to, and written authorization is obtained from, Dramatists Play Service.
>
> Authorization [to produce a play handled by Dramatists Play Service], when granted, is subject to the following conditions: (A) the title of the play may not be altered; (B) *there may be no deletions, alterations or changes of any kind made to the text* [emphasis mine]; (C) proper authorship, and other credits required in contract, must be given in all programs and advertisements; and (D) the program must include the following statement, "Produced by special arrangement with Dramatists Play Service, Inc."

MUSIC THEATRE INTERNATIONAL
www.mtishows.com/

To illustrate the conditions publishers–leasing agents place on scripts we lease from them, consider MTI's position, typical of other companies. Click on Customer Support (or go there directly at <*www.mtishows.com/support.htm*>) and scroll down the nine points. As MTI says, "Built into each and every performance license is specific language which governs how the copyrighted work must be presented."

Music Theatre International makes clear that scripts cannot be changed:

> Some people think making "minor adjustments" to a show (such as changing the gender of a character or changing the name of a town to give it local significance) is inconsequential to its integrity, or believe they have the right to "experiment" with the authors' intentions as an expression of their artistic vision. This is simply not the case. When you are granted a performance license, by law the show you license must be performed "as is." *You have no right to make any changes at all unless you have obtained prior written permission from us to do so* [emphasis mine]. Otherwise, any changes violate the authors' rights under federal copyright law. Without prior permission from

MTI, your actions will subject you to liability—not only to the authors, but also to us—for breaching the terms of your license agreement, which clearly forbid you to make any changes or deletions.

DRAMATIC PUBLISHING

www.dramaticpublishing.com/

Some theatre people profess to believe that they have a "right" to cut a show. One even hears of class instructors who tell their directing students to take a full-length play and present a 10-minute scene from it in a public performance. Bad education, not to mention poor ethics. That violates copyright law. Dramatic Publishing makes clear the process of obtaining approval, in advance, to make cuts. From its home page click on FAQs and you'll see its position:

> The process of·cutting a show or musical can be very simple or complicated, depending on the play you have chosen, the cuts you wish to make, and the amount of time you provide us for approval. Please remember that not all authors will allow their works to be cut. Some authors feel so strongly about presenting their show in its entirety that they will not approve cuttings of any kind, whereas other authors will approve a cutting for competition only and still others are happy to oblige cutting requests of any kind. As such, *all cuttings require our written approval* [emphasis mine].
>
> Dramatic Publishing defines a cutting as whole, unedited excerpts of a show, including an act or scene(s) of a play or all of the text from one page through another page. When an approved cutting is performed, the play must be billed as "Scenes from [Play] by [Playwright]" in all promotional material generated by the producing organization. All cuttings must be licensed by Dramatic Publishing and adhere to these guidelines. Any changes made after a cutting has been approved must be approved under a separate request.

Dramatic Publishing also discusses the old canard that permission isn't required if there is no charge for admission. This statement echoes what other publishers–leasing agents say:

> A royalty must be paid every time a play is performed regardless of whether it is presented for profit and whether admission is charged. A play is performed any time it is acted before an audience.

COPYRIGHT FOR THE HIGH SCHOOL/AMATEUR THEATRE PRODUCER

www.angelfire.com/or/Copyright4Producers

AUTHOR'S CHOICE This is an excellent site by Kevin N. Scott. The only complaint I have is that the title is too limited. These materials are not just for high schools; they also are directly relevant to college and university theatres, community theatres, regional theatres—all theatrical organizations. That aside, what he says is precisely correct, well researched, thoughtfully presented, and on target. Every producer, director, artistic director, teacher, and would-be director should visit this site.

One Exception: Face-to-Face Classroom Education

Under very specifically stated circumstances—an educational exception—performances are permitted without obtaining permission. The copyright code (U. S. Code XX110) allows for:

> performance or display of a work by instructors or pupils in the course of *face-to-face teaching activities* [emphasis mine] of a nonprofit educational institution, in a classroom or similar place devoted to instruction.

Clearly, this exception will not permit an educational institution to avoid obtaining permission for a major, faculty-directed mainstage production; calling it "face-to-face teaching" obviously is incorrect. Nor can this exception permit a student-directed production outside of the actual class environment.

Equally clearly, it does allow certain presentations inside the classroom situation, *if limited to the class instructor and members of that particular class*. One thinks of examples such as members of an acting class presenting scenes for the instructor and members of that class. In that limited environment, use of copyrighted materials "in connection with 'teaching activities' of the institution is protected" (*Copyright Law Reports* a:xx2125).

But what if others are invited to see the activity? Says the same Law Reports, "Performances or displays for entertainment or recreational purposes are not among those protected by the exemption." If an "audience" is invited or permitted—once again, whether admission is charged is not a factor—there no longer is face-to-face teaching. Instead an "entertainment" is in progress. The spectators are not being instructed by the teacher. They are not enrolled in that particular course. Therefore, getting permission is mandated.

Fair Use

The concept of fair use allows *certain*—not unlimited—use of copyrighted materials without permission. Easy-to-understand examples would include citation of copyrighted materials in a critical or scholarly review. It also allows parodies: A playwright could use bits of a play by, say, Beckett to poke fun. For example, in 1994 the Supreme Court ruled that a rap parody of Roy Orbison's song "Pretty Woman" was a fair use, noting that the markets for the original and the transformative work may be different.

It is my understanding that fair use doctrine has little other application to theatrical production, but others may disagree.

COPYRIGHT AND FAIR USE

http://fairuse.stanford.edu

Stanford University Libraries provides this list of links dealing with fair use. Although one may hear theatre people claiming *fair use* is a technique to avoid obtaining permission to present a play or to perform only extracts from one, I see no application of *fair use* to theatre or dance.

It seems to me one thing should be clear from the foregoing discussions. The copyright laws say that a playwright owns his or her play with precisely the same legal certainty as a person owns a car or someone owns an apartment complex. Can you "borrow" that car without the owner's permission for a five-week cross-country trip? Can you arbitrarily decide to "remodel" an apartment that you rent, knocking out a wall here, rearranging this door to be in that other wall, or walling off that window and cutting a new one? Of course not. When you get hauled into court, even a dream team of lawyers won't help much.

So, in theatre, do directors have a right to "borrow" a play by producing it without permission of the legal copyright holder or his or her representative? Can directors remodel a play by shifting scenes, changing characters, deleting or adding lines, or excerpting a small scene from a whole play? No. Not legally. If directors are free to take such actions, we're forced to believe that a car thief is "liberating" a car or the apartment vandal is showing "free expression."